D0024652

the déjà vu experience

ESSAYS IN COGNITIVE PSYCHOLOGY

North American Editors:
Henry L. Roediger, III, *Washington University in St. Louis*
James R. Pomerantz, *Rice University*

European Editors:
Alan Baddeley, *University of Bristol*
Vicki Bruce, *University of Edinburgh*
Jonathan Grainger, *Université de Provence*

Essays in Cognitive Psychology is designed to meet the need for rapid publication of brief volumes in cognitive psychology. Primary topics will include perception, movement and action, attention, memory, mental representation, language and problem solving. Furthermore, the series seeks to define cognitive psychology in its broadest sense, encompassing all topics either informed by, or informing, the study of mental processes. As such, it covers a wide range of subjects including computational approaches to cognition, cognitive neuroscience, social cognition, and cognitive development, as well as areas more traditionally defined as cognitive psychology. Each volume in the series will make a conceptual contribution to the topic by reviewing and synthesizing the existing research literature, by advancing theory in the area, or by some combination of these missions. The principal aim is that authors will provide an overview of their own highly successful research program in an area. It is also expected that volumes will, to some extent, include an assessment of current knowledge and identification of possible future trends in research. Each book will be a self-contained unit supplying the advanced reader with a well-structured review of the work described and evaluated.

Titles in preparation

Gallo: *Associative Illusions of Memory*
Gernsbacher: *Suppression and Enhancement in Language Comprehension*
McNamara, *Semantic Priming*
Park: *Cognition and Aging*
Cowan: *Limits to Working Memory Capacity*
Mulligan: *Implicit Memory*

Recently published

Brown: *The Déjà Vu Experience*
Coventry & Garrod: *Seeing, Saying and Acting: The Psychological Semantics of Spatial Prepositions*
Robertson, *Space, Objects, Minds, & Brains*
Cornoldi & Vecchi, *Visuo-spatial Representation: An Individual Differences Approach*
Sternberg et al., *The Creativity Conundrum: A Propulsion Model of Kinds of Creative Contributions*
Poletiek, *Hypothesis Testing Behaviour*
Garnham, *Mental Models and the Interpretation of Anaphora*
Engelkamp, *Memory for Actions*

For continually updated information about published and forthcoming titles in the Essays in Cognitive Psychology series, please visit: **www.psypress.com/essays**

the déjà vu experience

ALAN S. BROWN

PSYCHOLOGY PRESS
NEW YORK • HOVE

Published in 2004 by
Psychology Press
29 W 35th Street
New York, NY 10001
www.psypress.com

Published in Great Britain by
Psychology Press
27 Church Road
Hove, East Sussex
BN3 2FA
www.psypress.co.uk

Psychology Press is an imprint of the Taylor & Francis Group.
Printed in the United States of America on acid-free paper.

10 9 8 7 6 5 4 3 2 1

Library of Congress Cataloging-in-Publication Data

Brown, Alan S.
  The déjà vu experience / by Alan S. Brown.
    p. cm. — (Essays in cognitive psychology)
  Includes bibliographical references and index.
  ISBN 1-84169-075-9 (hard : alk. paper)
  1. Déjà vu. I. Title. II. Series.
  BF378.D45B76 2004
  153.7—dc22
                                            2003021979

CONTENTS

Preface   xi

Chapter **1**   **Introduction**   **1**
Why Study the Déjà Vu Experience?   3
   Widespread Cultural Awareness   3
   Pure Metacognition Phenomenon   4
   Occult and Psychodynamic Encapsulation   5
   Emerging Links to Scientific Cognitive Research   5
Summary   6

Chapter **2**   **Defining the Déjà Vu Experience**   **9**
A Phenomenon in Search of a Term   9
Defining the Déjà Vu Experience   12
Changes in the Referent Use of "Déjà Vu"   16
Summary   17

Chapter **3**   **Methods of Investigating Déjà Vu**   **19**
Retrospective Reports   19
   Problems with Survey Design and Administration   21
      Unrepresentative Samples   21
      Association with the Paranormal   23
      Association with Anomalous or Pathological
       Phenomena   25
      Reliability of Self-Reports   26
   Other Surveys with Déjà Vu Items   27
Prospective Surveys   28
Summary   30

Chapter **4**   **General Incidence of Déjà Vu**   **31**
Subjective Evaluation   31

Objective Evaluation   32
   Frequency and Recency of Déjà Vu   38
      Absolute Frequency   38
      Relative Frequency   39
      Temporal Frequency   39
Types of Déjà Vu   41
Chronic Déjà Vu   42
Summary   42

Chapter 5   **Nature of the Déjà Vu Experience**   **45**
Specific Triggers   46
Stress, Fatigue, Anxiety, and Illness   47
Context of the Déjà Vu Experience   48
   Physical Setting   49
   Activity   49
   Social Setting   50
Duration   51
Time of Occurrence   52
   Time of Day   52
   Day of the Week   53
   Month of the Year   53
Emotional Reaction   54
Physical Response   56
Subjective Sense of Time and Space   56
Time Since Original Experience   57
Literary Descriptions   58
Summary   58

Chapter 6   **Physical and Psychological Variables Related
to Déjà Vu**   **61**
Age   61
   Lifetime Incidence Changes with Age   62
   Frequency Changes with Age, Among Experients   63
   Age at First Experience   65
   "Cause" of the Adult Age-Related Decline in Déjà Vu 66
Education   67
Socioeconomic Status   69
Gender   70
Race   72
Travel Frequency   73
Religious Belief   74
Political Orientation   74

Dreams and Related Phenomena   75
  Daydreams   76
  Childhood Fantasy   77
Belief in Déjà Vu   77
Summary   79

Chapter 7 **Physiopathology and Déjà Vu**   **81**
Is Déjà Vu Diagnostic of Epilepsy?   82
Association with Preseizure Aura   83
Eliciting and Recording Déjà Vu Experiences   85
Hemispheric Origin of Seizure in TLEs with Déjà Vu   86
Hemispheric Laterality and Déjà Vu   88
Brain Structures Associated with Déjà Vu   89
Other Neuropathology   91
Drugs   92
Summary   94

Chapter 8 **Psychopathology and Déjà Vu**   **95**
Schizophrenia   95
  Other Recognition Disorders Associated with
    Schizophrenia   97
Neurotic Conditions   98
Depersonalization   100
Dissociation   101
Summary   102

Chapter 9 **Jamais Vu**   **103**
Incidence of Jamais Vu   104
Jamais Vu and Temporal Lobe Epilepsy   105
Relationship Between Déjà Vu and Jamais Vu   106
Explanations of Jamais Vu   107
Capgras' Syndrome   110
Summary   111

Chapter 10 **Parapsychological Interpretations of Déjà Vu**   **113**
Relationship Between Déjà Vu and Belief in the
  Paranormal   114
Precognition   116
Telepathy   117
Reincarnation   118
  Hereditary Transmission   118
Summary   119

Chapter **11 Psychodynamic Interpretations of Déjà Vu**   **121**
    Ego Defense   121
        Repressed Memories   122
        Intrapsychic Conflict   123
    Wish Fulfillment   124
    Dissolution of Boundaries   124
    Freud and Déjà Vu   125
    Comment   125
    Summary   126

Chapter **12 Dual Process Explanations of Déjà Vu**   **127**
    Spontaneous Activation   128
        Retrieval and Familiarity   128
        Retrieval and Temporal Tags   129
    Merged Processes   129
        Encoding and Retrieval   130
        Perception and Encoding   130
        Sensation and Recollection   131
    Separated Processes   132
    Background Processing Comes to the Fore   133
        Dual Consciousness   133
        Supraliminal and Subliminal Awareness   134
    Summary   135

Chapter **13 Neurological Explanations of Déjà Vu**   **137**
    Spontaneous Brain Activity   137
        General Seizure Activity   138
        Inappropriate Parahippocampal Firing   138
    Alteration of Neural Transmission Speed   139
        Single Pathway   140
            Slowed Transmission   140
            Speeded Transmission   140
        Two Pathways   141
            Secondary Pathway Delay   141
            Primary Pathway Delay   144
    Summary   144

Chapter **14 Memory Explanations of Déjà Vu**   **147**
    Episodic Forgetting   148
        Early Childhood Experience   148
        Literature   149
        Media   150
        Hypnotic Analogue   151

Duplication of Processing   154
Single Element Familiarity   154
    Imagined Elements   157
        Implanted Memories   159
        False Memory Effect   159
    Poetzl Phenomenon   160
    Multiple Element Familiarity   160
    Redintegration and Restricted Paramnesia   161
Processing Fluency   162
Affective Association   164
    Positive Affect as Familiarity   164
    Negative Affect Masked by Familiarity   165
    Subliminal Mere Exposure   167
Gestalt Familiarity   168
Summary   170

Chapter **15 Double Perception Explanations of Déjà Vu**   **173**
Perceptual Gap   174
    Mentally Induced Gap   175
    Revelation Effect   176
Degraded Initial Perception   177
    Perceptual Occlusion   177
    Diminished Attention   180
Indirect Initial Perception   181
    Inattentional Blindness   181
    Perceptual Inhibition   183
Emotional Reverberation   184
Subjective Interpretations   184
Summary   185

Chapter **16 It's Like Déjà Vu All Over Again**   **187**
Summary: Déjà Vu Findings   187
Important Issues Concerning Déjà Vu   188
    Déjà Vu in Unique Versus Ordinary Settings:
        Different Mechanisms?   188
    Why Does Déjà Vu Happen during Mundane
        Activities?   188
    Are Auditory and Visual Déjà Vu Experiences
        Comparable?   189
    What Elicits the Subjective Sense of Precognition?   189
    Why Does Déjà Vu Decrease with Age?   189
    How Does Déjà Vu Relate to Memory Deficits?   190
    How Are Individual Differences to Be Explained?   190

Can Drugs Reliably Elicit Déjà Vu?	190
Questionnaire Development	191
Future Laboratory Research	192
Memory Approaches	193
Double Perception Approaches	194

Appendix **A Descriptions of Déjà Vu Experiences**   **197**
Routine Examples	197
Clinical Case Study Examples	197
Psychoanalytic Examples	198

Appendix **B Summary of Scientific Explanations of Déjà Vu**   **199**
Dual Processing	199
Neurological	199
Memory	200
Double Perception	201

References   **203**

Author Index   **221**

Subject Index   **229**

PREFACE

The déjà vu phenomenon has established a strong presence in our popular culture. A recent search of the Internet using the keyword "déjà vu" brought up over 400,000 sites. This profound infusion of the term in our everyday experience stands in marked contrast to the relative paucity of attention given to the phenomenon in the scientific literature. Several published articles (Burnham, 1889; Kohn, 1983; Sno, 2000; Sno & Linszen, 1990), book chapters (Ellis, 1911; MacCurdy, 1925) and a book (Neppe, 1983e) review the literature on déjà vu, but none attempts a serious connection with the literature from the rapidly expanding areas of research in human perception, cognition, and neurophysiology. A recent article summarizing the déjà vu experience (Brown, 2003) emphasizes that scientific discoveries and theorizing over the past few decades provide a rich potential for explaining the déjà vu experience, and this book is an expansion and extension of the material presented in the article.

The literature on déjà vu consists of an unusually broad range of research based on a variety of measurement instruments, anecdotal reports, and personal reflections. The quality of the data varies from report to report, but the important message emerges in the consistency of the evidence across published articles. For example, the negative association of déjà vu incidence and stress/fatigue has been noted by many researchers. Although based primarily on their own personal observations, the consistency of such evidence from many scientists gives this assertion credibility. In short, the precision that research scientists normally demand may not be present in the individual investigations, but this is superceded by the reliability of outcomes across numerous studies.

Another distinctive feature of the research on déjà vu is that it derives from individuals from a variety of professional orientations and background training: philosophy, religion, neurology, sociology, and psychology. And furthermore, within psychology, research on déjà vu emanates from many subdisciplines, including social behavior, memory, perception, experimental clinical, psychopathology, and psychopharmacology.

There is a large body of non-English language literature written by philosophers, psychologists, and physicians in France, Germany, and Holland during the late 19th and early 20th centuries. Some of this work is included in this book, but I rely on secondary sources for the translation of these works (Allin, 1896a, 1896b; Berrios, 1995; Burnham, 1889; Ellis, 1911; Funkhouser, 1983a; Neppe, 1983e; Sno & Draaisma, 1993).

The purpose of this book is to open avenues of research on déjà vu, rather than to produce the definitive characterization of the experience (cf. Brown, 2003). I have delighted in reading historical interpretations of déjà vu and being able to connect many of them to modern theories and findings in the broad realm of cognitive research. It is my sincere hope that this book will stimulate other researchers to contribute additional connections and inroads into exploring this curious cognitive glitch.

Introduction

"Last Wednesday, I was at home with both my parents around. I was revising a term paper, around 1 A.M. I felt a sensation that told me that I had revised that paper before. I felt strange because the minute I highlighted the word 'wander,' I got a sense that it had happened already. I even said out loud the word 'déjà vu' when I received that sensation."

"Last summer, I was in a program at Galveston. I was sitting with my roommate and we were talking about our problems. After a few minutes of talking, I experienced déjà vu. I don't know if I had dreamed that experience or what, but it felt as if it was recurring."

"We visited a discothèque in Downtown Disney, and were dancing with two girls from Brazil. Neither one of us had been there before, or had met the girls before. However, when a song played I felt as if I had lived the moment before. I couldn't remember exactly when or where, but I knew it wasn't my first time there and with them."

Research suggests that most of us have had a déjà vu experience at some point in our lives. As illustrated in the above stories, you are suddenly and inexplicably overcome with a feeling that you have done this exact same thing once before—been in this place, engaged in this activity, said that phrase. However, it is impossible because to the best of your recollection, you have *never* been in this place before, been with these particular people, or engaged in this particular activity at any time in your past. Reduced to the simplest form, the déjà vu experience represents the clash between two simultaneous and opposing mental evaluations: an objective assessment of unfamiliarity juxtaposed with a subjective evaluation of familiarity.

From moment to moment in our routine lives, we are accustomed to our cognitive impressions matching our objective evaluations. When we enter our own bedroom, it feels familiar; when we visit the Bronx Zoo for the first time, it feels unfamiliar. The sense of familiarity is so automatic, and consistently in sync with objective reality that we pay little attention to it until the two dimensions fail to correspond with each other.

Interest in the déjà vu experience is many centuries old, and one can find references to the phenomenon (if not by that name) as far back as the mid-1800s. There was a notable flurry of attention concerning the phenomenon during the late 1800s in the areas of philosophy and medicine. French scholars engaged in a lively debate concerning whether the déjà vu experience reflected mental pathology or the temporary memory dysfunction of normal individuals (Berrios, 1995). This intellectual conversation culminated in a special issue of *Revue Philosophique* in 1893 (Schacter, 2001). This topic became so "hot" and professionally important that some strange interpretations were proposed (e.g., Dugas, 1894) just so scholars could participate in a zeitgeist of theoretical speculation and avoid the "humiliation" of being caught without one's unique hypothesis about déjà vu (cf. Allin, 1896a).

As interest in déjà vu was beginning to work its way into the domain of psychology in the late 1800s and early 1900s, behaviorism was establishing a firm hold over psychological investigation. The déjà vu experience did not fit under this behavioristic, empirical framework because there were no consistently observable behaviors or clearly identifiable eliciting stimuli associated with it. Thus, it was bypassed by those in the mainstream of psychological research in America, Britain, and Germany where the behaviorist influence was clearly dominant. Since that time, the concept of déjà vu has never made a successful inroad into mainstream cognitive research and has been primarily viewed as a "symptom without a psychological function" (Berrios, 1995, p. 123).

Research on human memory and cognitive function grew dramatically during the 1900s, but most investigations focused on the panoply of variables that affect *routine* encoding and retention of information. Although memory errors were extensively examined by Bartlett (1932), most research followed the Ebbinghaus (1885) tradition where memory errors were viewed as nuisance variance to be controlled or eliminated (cf. Slamecka, 1985). Thus, even though early research on perception focused on errors and illusions, memory investigators have summarily ignored such effects (Roediger & McDermott, 2000). In his review of the limited literature on memory illusions, Roediger (1996) laments how little progress we have made over the past century of research toward clarifying the nature of memory illusions such as déjà vu.

The purpose of this book is to summarize scientific findings and theoretical speculation concerning déjà vu presented over the past century and a half. The first portion of this book is aimed at clarifying the manner in which the déjà vu experience is defined (Chapter 2) and investigated (Chapter 3), followed by details on the incidence of the experience (Chapter 4) and its nature (Chapter 5). Various demographic, behavioral, and physical variables (Chapter 6) have been examined as related (or unrelated) to déjà vu, and the connection between déjà vu and both epilepsy (Chapter 7) and psychopathology (Chapter 8) have come under more careful scrutiny. Jamais vu, which some consider to be the opposite of déjà vu, consists of a momentary sense of unfamiliarity in a very familiar environment (Chapter 9). The third portion of the book focuses on the various explanations of déjà vu. Parapsychological (Chapter 10) and psychodynamic (Chapter 11) interpretations are given brief coverage, and more credible interpretations are based on two cognitive functions momentarily out of synchrony (Chapter 12), a neurological glitch (Chapter 13), memory dysfunction (Chapter 14), and double perception (Chapter 15). The final chapter of the book involves a recap of research and speculation, along with suggestions for future scientific exploration of déjà vu (Chapter 16).

☐ Why Study the Déjà Vu Experience?

Prior to a detailed review of the déjà vu experience, it is worth considering why psychologists should devote their energies attempting to explore, evaluate, and understand the déjà vu phenomenon.

Widespread Cultural Awareness

Déjà vu is widely experienced by the general public and oft-cited in the popular literature (Sno, Linszen, & De Jonghe, 1992a). As Searleman and Herrmann (1994) point out, déjà vu is "… the most well-known anomaly of memory" (p. 326). Few memory phenomena are referenced by the general public, and this short list includes forgetting, memory blocks (tip-of-the-tongue state) and the déjà vu experience. One can personally verify the general infusion of the concept of déjà vu into our culture by the hundreds of thousands of hits from a Web search with that key word. Although many of these sites do not refer directly to the memory anomaly, it none the less illustrates how the concept has become a mainstay of popular vernacular. Further confirmation of this widespread usage can be found in Microsoft's Word software program. It will automatically add the appropriate accents if one simply types in the phrase "deja vu."

Although popular attention and usage alone do not justify doing research on a topic, it would also be ill-advised to ignore such a phenomenon. Neisser (1982) expressed a concern that "if X is an interesting or socially significant aspect of memory, then psychologists have hardly ever studied X" (p. 4). There has been some response to this criticism by the field as a whole, reflected in the appearance of new journal outlets for accommodating applied research topics (e.g., Applied Cognitive Psychology), but there is still an unfortunate tendency for memory researchers to sidestep common experiences that may be less amenable to experimental control.

Pure Metacognition Phenomenon

Metacognition pertains to the ways in which we are aware of, monitor, and resolve our personal cognitive experiences. Roediger (1996) suggests that "two of the most famous illusions of memory—déjà vu and jamais vu—are illusions of metacognition" (p. 95). What makes déjà vu unique among metacognitive phenomena is that the experience has no clearly identifiable cause, and *no* objective behaviors against which it can be verified. In other words, the experience is purely a mental conflagration between diametrically opposed evaluations of a momentary experience, with no way objectively to resolve or evaluate the accuracy of this conflict.

Other metamemory phenomena have some connection to objective reality, both in the identification of the triggering stimuli and a behavioral resolution, or avenue to evaluate the accuracy of one's assessment of learning or memory performance (cf. Metcalfe, 2000). For example, in judgments of learning (JOL) research, participants make evaluations of their ability to remember the material that they are presently learning, and these subjective assessments can be compared later to the objective indices of memory performance—recall or recognition (Nelson & Dunlosky, 1991, 1992; Simon & Bjork, 2001). Similarly, both feeling of knowing (FOK) ratings on the likelihood of later remembering inaccessible or unrecallable material (Blake, 1973), and tip-of-the-tongue (TOT) judgments on imminently recallable but momentarily inaccessible words (Brown, 1991), are clearly connected with the eliciting definitions or cue stimuli, and the accuracy of one's personal cognitive evaluations can be objectively evaluated against the later likelihood of retrieving or identifying the target word.

In contrast to JOL, FOK, and TOT, déjà vu lacks any identifiable eliciting stimulus or verifiable behavioral response to corroborate the subjective state. Thus, it is a "pure" metamemory experience unconnected with the empirical world, and presents a unique challenge for this area of research. In fact, simply identifying those conditions that consistently trigger a déjà vu may be the key to understanding the phenomenon.

Occult and Psychodynamic Encapsulation

Much of the published literature on the déjà vu experience has stemmed from either psychodynamic or parapsychological perspectives, and this is understandable given the unusual subjective nature of the déjà vu experience. The impression that something is stored in memory, but the only accessible vestige is a feeling about its existence, is certainly bound to encourage speculation about a psychodynamic conflict involving repression of prior emotionally charged experiences. This feeling that one is tapping into a prior experience missing from the library of our personal past also could suggest to a creative mind a parapsychological experience involving past lives or precognition. Psychodynamic interpretations may ultimately hold some explanatory potential, but these remain generally complex and cumbersome in light of simpler scientific explanations.

The main problem with parapsychological and psychodynamic interpretations is that they put off serious scientific inquiry. A reputable researcher may have second thoughts before embarking on a research program on déjà vu because of the nonscientific framework that has built up around the phenomenon. When Funkhouser (1983a) surveyed the prior literature on déjà vu, he speculated that the paucity of published reports is because of the widespread notion that déjà vu supports the concept of reincarnation. The parapsychological and psychodynamic interpretations are covered for the sake of historical completeness (Chapters 10 and 11), but there exist a number of scientifically based perspectives in the areas of cognition and neuroscience that have considerable potential to explain and demystify the déjà vu experience (Chapters 12 through 15).

Emerging Links to Scientific Cognitive Research

A survey of textbooks on memory and cognition published over the past 30 years reveals a nearly uniform silence on the topic of déjà vu. An informal sample of general-coverage memory/cognition books reveals no mention (in the index) of the topic of déjà vu in 39 books (B. F. Anderson, 1975; J. R. Anderson, 1980; Ashcraft, 2002; Baddeley, 1976, 1990; Best, 1986; Bourne, Dominowski, & Loftus, 1979; Crowder, 1976; Dawson, 1998; Dodd & White, 1980; Ellis & Hunt, 1972; Greene, 1992; Gregg, 1986; Haberlandt, 1994; Horton & Turnage, 1976; Houston, 1981; Hulse, Deese, & Egeth, 1975; Kausler, 1974; Kintsch, 1970; Klatzky, 1975; Loftus & Loftus, 1976; Martindale, 1991; Matlin, 1983; Medin & Ross, 1992; Murdock, 1974; Neath & Surprenant, 2003; Norman, 1969; Parkin, 1993; Payne & Wenger, 1998; Posner, 1973; Reed, 1982; Reisberg, 1997; Reynolds & Flagg, 1983; Seamon, 1980; Solso, 1979; Stern, 1985; Sternberg, 2003; Tarpy & Mayer, 1978; Zechmeister & Nyberg, 1982). Three textbooks touch on this phenomenon in passing, and two are by the same author (Glass, Holyoak, & Santa, 1979, p. 63; Wickelgren, 1977, p. 360, 396; Wickelgren, 1979, p. 250). The only textbooks to devote a section to the déjà vu phenomenon are Searleman and Herrmann (1994, p. 326) and Wingfield (1979, pp. 290–291). Although originally published for the trade market, two recent books by Schacter (1996, 2001) have become popular alternative textbooks and have given the déjà vu phenomenon a new level of exposure among professionals and the public alike (Schacter, 1996, pp. 172–173; Schacter, 2001, pp. 88–91).

The déjà vu experience has recently been connected to findings in several different areas of scientific research on cognition, including repetition priming (Schacter, 1996), perceptual fluency (Bernstein & Welch, 1991; Jacoby & Whitehouse, 1989; Roediger, 1996), source attribution (Hoffman, 1997) and subliminal mere exposure (Seamon, Brody, & Kauff, 1983b), and these links will be discussed in detail later in Chapters 14 and 15. With the exception of Jacoby and Whitehouse (1989) and Bernstein and Welch (1991), these connections are only peripheral, involving possible extensions of the empirical outcome. But these cognitive paradigms provide possible frameworks for understanding déjà vu, and can help shape a systematic exploration of the phenomenon in the laboratory. New findings in the area of brain function also may hold considerable promise for understanding déjà vu (see Chapters 7 and 13).

☐ Summary

Whereas research on the déjà vu experience has a long history reaching back into the mid-1800s, it has struggled for serious consideration by the scientific community. Its emergence as a legitimate topic in the late 1800s was summarily halted by the behavioristic movement, and the abundance of parapsychological and psychodynamic interpretations of déjà vu has made the topic a "hot potato" for scientists. Research efforts also have been handicapped by the lack a clearly identifiable eliciting stimulus or observable behavioral response related to the phenomenon. Much of the prior literature on the déjà vu experience has been published in journals and books that do not connect with mainstream scientific research, probably because of the difficulty in gaining acceptance for déjà vu as a legitimate research topic. Despite this, there are sufficient data and speculation available to formulate a nascent picture of the déjà vu experience. And, as Roediger and McDermott (2000) suggest, "… distortions of memory provide a fertile ground for studying interesting and important psychological phenomena" (p. 123). A goal of this book is to summarize clearly an extensive but fragmented literature, and to stimulate constructive ideas from researchers in the clinical, neuropsychological, and cognitive areas.

Defining the Déjà Vu Experience

It took nearly a century to settle on a common term for the déjà vu experience, an understandable difficulty given the strange nature of the experience. The diametrical opposition of one's objective (new) and subjective (old) evaluations of a personal experience has no cognitive parallel, and leaves an individual searching for a succinct label for this baffling experience. One of the primary reasons for the continued use of a French term introduced in the late 1800s is that there is no adequate English descriptor (Neppe, 1983e). A number of English terms have been put forth (see later), but they are generally cumbersome alternatives that tend to be more confusing than clarifying.

☐ A Phenomenon in Search of a Term

From the mid-1800s to the mid-1900s, researchers used a variety of different words and phrases in different languages to describe the déjà vu experience, and a collection of English terms is presented in Table 2.1. Sno and Linszen (1990) provide an additional five German and four French terms (other than déjà vu) to describe the phenomenon, and Neppe (1983e) gives a chronology of the evolution of various words and phrases used to label the experience.

TABLE 2.1. English Terms Used to Describe the Déjà Vu Experience

"been-here-before feeling" Burnham (1889), Calkins (1916)
"double memory" Ribot (1882), Burnham (1889), Smith (1913)
"double perceptions" Jensen (1868, cited in Marková & Berrios, 2000)
"feeling of familiarity in a strange place" Tiffin, Knight, and Asher (1946)
"feeling of familiarity in strange situations" Morgan (1936)
"feeling of having been there before" Humphrey (1923)
"has-been-experienced-before-illusion" Warren and Carmichael (1930)
"identifying fallacy" Kraepelin (1887, cited in Parish, 1897)
"illusion of having been there before" Woodworth (1940)
"illusion of having already seen" Conklin (1935)
"illusion of the already seen" Gordon (1921)
"illusion of memory" Osborn (1884)
"identifying paramnesia" Burnham (1889), Geldard (1963)
"inexplicable sense of familiarity and recognition" Hodgson (1865)
"known againness" Allin (1896a)
"mental mirage" Neumann (cited in Burnham, 1889)
"memory beforehand" Myers (1895)
"memory deception" Sander (1874, cited in Marková & Berrios, 2000)
"mental diplopia" Taylor (1931)
"paradoxical recognition" Wingfield (1979)
"paramnesia" Drever (1952), Pillsbury (1915), Titchener (1928)
"phantasms of memory" Feuchtersleben (1847)
"perplexity psychosis" MacCurdy (1925)
"promnesia" Myers (1895)
"sentiment of preexistence" Scott (in Berrios, 1995), Wigan (1844)
"sense of preexistence" James (1890)
"sense of prescience" Crichton-Browne (1895)
"sensation of reminiscence" Jackson (1888)
"sentiment of preexistence" Wigan (1844)
"recognition of the immemorially known" Jung (1963, cited in White, 1973)
"reduplicative paramnesia" Arnaud (1896)
"wrong recognition" Titchener (1928)

An extensive debate by French researchers and philosophers concerning the appropriate label for the experience (and different subtypes) appeared in the journal *Revue Philosophique* in the late 1890s. Marková and Berrios (2000) present a detailed account of this lively debate, which incidentally did not end up resolving the issue (cf. Neppe, 1983e; Schacter, 2001).

One problem with the early use of terms such as "false memory," "false recognition," "reminiscence," and "paramnesia" was that these assumed that the phenomenon was a memory dysfunction, as opposed to a neurological, perceptual, or attentional problem (Stern, 1938; Ward, 1918). Another problem is that one of the more popular English terms, paramnesia (Burnham, 1889), was used inconsistently by various authors (Funkhouser, 1983a; Smith, 1913). Some saw paramnesia as directly and exclusively referring to déjà vu (Dashiell, 1928, 1937; Gordon, 1921; Murphy, 1951; Pillsbury, 1915). Others interpreted paramnesia as a general term for a wide range of memory dysfunctions and pathologies, among which was déjà vu (Breese, 1921; Calkins, 1916; Myers, 1895; Phillips, 1913; cf. Berrios, 1995). For example, paramnesia was defined as perversion of memory where facts and fantasies are confused (Chari, 1962, 1964; Ellis, 1911), or a collection of memory errors of both omission and commission (Simmons, 1895).

To further add to the confusion, Pickford (1942a) suggested that paramnesia describes a recognition failure for a specific item (object, picture), whereas déjà vu consists of an amorphous familiarity for an *entire* setting, and a paramnesia can be traced back to a prior experience, whereas a déjà vu can not. Myers (1895) pushed "promnesia" as a more precise substitute for paramnesia, but his suggestion lost out to déjà vu probably because considerable early research was done by French researchers, and the term déjà vu was more theoretically neutral (Arnaud, 1896; Berrios, 1995).

Kraepelin's (1887) distinction between total and partial paramnesias (cf. Sno, 2000) was used by some scholars to differentiate déjà vu from related phenomena (Berrios, 1995; Burnham, 1889). Although partial paramnesia is a distortion of present reality, a total paramnesia refers to an experience independent of present reality and can be divided into three subtypes (Sno, 2000): *simple* (spontaneous image that appears as memory), *associating* (present stimuli evoke memories by association), and *identifying* (new experience appears to duplicate a previous one). Thus, déjà vu is a total paramnesia of the identifying type. A thorough discussion of the various ways that the term paramnesia has been applied, and how déjà vu fits with each perspective, can be found in Sno (2000).

Typical of the intellectual combat related to the emergence of the term déjà vu is the lack of consensus among scholars concerning the first use of that term. Berrios (1995) and Findler (1998) suggest that déjà vu was originally used in the late 1890s in a statement by Arnaud (1896), whereas Cutting and Silzer (1990) point to the first use by Jackson (1888). Sno (1994), Neppe (1983e), and Funkhouser (1983a) claim that Boirac (1876) first used the term déjà vu ("le sentiment du déjà vu") in a letter to the editor, while Krijgers Janzen (1958) suggests that Wigan (1844) was the first to write about the déjà vu experience. Finally, Dugas (1894) argues that the first occurrence of the term was in Lalande's (1893) article about paramnesias. Although the origin is unclear, we can be sure that the first use of the term déjà vu was in the late 19th century, and that a consensus regarding the use of the term déjà vu did not evolve until the middle of the 20th century (see Table 2.1).

☐ Defining the Déjà Vu Experience

The difficulty in coming to grips with the nature of the déjà vu experience is reflected in the definitional diversity found in text and trade books published from the late 1800s through the mid-1900s. The quotes presented in Table 2.2 illustrate the difficulty that well-trained behavioral scholars had in describing this amorphous experience. Perhaps this underscores why research on déjà vu has been so slow to evolve—simply arriving at a clear and consistent operational definition of the experience has been problematic.

This set of descriptions illustrates several consistencies in how the déjà vu experience is informally described and defined. First, many include some reference to *feeling*, suggesting an affective component. Of 53 definitions, nearly two thirds (34) mention feelings, while cognitive terms such as conviction, impression, appearance, sensation, or awareness appear in only 10. A number of definitions make reference to the *suddenness* of the onset and demise of the experience (Humphrey, 1923; Maeterlinck, 1919; Murphy, 1951; Osborn, 1884; Ward, 1918; Wigan, 1844), and similar characterizations include "overwhelm" (Calkins (1916), "take possession of the mind" (Crichton-Browne, 1895), "shock" (Hearn, 1927) and "all at once … flashes through us" (Holmes, 1891). The concept of *strange* also occurs repeatedly (Chapman & Mensh, 1951; Hearn, 1927; Maeterlinck, 1919), reflected in such terms as weird (Hearn, 1927; Woodworth, 1940), mysterious (James, 1890), uncanny (Freud, 1901), baffling (Humphrey, 1923), inexplicable (Ferenczi, 1969), eerie (Murphy, 1951; Sutherland, 1989) and bewilderment (Ward, 1918). A few incorporate *precognition* into their definition, describing the sense that one appears to be able to anticipate what will happen next (Carrington, 1931; Jensen, 1868; Myers, 1895; Titchener, 1928; Ward, 1918). Many of the researchers classify déjà vu as a disorder, illusion (Burnham, 1889; Drever, 1952; Ellis, 1911; Harriman, 1947; Osborn, 1884; Pillsbury, 1915; Warren, 1934) or hallucination (Burnham, 1889; Sully, 1887) of memory (Walter, 1960). Sno (1994, p. 145) even suggests a statistical analogy, that the déjà vu experience is "… a type I error based on the incorrect rejection of the null hypothesis."

A definition proposed by Neppe (1983b, 1983e) has become the standard in research on déjà vu: "*any subjectively inappropriate impression of familiarity of a present experience with an undefined past*" (Neppe, 1983e, p. 3). Neppe (1983b, 1983e) presents an exhaustive analysis of this particular definition and why it is superior to other alternatives. He explains each word of the definition and the importance of clearly ruling out other memory phenomena that could be confused with déjà vu, such as flashback, cryptomnesia, pseudopresentiment, vivid memory, precognition, and hallucination.

TABLE 2.2.   Definitions of the Déjà Vu Experience

"… conviction of having been before in the same place or in the same circumstances as those of the present presentation, but, nevertheless, can recall no other circumstances that confirm the conviction. The places or circumstances appear perfectly familiar, though we know we have never seen them before." Allin (1896b, p. 245)

"… an impression that we have previously been in the place where we are at the moment, or a conviction that we have previously said the words we are now saying, while as a matter of fact we know that we cannot possibly have been in a given situation, nor have spoken the words." Angell (1908, p. 235)

"The curious feeling of familiarity that we sometimes experience in the midst of surroundings really quite new …" Baldwin (1889, p. 263)

"The situation is vaguely felt to have been experienced before although one is also certain that it has not. It is probably that parts of the situation are similar or identical with situations previously encountered and that these parts call out motor imagery associated with the previous experience." Boring, Langfeld, & Weld (1935, p. 364)

"… the feeling of familiarity often accompanies experiences, that are not reproductions or repetitions of the past. Its commonest form is the 'been-here-before' feeling that sometimes overwhelms us when we enter places that are strange to us and scenes that are new." Calkins (1916, p. 260)

"… a novel experience carries with it a false feeling of familiarity. … The report, 'It seems to me that I have been here before,' given when an individual is visiting a new place is an example of this phenomenon." Carmichael (1957, p. 123)

"… the experience of suddenly feeling that he has lived through the present moment before—that he has seen the same sights, heard the same words, performed the same actions, etc., that everything is somehow familiar to him, and that he can almost tell just what is about to happen next." Carrington (1931, p. 301)

"… a person as he is doing something or seeing something has the strange feeling that somehow he has done or seen this before, when really it seems impossible that he has done it or seen it before." Chapman & Mensh (1951, p. 165); Richardson & Winokur (1967, pp. 622–623)

"… an impression suddenly taking possession of the mind that the passing moment of life has been once lived before or must be once lived again—that surrounding objects have been seen once before exactly in the relations in that they at the instant present themselves." Crichton-Browne (1895, p. 1)

"an illusion of recognition … when one experiences a new experience as if it had all happened before." Drever (1952, p. 62)

"… the illusion that the event that is at the moment happening to us has happened to us before." Ellis (1911, p. 230)

"the inexplicable feeling of familiarity conjured up by something that is met for the first time, as if it had been known already for a long time or previously experienced in exactly similar fashion …" Ferenczi (1969, p. 422)

"… when a person feels as if a situation in which he actually finds himself had already existed at some former time …" Feuchtersleben (1847)

"we must include in the category of the miraculous and 'uncanny' the peculiar feeling we have, in certain moments and situations, of having had exactly the same experience once before or of having once before been in the same place, though our efforts never succeed in clearly remembering the previous occasion that announces itself in this way." Freud (1901, pp. 265–266)

"the sensation that an event had been experienced, or a place had been visited, before." Gaynard (1992)

"a person comes across a place or situation that seems familiar, but which the person has never encountered before." Glass et al. (1979, p. 63)

"the illusion of having previously seen something that, actually has never been encountered before." Harriman (1947, p. 98)

"… the feeling of having already seen a place really visited for the first time. Some strange air of familiarity about the streets of a foreign town or the forms of a foreign landscape comes to mind with a sort of a soft, weird shock." Hearn (1927, pp. 492–493, cited in Neppe, 1983e, p. 1)

TABLE 2.2. Definitions of the Déjà Vu Experience (Continued)

"a state, with equal sudden onset and disappearance, during which we have the feeling that we have experienced the present situation on some occasion in a distant past in precisely the same manner down to the very last detail." Heymans (1904, cited in Sno & Draaisma, 1993)

"all at once a conviction flashes through us that we have been in the same precise circumstances as at the present instant, once or many times before." Holmes (1891, p. 73)

"this is one of the baffling and elusive experiences of everyday life. We are in a strange place, perhaps on holiday for the first time at a hotel. Suddenly, without warning, a certain feeling of familiarity seems to create itself. At once we seem to know the whole scene, windows, doors, pictures, and view from the windows. We recognize the person with whom we are speaking, although … we have never seen him to this minute. We even recognize the words he is saying, though it is impossible to know what he is going to say. We have the feeling of having been through everything before! Then, in a flash, the illusion vanishes." Humphrey (1923, p. 137)

"On the one hand, a present event is recognized as having been witnessed before. On the other hand, there is certainty that this event has not been witnessed before." Hunter (1957, p. 39)

"the experient has the conviction that a given place has been seen before yet knows that this could not possibly have been the case." Irwin (1996, p. 159)

"… the feeling that the present moment in its completeness has been experienced before—we were saying just this thing, in just this place, to just these people, etc. This 'sense of pre-existence' has been treated as a great mystery and occasioned much speculation." James (1890, p. 675)

"occasionally, generally only fleetingly, there arises in us a vague awareness that this or other situation as it is occurring at present, has been experienced in exactly the same way before. We recall that our friend took exactly that stance, held his hands in that particular way, had the same expression, spoke the same words, etc. We are almost convinced that we can predict what he will do next, say next and how we ourselves will respond." Jensen (1868, p. 48)

"… the feeling … of the particular set of circumstances or environment in that we find ourselves at the moment having occurred before or been experienced before, on a long previous occasion." Kinnier Wilson (1929, p. 61)

"… an inappropriate feeling of familiarity with new events or with new surroundings" Kohn (1983, p. 70)

"… qualitative disturbance of reproduction, that causes a whole situation to appear as the exact repetition of a previous experience …" Kraepelin (1887, cited in Parish, 1897, p. 280)

"some actual perception, usually visual or auditory, is suddenly felt to have been experienced before, although its previous occurrence cannot be explicitly remembered." MacCurdy (1925, p. 425)

"… a feeling of familiarity attaching to some bit of cognitive experience without being able to recall the antecedent experience of which the present one seems to be an identical reproduction." MacCurdy (1928, p. 113)

"… a man who finds himself in an unfamiliar country, in a city, a palace, a church, a house, or a garden, that he is visiting for the first time, is conscious of a strange and very definite impression that he 'has seen it before.' It suddenly seems to him that this landscape, these vaulted ceilings, these rooms and the very furniture and pictures that he finds in them are quite well-known to him and that he recollects every nook and corner and every detail." Maeterlinck (1919, p. 293)

"the experience of feeling 'I have been here before' or 'I have lived through this before', together with intellectual awareness that this is not so." McKellar (1957a, p. 200)

"do we not often find ourselves in a strange town, yet overcome with that curious feeling: 'I have been here before'? Do we not in the midst of a conversation suddenly have the eerie feeling that the whole conversation has run the same course at some indefinable time in the past?" Murphy (1951, p. 268)

"the feeling …' I have lived through all this before, and I know what will happen this next minute.'" Myers (1895, p. 341)

"… a person has the feeling that he has seen a part or the whole of a certain setting before … or that he has said something before …" Oberndorf (1941, p. 316)

"have you come suddenly upon an entirely new scene, and while certain of its novelty felt inwardly that you had seen it before—with a conviction that you were revisiting a dimly familiar locality?" Osborn (1884, p. 478)

TABLE 2.2. Definitions of the Déjà Vu Experience (Continued)

"... a very odd sentiment that sometimes comes over us in the ordinary run of thought and action—that the entire present situation is not new, but merely the repetition of a former one." Osborn (1884, p. 476)

"... the strong feeling or impression that you had been some place or in the same situation before, even though you had never actually been there before or were experiencing the event for the first time in 'real life.'" Palmer (1979, p. 233)

"... subject feels strongly that he has seen or done something before, but usually remains logically convinced that he has not." Pickford (1940, p. 152)

"One occasionally feels, when in a new place, that one has been there before. The whole setting and many of the details of the place are familiar, yet one is certain that this is the first visit." Pillsbury (1915, p. 210)

"... the feeling of recognition accompanying perception of a scene or event that in fact has not been experienced previously." Reed (1974, p. 106)

"I have found myself in a new position with a distinct sense that I had been there or experienced it before." Riley (1988, p. 449)

"the subjective sense that a present novel experience has been gone through subjectively." Rycroft (1968, p. 28)

"... a feeling of already having lived through an event that is occurring ostensibly for the first time." Schacter (1996, p. 172)

"People ... report feeling *subjectively* that they have already experienced a situation, while *objectively* they know that they have never encountered this particular situation before." Searleman and Herrmann (1994, p. 326)

"a feeling, usually eerie, of familiarity, when in fact the experience is new and has never previously occurred." Sutherland (1989, p. 110)

"... a definite 'feeling that all this has happened before,' sometimes connected with a 'feeling that we know exactly what is coming'—a 'feeling' that persists for a few seconds and carries positive conviction, in spite of the fact and the knowledge that the experience is novel." Titchener (1928, p. 187)

"... in certain so-called illusions of memory, we may suddenly find ourselves reminded by what is happening at the moment of a preceding experience exactly like it—some even feel that they know from what is thus recalled what will happen next. And yet, because we are wholly unable to assign such representation a place in the past, instead of a belief that it happened, there arises a most distressing sense of bewilderment, as if one were haunted and had lost one's personal bearings." Ward (1918, p. 208)

"an illusion of recognition in which a new situation is incorrectly regarded as a repetition of a previous experience" Warren (1934, p. 71)

"... the individual, although doing something for the first time, feels that he has done the act before." Warren & Carmichael (1930, p. 221)

"... one feels in the middle of a situation that what is happening has all happened before, even though one knows full well, on other grounds, that this could not possibly be so. This strong feeling of false familiarity occurs for places and, more strikingly, for events." Wickelgren (1977, p. 396)

"sudden feeling, as if the scene we have just witnessed (although, from the very nature of things it could never have been seen before) had been present to our eyes on a former occasion, when the very same speakers, seated in the very same positions, uttered the same sentiments, in the same words—the postures, the expression of countenance, the gestures, the tone of voice, all seem to be remembered, and to be now attracting attention for the second time." Wigan (1844, p. 84).

"... a weird feeling that one has been through all this before, as if time had slipped a cog and were now repeating itself." Woodworth (1940, p. 357)

There are various subtypes of déjà vu referred to in the literature. In the narrow, technical sense, déjà vu means "already seen." However, general usage has expanded the phrase's connotation to the more general "already experienced." This leaves open a wide variety of possible experiences that

TABLE 2.3. Subtypes of the Déjà Vu Experience

Déjà arrivé:	happened	Déjà pressenti:	sensed
Déjà connu:	known (personal)	Déjà raconté:	told
Déjà dit:	said (spoken)	Déjà recontré:	encountered
Déjà entendu:	heard	Déjà rêvé:	dreamed
Déjà eprouvé:	experienced	Déjà senti:	felt, smelt
Déjà gôuté:	tasted	Déjà su:	known (intellectually)
Déjà fait:	done	Déjà trouvé:	found (met)
Déjà lu:	read	Déjà vécu:	lived
Déjà parlé:	spoken	Déjà visité:	visited
Déjà pensé:	thought	Déjà voulu:	desired

can appear to be duplicated, and déjà vu has become an umbrella for all of these. Table 2.3 presents these variations (cf. Neppe, 1983b, pp. 79–82) and, in each case, the term "already" is implied by "déjà."

There is little empirical literature or speculation on these subtypes of the more general déjà vu experience, although Neppe (1983e) includes 10 separate (rather than one) déjà vu questions in his questionnaire: place, situation, doing, happening, meeting, saying, hearing, thinking, reading, dreaming, and other. His concern is that an individual may have experienced only one subtype of "déjà," and this may be missed by using a single generic and all-inclusive question. Thus, a respondent is considered to have experienced a déjà vu if he/she gives a positive response to any variety of the déjà vu experience.

Neppe (1983d) further argues that a better technique would be to allow the participant to describe their experience in an open-ended question that is later coded by the researcher. However, given the amorphous nature of déjà vu, Neppe's (1983e) definitional segmentation may be problematic. An individual often experiences déjà vu as a global reaction to an experience that is an amalgam of multiple stimulus dimensions (place, persons, verbal exchange), and it may be difficult for a person to identify precisely what they are responding to (see Chapter 5). This segmentation of déjà vu into subtypes is rare (Buck, 1970; Buck & Geers, 1967; Chari, 1962, 1964; Gaynard, 1992; Zangwill, 1945), with most investigators simply inquiring about an apparently unitary experience.

☐ Changes in the Referent Use of "Déjà Vu"

Over the last two decades, there has been a gradual shift in how the term déjà vu is used in the popular culture. Presently, déjà vu is often used as defining the repetition of a prior trend. When a previous fashion (bell-bottom pants) comes into vogue again, it is a "déjà vu" of the prior trend.

When a sports team repeats last year's playoff victory, it is a "déjà vu" of the year before (cf. Neppe, 1983e). Because use eventually establishes definition in language, the meaning of déjà vu may be evolving.

> Whereas this kind of improper use of déjà vu may ultimately be regarded by lexicographers as alternative usage and not misuse, the scientist must still tread well-worn pathways of applying conventional, research appropriate definitions to borderline instances of this inappropriate impression. (Neppe, 1983b, p. 8)

The other way that the term déjà vu has changed relates to the humorous misstatement attributed to Yogi Berra: "It's like déjà vu all over again." Whereas the original statement was a brilliant example of irony, this particular statement is beginning to replace the standard phrase as definitional. Most cute statements have a relatively short half-life ("Where's the beef?"; "I can't believe I ate the whole thing"), but this one has been firmly planted in the lexical landscape and continues to grow, and a new generation of mass media consumers are beginning to take the misstatement as veridical. This trend is reflected in a recent comparison of two Web-based searches using Google. Using the keyword "déjà vu" turned up over 400,000 hits, while a second search using the phrase "déjà vu all over again" yielded over 100,000 hits. Thus, much of the Web-based usage is specifically (if erroneously) tied to Mr. Berra's reformulation of the term, and as a culture we may be at risk of losing touch with the original meaning of the phrase.

☐ Summary

The déjà vu experience has been given a variety of different labels, in various languages. The amorphous nature of the experience is in part responsible for the difficulty in settling on a specific label, and the varied manner in which the experience is defined reflects this problem. Paramnesia almost caught on, but the term's inconsistent use across researchers led to its demise: some viewed it as synonymous with the déjà vu experience, while others considered déjà vu to be a subtype of paramnesia. Throughout the past century and a half, a broad array of definitions of déjà vu have focused on feelings (rather than cognitions), and many emphasize its sudden and strange qualities. Recently, a definition proposed by Neppe (1983e) has become the accepted standard: "any subjectively inappropriate impression of familiarity of a present experience with an undefined past." The meaning of the term déjà vu has recently shifted to include a more generic repetition of an episodic experience, rather than the state of confusion where an episodic recollection is missing.

Methods of Investigating Déjà Vu

A variety of different techniques have been used to gather information on the nature of the déjà vu experience. The primary methods involve retrospective and prospective questionnaires (present chapter), although researchers have used case studies for the detailed exploration of psychodynamic interpretations of déjà vu (Chapter 11). Group comparisons also have been used to determine if the incidence and nature of the déjà vu experience varies as a function of brain pathology (Chapter 7) and psychological maladjustment (Chapter 8).

☐ Retrospective Reports

Much of the research on déjà vu has used retrospective evaluations of two different varieties: short surveys assessing the incidence of déjà vu, and longer questionnaires evaluating multiple dimensions of the déjà vu experience. The short surveys involve either a *single* yes/no question concerning whether the respondent has ever experienced a déjà vu (Gallup & Newport, 1991; Green, 1966; Greyson, 1977; Leeds, 1944; McKellar, 1957; McKellar & Simpson, 1954; Myers & Grant, 1972; van Paesschen, King, Duncan, & Connelly, 2001; Zuger, 1966) or a multipoint scale addressing déjà vu frequency (with one response option being "never") (Ardila, Niño, Pulido, Rivera, & Vanegas, 1993; Brauer, Harrow, & Tucker,

TABLE 3.1. Wording of Questionnaire Items Concerning Déjà Vu

"Do you sometimes get the feeling that you have experienced something or been some place before even though you know you have not?" Ardila et al. (1993, p. 138)

"Have you ever had the feeling of déjà vu and felt you had been somewhere or done something before?" Gallup and Newport (1991, p. 141)

"Have you ever had the feeling—'I have experienced this before'?" Green (1966, p. 357)

"Have you ever had an experience that seemed to have happened exactly the same way, once before?" (or) "Have you ever been to a place for the first time, yet something about it made you feel that you had been there once before?" Leeds (1944, p. 40)

"Have you ever thought you were somewhere you had been before, but knowing that it was impossible?" NORC (1973, 1984, 1988, 1989)

"Have you ever come suddenly upon an entirely new scene, and while certain of its novelty felt inwardly that you had seen it before—with a conviction that you were revisiting a dimly familiar locality?" Osborn (1884, p. 478)

"Have you thought you were somewhere you had been before but knew that it was impossible?" McClenon (1988, p. 425)

"Have you ever been in a new place and felt as if you have been there before?" Neppe (1983e, p. 225)

"Have you ever had the strong feeling or impression that you had been some place or in the same situation before, even though you had never actually been there before or were experiencing the event for the first time in 'real life'?" Palmer (1979, p. 233; cf. Kohr, 1980)

"Do you sometimes get the feeling that you have experienced something or been someplace before even though you know you have not?" Roberts et al. (1990, p. 83)

"the feeling that what is happening to you has happened before." Ross & Joshi (1992, p. 145)

"Have you ever had the feeling of having experienced a sensation or situation before in exactly the same way when in fact you are experiencing it for the first time?" Sno, Schalken, de Jonghe, & Koeter (1994, p. 28)

"… having been in a place for the first time and experiencing the strange feeling of having been there before, or of doing something for the first time and experiencing the strange feeling of having done it before." Zuger (1966, p. 193)

1970; Buck, 1970; Buck & Geers, 1967; Harper, 1969; Kohr, 1980; McClenon, 1988; McCready & Greeley, 1976; NORC, 1984, 1988, 1989; Palmer, 1979; Roberts, Varney, Hulbert, Paulsen, Richardson, Springer, Shepherd, Swan, Legrand, Harvey, & Struchen, 1990; Silberman, Post, Nurnberger, Theodore, & Boulenger, 1985; Zuger, 1966). Both Chapman and Mensh (1951) and Richardson and Winokur (1967) used similar two-tier question sets, with a yes/no initial question followed up by additional questions on the frequency/recency of déjà vu. These short surveys have been administered orally in person (Chapman & Mensh, 1951; Greyson, 1977; Harper, 1969; Leeds, 1944; Richardson & Winocur, 1967; van Paesschen et al., 2001; Zuger, 1966), orally over the telephone (Gallup & Newport, 1991), through the mail (Kohr, 1980; Palmer, 1979; Palmer & Dennis, 1975), and written in a group setting (Gaynard, 1992; Green, 1966). Examples of the short survey questions appear in Table 3.1 (also see Table 2.2 for Chapman & Mench, 1951; Heymans, 1904, 1906; Richardson & Winocur, 1967).

Several researchers have developed longer retrospective questionnaires, aimed at assessing physical and psychological circumstances surrounding the déjà vu experience. Neppe (1983e) developed both quantitative (frequency; duration) and qualitative (emotional intensity; clarity of experience) questionnaires to be administered in an interview format. Sno et al. (1994) later refined and extended Neppe's (1983e) questionnaires, and included additional questions from Heymans (1904) and Chapman and Mensh (1952), resulting in their own 23-item questionnaire. Both instruments focused on defining the content (setting, your actions, words spoken), frequency (how often, first experience), personal circumstances (where, when, doing what), physical state (fatigued, angry, intoxicated), and psychological reaction (emotions, time sense, body awareness) related to the déjà vu experience, as well as auxiliary psychological dimensions (dream memory) and personal habits (travel frequency).

Problems with Survey Design and Administration

Although many instruments have been used to evaluate the déjà vu experience, the research is plagued with numerous problems. One is a failure to report some of the basic details of the research, such as the actual survey question (Brauer et al., 1970; Buck, 1970; Buck & Geers, 1967; Dixon, 1963; Gaynard, 1992; Greyson, 1977; Harper, 1969; Kohr, 1980; McKellar, 1957; McKellar & Simpson, 1954; Myers & Grant, 1972; Palmer, 1979), the exact nature of the response scale(s) (Brauer et al., 1970; Buck, 1970; Buck & Geers, 1967; Green, 1966; Harper, 1969; McKellar, 1957; Myers & Grant, 1972; Osborn, 1884) or the déjà vu incidence found through this query (Dixon, 1963; Osborn, 1884; Sno et al., 1994). It is also not uncommon for the details of the sample, such as the mean age (Brauer et al., 1970; Buck, 1970; Buck & Geers, 1967) or sex distribution (Brauer et al., 1970), to be missing from the report (See Table 4.2).

Leeds (1944) even admits to his lack of survey precision: "In interviewing, I made no attempt to standardize my method of approach. I tried to work on a personal basis and encouraged the individual to talk informally on the subject" (p. 40). One of the more thorough déjà vu questionnaires, developed by Sno et al. (1994), provided considerable detail on the test-retest and interitem reliability, as well as face and construct validity. Surprisingly, they did not publish the actual questionnaire *or* any descriptive statistics on the déjà vu responses derived from four subgroups of individuals (schizophrenics, depressed, complex seizure prone, and normals).

Unrepresentative Samples

The samples used in déjà vu survey research are frequently unrepresentative. In a review of 16 prior déjà vu survey studies, Neppe (1983d) stated that only one (McCready & Greeley, 1976) used adequate sampling. Although this situation has improved since then, methodological problems still pervade this literature. Often, a sample of "convenience" is used, with researchers selecting a group of individuals from the place they work or do research. Leeds (1944) sampled individuals in a shop where he worked. Osborn (1884) selected people "at Princeton and elsewhere" (without further clarification), while Harper (1969) queried workers in a public health department, but admitted that "no attempt was made to make this a representative sample of the normal population ..." (p. 69). Kohr (1980) polled members of a paranormal society to which he belonged (Association for Research and Enlightenment), but admits that his "... respondents represent an atypical population of individuals, who are attracted to an organization like the A. R. E. because of their own psi experiences ..." (Kohr, 1980, p. 396). Many of the studies were conducted by psychotherapists who surveyed their own patients (Auger, 1966; Zuger, 1966), or physicians who used inpatients at the hospitals where they worked (Chapman & Mensh, 1951; Richardson & Winocur, 1967). Gaynard (1992) queried students at a university who were aware of his course on "Aspects of the Paranormal" and his personal bias toward such phenomena, and gave questionnaires to 40 tutors to pass out during their 1-hour sessions to "any ten pupils willing to complete them" (p. 167).

That most previous surveys "... involved preselected samples that might be atypical of a broadly representative population" troubled Palmer (1979, p. 221) who attempted to rectify this by using a broader sample of community dwellers in a university town (Charlottesville, Virginia) to compare with his university student sample. Palmer's (1979) detailed efforts to construct a representative sample are included in his report, but Neppe (1983d) takes issue with the adequacy of his sample, arguing that the small university town is overrepresented with intellectually and culturally superior individuals.

Samples are sometimes made unrepresentative in the way respondents are interviewed. Leeds (1944) was convinced that the déjà vu experience is essentially universal, so he "pressed" those individuals who originally claimed no déjà vu experience and got about half of these to change their mind on his second query. In fact, it is quite likely that respondents in many studies could become confused about exactly what is being asked in the déjà vu question, as reflected in the wide diversity in the wording of questionnaire items (see Table 3.1).

This problem of an inadequate and restricted sample is particularly disappointing in Neppe's (1983e) study, one of the most extensively documented survey projects on déjà vu. He included five groups: schizophrenics, temporal lobe epileptics, nontemporal lobe epileptics, paranormal experients, and paranormal nonexperients. The latter two groups were comprised of those who have and have not (respectively) had a paranormal experience. His "normal" control group, the paranormal nonexperients, consisted of only 10 people, five of whom had experienced déjà vu. Thus, dozens of pages of descriptive statistics and analyses in his book are based on these five persons. Neppe (1983e) repeatedly bemoans the lack of statistical power and the limits this placed on comparisons across his groups, and admits throughout this book (Neppe, 1983e) and elsewhere (Neppe, 1983d) that his results are not conclusive or generalizable and should serve only as a guideline for future research. It is truly unfortunate that such a great effort was expended on presenting the results from so few individuals. It is also problematic that important details of his research are missing from the book, and the reader is directed to his unpublished dissertation for clarification. To make matters worse, the specific composition of the various samples is unclear and confusing, and the number of individuals in his "normal" sample appears to change at different points throughout the book without clear explanation. There is also reference to a pilot and main study, but these are not clearly differentiated.

Association with the Paranormal

Another bias in many déjà vu surveys is a déjà vu item that is embedded among ones evaluating paranormal experiences. A listing of the types of paranormal items associated with the déjà vu item appears in Table 3.2.

The information presented in this table clearly indicates that many of those conducting déjà vu surveys assume that the experience falls somewhere outside of the realm of normal cognitive experience. In fact, 19 of the 57 survey outcomes on déjà vu incidence evaluated later in Chapter 4 include this bias. Typical of such thinking, one of Palmer's (1979) primary objectives was to estimate the proportion of Americans having psychic experiences, and in this process he assumed that déjà vu was paranormal. Interestingly, Ross and Joshi (1992) removed the déjà vu question from their analyses of 15 paranormal questions because the déjà vu incidence was much higher than the other items, making it difficult for them to view déjà vu as comparable to the other (much rarer) paranormal experiences. A particularly unfortunate example of this bias is in the General Social Survey (GSS) done by the National Opinion Research Center (NORC) at the University of Chicago. NORC uses exceptionally good sampling procedures, yet imbed the déjà vu question with four questions evaluating parapsychological phenomena: ESP, OBE, clairvoyance, and contact with the dead. Similarly, a Gallup Poll (Gallup & Newport, 1991) placed the déjà vu item among questions about ESP, astrology, ghosts, clairvoyance, witches, and devils.

TABLE 3.2. Questions Accompanying the Déjà Vu Item in Surveys

Apparitions—Gaynard (1992), Greyson (1977)

Clairvoyance—Gallup & Newport (1991), Greyson (1977), McCready & Greeley (1976), NORC (1984, 1988, 1989), Sobal & Emmons (1982)

Contact with dead—Gallup & Newport (1991), Kohr (1980), McClenon (1988, 1994), McCready & Greeley (1976), NORC (1984, 1988, 1989), Palmer (1979), Ross & Joshi (1992), Ross, Heber, Norton, Anderson, Anderson, & Barchet (1989)

Extra sensory perception—Green (1966), Kohr (1980), Palmer (1979), McClenon (1988, 1994), McCready & Greeley (1975), NORC (1984, 1988, 1989), Sobal & Emmons (1982)

Ghosts—Gallup & Newport (1991), Gaynard (1992), Ross & Joshi (1992), Ross et al. (1989), Sobal & Emmons (1982)

Hallucinations—Green (1966)

Haunting—Kohr (1980), Palmer (1979)

Lucid dreaming—Green (1966), Greyson (1977), Kohr (1980), Palmer (1979)

Mystical experience—Kohr (1980), McCready & Greeley (1976), NORC (1984, 1988, 1989), Palmer (1979)

Night paralysis—McClenon (1994)

Out-of-body experience—Kohr (1980), Gaynard (1992), Green (1966), Greyson (1977), Irwin (1993), McClenon (1988; 1994), Myers & Austrin (1985), Palmer (1979)

Past-life memory—Kohr (1980), Palmer (1979), Ross & Joshi (1992), Ross et al. (1989)

Poltergeists—Gaynard (1992), Kohr (1980), Palmer (1979), Ross & Joshi (1992), Ross et al. (1989)

Precognition—Gaynard (1992), Greyson (1977), Ross & Joshi (1992), Ross et al. (1989), Sobal & Emmons (1982)

Psychic healing—Gallup & Newport (1991)

Psychokinesis—Gallup & Newport (1991), Gaynard (1992), Ross & Joshi (1992), Ross et al. (1989)

Reincarnation—Gallup & Newport (1991), Kohr (1980), Palmer (1979)

Spirit possession—Greyson (1977), Ross & Joshi (1992), Ross et al. (1989)

Telepathy—Gaynard (1992), Ross & Joshi (1992), Ross et al. (1989)

Unidentified flying object—Gaynard (1992)

Respondents in both of these large national surveys are given the clear message that déjà vu is paranormal. Gallup and Newport (1991) even acknowledge that most psychologists do not consider déjà vu as psychic or paranormal, yet their survey format implies this to respondents. Similarly, Gaynard (1992) opines that déjà vu may have a perfectly acceptable physiological explanation, but he (unconvincingly) rationalizes including déjà vu among paranormal questions to allow respondents to differentiate between precognition and déjà vu. Gaynard (1992) suggests that respondents may be embarrassed to admit a belief in the paranormal, which logically should lower the response rate for a déjà vu item affiliated with these paranormal topics. Irwin (1993) even speculates that having paranormal questions may lower the overall questionnaire return rate because respondents are unwilling to disclose details of the "anomalous phenomenon" (OBE) accompanying the déjà vu question.

Similarly, Palmer (1979) was concerned that those who answer surveys that include paranormal items are unrepresentative of the general population, and the incidence of déjà vu (and other "paranormal experiences") would be higher in such respondents than in nonrespondents. To evaluate this, he compared incidence rates in those who responded to the initial mailing (N = 183) with those who responded after one reminder (N = 112) and after two reminders (N = 59). He was comforted by the fact that the incidence rate for survey items, including déjà vu, did not vary across these three subsamples. However, his definition of "nonresponders" as later-responders (or nagged responders) may not provide the cleanest control group to address this issue.

Association with Anomalous or Pathological Phenomena

Aside from an association with parapsychological phenomena, other questionnaires imply a relationship between déjà vu and various types of anomalous behaviors and mild forms of psychopathology. Several surveys have included questions on *depersonalization*, a sense of unreality about one's personal existence (Buck, 1970; Buck & Geers, 1967; Brauer et al., 1970; Harper & Roth, 1962; Myers & Grant, 1972) and on *derealization*, a sense of unreality about the environment (Brauer et al., 1970; Harper, 1969; Harper & Roth, 1962). Both psychological disturbances have a superficial resemblance to déjà vu, but their inclusion in a questionnaire could suggest that déjà vu is connected with a global and serious disturbance of reality perception.

Questionnaires surveying the déjà vu experience also have contained items on belief in the Loch Ness Monster and Bigfoot (Sobal & Emmons, 1982), participation in cult activities (Ross & Joshi, 1992), experiencing crystal/pyramid healing and channeling (Gallup & Newport, 1991), astrology (Sobal & Emmons, 1982), and visits to a psychic, astrologer, and haunted house (Gallup & Newport, 1991). Also accompanying déjà vu items are ones on *agoraphobia*, an all-encompassing fear of the outside world (Myers & Grant (1972), *synesthesia*, the experience of one sensory dimension in another (tasting the color red; smelling a musical note) (Buck, 1970; Buck & Geers, 1967; McKellar, 1957), and *hypnogogic* and *hypnopompic imagery*, those dreamy periods preceding and following (respectively) sleep (Buck, 1970; Buck & Geers, 1967; McKellar, 1957; McKellar & Simpson, 1954). Although some dimensions, such as hypnogogic and hypnopompic imagery, do not connote psychological problems, they are still exotic experiences that may frame déjà vu as anomalous or bizarre by association. As McKellar and Simpson (1954, p. 268) so cogently point out,

> It was thought justifiable to inform subjects that what was being investigated was an experience undergone by a large number of

people who were not apparently maladjusted or psychotic. Despite this, it seems likely that superficial investigation by questionnaire is more likely to underestimate than to overestimate the incidence of such experiences.

The disclaimer concerning the dissociation between déjà vu and psychopathology is limpid, at best, but at least it is presented (unlike other such surveys). McKellar and Simpson's (1954) disclaimer may actually bias the results in the high direction because of their assertion that déjà vu is experienced by a "large number of people."

Reliability of Self-Reports

A final concern in survey research on déjà vu is the potential unreliability of self-report data. Harper (1969) suggests that the incidence of déjà vu may simply be "… an artefact of the interview situation and measures only the willingness of an individual to admit to an experience that may be universal …" (p. 70) (cf. Chapman & Mensh, 1951). Somewhat troubling is Harper's (1969) comparison of oral versus card sort techniques for assessing the incidence of déjà vu. Following an initial face-to-face interview about the déjà vu experience, he asked the *same* respondents to sort cards containing an assortment of personal experiences (including déjà vu) into two piles—true or false—with respect to their own experience. Harper (1969) discovered that over a fifth of his respondents (22%) gave different answers in the two formats, with the interview yielding a higher incidence than the card sort. The oral interviewer may have positively biased the respondents, or the card sort may have been confusing, but it is troubling that substantially different estimates of déjà vu are derived from the same people in the same session with different query formats.

Another issue in this research is the reluctance of some individuals to admit to having a déjà vu. Although there is no direct evidence that the general public views déjà vu with suspicion, Crichton-Browne (1895) suggested that individuals who had déjà vu were reticent to talk about it because they believed the experience to be "somehow morbid," and Harper (1969) notes that interviewees may be reluctant to volunteer reports of this experience for fear of being labeled as "abnormal." Harper advises that providing respondents with the description first, rather than requesting personal descriptions, is a better technique.

Taking the opposite perspective concerning survey report bias, Neppe (1983d) suggests that the typical survey may *underestimate* déjà vu incidence because such experiences "… may have become so routinized that they are not recalled" (p. 96). He suggests that we may have become so jaded by the commonplace memory illusion of déjà vu that we tend to underreport it. Leeds (1944) concurs that déjà vu is much more frequent than commonly reported because it is "… quickly lost in the welter of normal waking experience" (p. 31). Such speculation, however, seems unlikely. From all other indicators in the published research, the experience of a déjà vu is very attention-grabbing.

A final problem centers on the questionable skills that the typical person brings to their own self-monitoring processes. Whereas most of us have experienced a variety of memory problems in general and recognition problems in particular, the precise assessment of the déjà vu experience may be especially problematic because it involves the simultaneous monitoring two opposing cognitions: an objective evaluation of newness and a subjective evaluation of oldness. Given that individuals are less than impressive in monitoring their personal cognitive/emotional states (Nisbett & Wilson, 1977), the simultaneous monitoring of two different cognitive evaluations may be even more problematic.

Another self-evaluation difficulty is that the lack of an objective criterion against which to validate the existence of a déjà vu experience (see Chapter 1) may cause different individuals to judge the same identical subjective experience differently. As Neppe (1983d) proposes, if you walk into a new room and have a familiarity response, one person might rationalize it as a resemblance to another friend's apartment and another might interpret it as déjà vu.

Other Surveys with Déjà Vu Items

There exist longer surveys that contain a déjà vu item, and these include the Questionnaire for Episodic Psychic Symptoms (Ardila et al., 1993; Roberts et al., 1990), Anomalous Experiences Inventory (Gallagher, Kumar, & Pekala, 1994), Dissociative Disorders Interview Schedule (Ross et al., 1989), and Silberman-Post Psychosensory Rating Scale (Silberman et al., 1985). Most published research provides no separate data on the déjà vu question (Gallagher et al., 1994; Ross et al., 1989), with the déjà vu item combined with others into a total score, or correlated with a particular scale or other measurement instrument (Gallagher et al., 1994). In most of these instruments, the implication is that déjà vu is a type of psychic, anomalous, or dissociative experience, rather than a more mundane cognitive dysfunction. It should be noted that inventories on anomalous and paranormal experiences designed by psychologists generally do not include an item on déjà vu (Davis, Paterson, & Farley, 1974; Grimmer & White, 1990; Tobacyk & Milford, 1983).

☐ Prospective Surveys

Retrospective estimates of déjà vu frequency are problematic primarily because it is a relatively rare event (Adachi, Adachi, Kimura, Akanuma, Takekawa, & Kato, 2003). One could argue that infrequency is likely to create a distinctive mnemonic impression, similar to a flashbulb memory that occurs with a surprising event such as the Columbia disaster or the death of Princess Di (Brown & Kulik, 1977). However, a déjà vu is often experienced in a mundane context, which would make remembering the specific physical and psychological details surrounding the déjà vu experience difficult. As Holmes (1891, p. 94) suggests, "... the impression is very evanescent, and that it is rarely... recalled by any voluntary effort, at least after any time has elapsed." This problem can be addressed by prospective evaluations, but only Heymans (1904, 1906) has used this methodology. The rarity of such research is probably due to the time span required to collect an adequate behavioral sample. Whereas a month may be sufficient for other memory dysfunctions, like the tip-of-the-tongue experience (Burke, MacKay, Worthley, & Wade, 1991; Reason & Lucas, 1984), a year (or more) may be required for several déjà vu experiences to occur.

In two separate studies, Heymans (1904, 1906) had college students record the details of each déjà vu they experienced during an academic year. In the original reports, written in Dutch and translated into English by Sno and Draaisma (1993), Heymans' primary goal was to determine the relationship between déjà vu and depersonalization, as well as a variety of physical (sleeping pattern, diurnal rhythm, working rhythm, activity pattern), emotional (emotional sensitivity, mood fluctuations), social, and cognitive (imaginative facility, absent-mindedness, math and language aptitude) dimensions. In Heymans's study, whenever a participant had a déjà vu, they documented the circumstances at the time of the experience and immediately prior to it, including time of day, environmental familiarity, social setting (alone/with others), speaking or listening activities, physical (fatigued/relaxed) and mental state, recent consumption of food or alcohol, and so on.

In the first investigation (Heymans, 1904), 6 of 42 students (14%) had a total of 13 déjà vu experiences during the year. The prospective incidence of déjà vu is more difficult to extract from the second study (Heymans, 1906) because déjà vu and depersonalization experiences are reported in combination. However, it appears that 55 of 88 respondents (62%) had a déjà vu during the year, and a total of 59 déjà vu episodes were reported by these individuals. The discrepancy in the prospective incidence between the two investigations is troubling, and an explanation for this difference is not readily apparent.

This combined reporting of déjà vu and depersonalization experiences in Heymans (1906) highlights a consistent theme in early investigations of déjà vu. Many researchers assumed that déjà vu was a symptom of a mood or personality disorder, rather than a routine cognitive dysfunction. Thus, they were *primarily* interested in documenting the relationship between déjà vu and other moderate to severe psychological disturbances (depersonalization), psychopathology (schizophrenia) and ongoing personal dispositions (mood fluctuations, working rhythms, emotional sensitivity), and relatively uninterested in gathering systematic and objective information on the details of the déjà vu experience (where, when, how long, personal reaction).

One other published article employed a prospective procedure, but of a different sort. Leeds's (1944) struggle with his own frequent and recurrent déjà vu experiences motivated him to make an extensive personal log. Across 12 months, he recorded 144 déjà vu experiences, an average of one every 2½ days! After stopping for a year, he picked up again for another 2 months (at the request of a friend) and recorded an additional 14 déjà vu experiences during this period. The record Leeds kept is truly impressive. For each déjà vu experience, he included the date and time, an assessment of intensity and duration (both on a 4-point scale), as well as a description of the physical setting, his behaviors, the psychological nature of the experience, and his physical state. In addition, he added an "x" beside the intensity-duration evaluation when he believed that some element(s) in the present setting duplicated one experienced previously. Below is an example of one of these records (No. 135):

> Feb. 18. Wed., 9:10 A.M. 4-4x Standing on a bin in aisle at work. Paused in work for a moment. The feeling came and went, and came again. Quite wide awake, but still slightly tired. Had only had 6 1/2 hours sleep. (Leeds, 1944, p. 26)

Leeds provided extensive graphical summaries of his déjà vu experiences (by month, week, time of day) and drew a number of conclusions based on his observations. First, the intensity and duration of the déjà vu experiences are directly related to each other. Second, the frequency of déjà vu is inversely related to intensity-duration—the more time that has passed since the previous déjà vu, the more intense and longer the present déjà vu experience is. Leeds further observed that déjà vu experiences tend to come in clusters, and that they occasionally occur in dreams (he recorded two such experiences). This diary document published by Leeds is fascinating, but it is difficult to draw any general conclusions because there is no other such behavioral record for comparison. In other words, it is unclear whether this extraordinary frequency of déjà vu is driven by the same mechanisms that underlie the typical, but infrequent, déjà vu experience.

☐ Summary

The primary techniques to assess the déjà vu phenomenon are retrospective and prospective surveys. Retrospective surveys have been used in nearly all of the research on déjà vu. Most retrospective surveys consist of a single item with either yes/no response ("have you ever experienced déjà vu?") or multipoint scale ("how often have you experienced déjà vu? never, seldom, occasionally, often"). Several longer retrospective surveys have been developed (Neppe, 1983e; Sno et al., 1994), but have not been used to gather extensive data on the incidence and nature of the déjà vu experience. Many problems exist in the current retrospective survey literature, including inconsistent or spotty reporting of the survey design and data, unrepresentative samples, and placing the déjà vu item in the context of items on paranormal and anomalous experiences. Prospective research would be more useful, but few of these efforts have been undertaken (Heymans, 1904, 1906; Leeds, 1944). The rarity of the experience makes prospective research a low-yield effort, but a thorough understanding of déjà vu experience ultimately demands such an undertaking.

CHAPTER

4

General Incidence of Déjà Vu

Given that the déjà vu experience does not appear to be universal, an evaluation of the incidence of the illusion separates into two questions. First, what proportion of individuals have experienced déjà vu? Second, of those who have had the experience, how often has it occurred?

□ Subjective Evaluation

Whereas the bulk of this chapter will address objective data on déjà vu incidence derived from surveys, there have been numerous subjective evaluations of déjà vu incidence. Most behavioral scientists who comment on the déjà vu experience describe it as both *common* and *universal* (cf. Greeley, 1975). Although anecdotal and subjective, such assessments from research scientists should be afforded some credibility because of their training in techniques of systematic and objective behavioral observation. Comments concerning the commonality and universality of déjà vu appear in Table 4.1, with italics added to emphasize these points. Most of these writers are well-educated, and one should keep in mind that evidence presented later (Chapter 6) suggests that déjà vu is more common among such individuals. Out of 38 comments, seven assert that déjà vu is universal and the remainder imply that the majority of persons have experienced déjà vu.

TABLE 4.1. Subjective Assessments of the Pervasiveness of the Déjà Vu Experience

Adachi et al. (1999, p. 380) "… probably a *universal* experience …"
Allin (1896b, p. 245) "We have *often* a very strong conviction …"
Angell (1908, p. 235) "… disturbance of memory, with which *most of us are familiar* …"
Antoni (1946, p. 16)"… *the majority*, recognize the sensation."
Breese (1921, p. 258) "… *every one* has at times experienced."
Burnham (1889, p. 439) "This form of paramnesia is *very common*."
Carrington (1931, p. 301) "*Almost everyone* … has had the experience …"
Chapman & Mensh (1951, p. 163) "… *relatively common* in adults."
Conklin (1935, p. 89) "Certainly it is a *common* phenomenon."
Crichton-Browne (1895, p. 1) "… a *universal* human experience."
Critchley (1989, p. 196) "*All people* … have the occasional…déjà vu …"
Greeley (1975, p. 10) "… *relatively common* in the population."
Harper (1969, p. 70) "… an experience that may be *universal* …"
Holmes (1891, p. 73) "… have *often* been struck by it."
Jackson (1876, p. 702) "… *not uncommon* in healthy people …"
James (1890, p. 675) "… a curious experience that *everyone seems to have had* …"
Kinnier Wilson (1929, p. 61) "… undoubtedly of *common occurrence* in normal persons …"
Leeds (1944, p. 24) "… the illusion of déjà vu … is, I believe, *almost universal*."
MacCurdy (1925, p. 425) "… déjà vu…[occurs] in *many* normal people …"
Maudsley (1889, p. 187) "… *almost everybody has had* more than once in his life …"
Maeterlinck (1919, p. 293) "It happens *fairly often* …"; "which of us but has, *at least once in his life*, vaguely experienced some such impression?"
Murphy (1951, p. 268) "… *often find ourselves* … overcome with that curious feeling …"
McKellar (1957, p. 54) "… the phenomenon occurs, and *very commonly* indeed."
Myers (1895, p. 341) "… the feeling that *many men* have experienced …"
Neppe (1983e, p. 51) "… occurring in an *extremely high proportion* of the population."
Reed (1974, p. 106) "… *not at all uncommon*."
Reed (1979, p. 13) "… experienced on occasion by the *majority* of normal people."
Schacter (1996, p. 172) "*Most people* have on some occasion …"
Schneck (1964, p. 116) "Déjà vu is a *common occurrence* …"
Smith (1913, p. 55) "… *very common* among normal individuals."
Sno & Linszen (1990, p. 1594) "… *ubiquitous* … *almost everyone* is familiar with it."
Spatt (2002, p. 6) "*Most people* at some times experience déjà vu …"
Titchener (1928, p. 187) "*Most of us*, probably, have an occasional acquaintance with …"
Walter (1960, p. 7) "… *most normal people* have had … or will have … déjà vu …"
Warren & Carmichael (1930, p. 221) "… a *common* and interesting abnormality …"
West (1948, p. 267) "… a *common* illusion of memory …"
Wickelgren (1977, p. 396) "… *most normal people* have also experienced déjà vu."

☐ Objective Evaluation

The percentage of individuals who have reported experiencing at least one déjà vu at some point in their lifetime through formal or informal surveys is provided in Table 4.2, with outcomes separated by clinical and nonclinical samples. These outcomes are listed in *decreasing* order of déjà vu incidence within each of these two categories. Also provided (where available) is the number of individuals sampled, the percent of females, age characteristics, and a short description of the sample. A graphical summary is provided in Figure 4.1, showing the number of outcomes falling within each incidence range (by 10% blocks). Where different subgroups of individuals were sampled within a single research report, these are presented as separate entries that may not appear adjacent to each other because of different incidences (Bernard-Leroy, 1898; Greyson, 1977; Harper & Roth, 1962; McClenon, 1994; Myers & Grant, 1972; Neppe, 1983e; Palmer, 1979; Richardson & Winokur, 1967; Silberman et al., 1985). With Neppe's (1983e) survey, two separate subgroups of individuals were combined (those who *did* and *did not* experience paranormal phenomena) because the sample size was extremely small in both subsamples (6 and 10, respectively). Most of the clinical samples consist of individuals with temporal lobe epilepsy (TLE) or psychiatric patients, and two studies used hospital inpatients as controls for psychiatric groups (Chapman & Mensh, 1951; Richardson & Winokur, 1967).

Across all 57 outcomes from 42 different studies presented in Table 4.2, the déjà vu incidence ranges from 10% to 100%, with a mean incidence of 67% and a median of 67%. Within the 41 *nonclinical* outcomes, the déjà vu incidence ranges from 30% to 100%, with a mean of 72% and a median of 69%. For the 16 *clinical* outcomes, the incidence ranges from 10% to 92%, with a mean of 53% and a median of 53%. In short, about two thirds of sampled individuals have experienced at least one déjà vu in their life. Clinical samples have a lower incidence than nonclinical samples, but this may be, in part, because of the diminished memory function often found in such individuals.

One of the most striking features of the déjà vu incidence is the extreme range across studies. There are probably a number of factors that contribute to this variability. How the question is worded may affect the percentage of positive responses. As suggested earlier (see Chapter 3), a déjà vu question appearing with items related to paranormal or anomalous experiences may receive fewer positive responses. Also, there has been an increase in the acceptability of the déjà vu phenomenon across recent decades (see Chapter 6), making déjà vu incidence related to survey year. In support of such speculation, the median publication year for the 27 outcomes *below* the median incidence rate (67%) is 1972, while the median publication year for the 28 outcomes *above* the median incidence rate is 1982 (two outcomes at the median were excluded). Also, there is a significant positive correlation between publication year and reported incidence, r (55) = .47. $p < .01$.

TABLE 4.2. Lifetime Incidence of Déjà Vu Experience

Nonclinical Sample	% Incidence	N	% Female	Age	Nature of Sample
Irwin (1993)	100	106	77	M = 37; R = 19–55	Students (of mature age) at the University of New England, Australia Mail survey; 63% return
Buck (1970)	98	49	67		College students enrolled in Introductory Psychology
Brown et al. (1994)	97	353	60	M = 20; R = 12–58	Students at Southern Methodist University
Buck & Geers (1967)	96	91	46		Students at Dowling College
Neppe (1979)	96	84	100	R = 40–70; 90% > 40	White South African, Christian, university graduates; members of a cultural society
Leeds (1944)	92	100	38	Most under 30	Coworkers (warehouse) and friends
Ardila et al. (1993)	91	2500	50	M = 24; R = 17–50	Students in different universities in Bogotá, Columbia
McClenon (1994)	89	214			Students at University of Maryland (in 1987); mail survey, 42% response
Palmer (1979)	88	268	40	99% < 31 yrs.	Students at University of Virginia; mail survey (in 1974); 89% response
McClenon (1994)	88	132			Students at Taukuba University, Japan (in 1989); mail survey, 33% response
Roberts et al. (1997)	87	484			Students at University of Iowa
McClenon (1994)	86	532	67		Students at University of North Carolina, Greensboro (in 1990); in-class survey, 98% response
Kohr (1980)	83	406	68	Mdn. = 45	Mail survey to 570 members of Association for Research and Enlightenment (a psi society) who volunteered to participate in research; 71% response; used Palmer's (1979) survey
Green (1966)	82	112	13		Students at Southhampton University, 97% response
Myers & Grant (1972)	80	66	55		Students at University of Newcastle; 2-tier sample: mail questionnaire, followed by interview invitation to those with depersonalization experience (76 of 891 respondents); 87% showed up

Citation	%	N	% female	Age	Sample description
McClenon (1994)	80	391			Students at East City State University (North Carolina), predominantly African American in-class sample, 99% response (in 1988)
Adachi et al. (2001)	77	73	49	M = 35	Citizens of Japan
Adachi et al. (2003)	76	386	51	M = 38	Citizens of Japan
Rhine (cited in White, 1973)	75				Estimate from repeated observation at talks
McKellar & Simpson (1954)	71	110	55		Students at Aberdeen University
McKellar (1957a)	69	182	59		Students at Aberdeen University
Neppe (1983e, pilot)	69	16			10 paranormal non-experients (50% incidence) + 6 paranormal experients (100% incidence)
Palmer (1979)	68	354	60	49% < 41 yrs.	Townspeople of Charlottesville, Virginia; mail survey; 51% response
Neppe (1981)	68	28			
NORC (1984)	67	1439		18+	General Social Survey (GSS); random sample from USA; 79% response
NORC (1989)	67	1456		18+	General Social Survey (GSS); random sample from USA; 77% response
NORC (1989)	64	990		18+	General Social Survey (GSS); random sample from USA; 78% response
McClenon (1988)	64	314			Students from 3 colleges in Xi'an People's Republic of China (in 1986); Northwestern Polytechnic University; Xi'an University of Medical Science, Shaanxi Finance and Economic Institute; mail survey (in 1986) 40% response
Heymans (1906)	63	88			College students
Harper (1969)	63	91	74	R = 18–65	Employees of a local authority health department; 61 normal or mild neurotic; 27 marked neurotic; 3 abnormal personality
Silberman et al. (1985)	63	30	47	M = 43	Out-patients in a hypertension clinic, National Heart, Lung and Blood Institute
McCready & Greeley (1976)	59	1467			NORC data from 1973
McClenon (1994)	59	339	20	M = 55	Scientists in American Association for the Advancement of Science (in 1981)
Gallup & Newport (1991)	57	1236		18+	Random sample by telephone interview
Ross & Joshi (1992)	55	502	63	M = 45	Random sample from city of Winnipeg

TABLE 4.2 Lifetime Incidence of Déjà Vu Experience (Continued)

Nonclinical Sample	% Incidence	N	% Female	Age	Nature of Sample
Myers & Grant (1972)	51	109	52		Students at University of Newcastle; two-tier sample: mail survey, followed by interview of those with no depersonalization experience (815 of 891 mail respondents); 130 invited for interview (84% showed up)
Osborn (1884)	50*				"Distributed at Princeton and elsewhere" (p. 478)
Bernard-Leroy (1898)†	50*	500 (app.)			Combination of mail survey and individual interview
Gaynard (1992)	48	340	48		Students at Wyke College; 85% response; combind event- and place-based déjà vu
Heymans (1904)	40	42	22		College students
Lalande (1893; in Ellis, 1911)	30	100		R = 20–25	
Clinical Individuals					
Brauer et al. (1970)	92	84			Schizophrenics (30%); personality disorder (31%); neurotic depression (15%); psychotic depression (13%); manic depressive (4%); other (7%)
Neppe (1983e)	86	14			Temporal lobe epileptics
Silberman et al. (1985)	73	44	61	M = 44	Major depressive disorder; 34 biplar; 10 unipolar
Neppe (1983e)	71	14			Patients with temporal lobe disease and non-temporal lobe epileptics
Zuger (1966)	66	58	45	R = 14–50; 43% < 25	Psychotherapy patients of Zuger; 54 psychoneurotics (mostly anxious and obsessive-compulsive-phobic), 4 psychotics, 3 manic-depressive, 1 pseudo-neurotic schizophrenic
Neppe (1983e)	65	20			Schizophrenics
Greyson (1977)	65	20			Psychiatric admits to University of Virginia Hospital: schizophrenics

Silberman et al. (1985)	54	37	45	M = 30	Epileptics with complex partical seizures; mainly out-patients
Greyson (1977)	51	68			Psychiatric admits to University of Virginia Hospital: nonschizophrenic, nonorganic
Richardson & Winokur (1967)	44	301	61	M = 43 (est.)	Psychiatric patients
Richardson & Winokur (1967)	41	161	42	M = 43 (est.)	Neurosurgery patients
Harper & Roth (1962)	40	30	77	M = 34	Phobic anxiety-depersonalization syndrome
van Paesschen et al. (2001)	34	50	68	Mdn. = 31; R = 16–49	Patients with intractable unilateral temporal lobe epilepsy
Champan & Mensh (1951)	33	220	50	M = 43 (est.)	White hospital inpatients
Harper & Roth (1962)	23	30	43	M = 37	Temporal lobe epileptics (déjà vu incidence NOT in aura)
Bernard-Leroy (1898)†	10*	60			Psychiatric patients interviewed at Sâlpetrière

M = age mean; Mdn. = age median; R = age range.
* Déjà vu experience was claimed by "about one-half" of those surveyed.
† Reported in Sno et al., 1992c (p. 156).

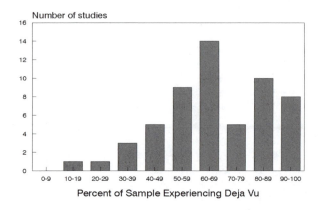

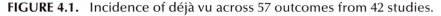

FIGURE 4.1. Incidence of déjà vu across 57 outcomes from 42 studies.

Still another important factor determining incidence rate is the mean age of the sample. One of the most pervasive findings in the déjà vu literature is the decline in the lifetime incidence with increasing age (see Chapter 6). For the 15 studies in Table 4.2 that provide mean age, there is a substantial but nonsignificant negative correlation between mean age of the sample and déjà vu incidence, r (13) = –0.44. Also, assuming college student samples are younger than the average adult samples, the 20 outcomes with college students have a higher mean (78%, versus 67% overall) and median (87%, versus 67% overall) incidence. Thus, déjà vu incidence appears to be directly related to the year the study was published and inversely related to the age of the sample. Both of these points are addressed in more detail in Chapter 6.

Frequency and Recency of Déjà Vu

The following section addresses both the frequency with which individuals experience déjà vu, and the recency of such experience. Because estimates of lifetime déjà vu incidence vary considerably across studies, the percentages in this section are computed *relative* to those individuals who have reported a lifetime déjà vu, also referred to as "experients." To illustrate, if a study found that 80% of respondents had experienced a déjà vu, and that 20% reported experiencing a déjà vu once a month, this yields a monthly rate of 25% (20%/80%) within experients.

Absolute Frequency

The frequency of déjà vu experiences has been measured in three different ways. Both Kohr (1980) and Palmer (1979) asked respondents to indicate the total number of lifetime déjà vu experiences. Kohr (1980) found 7% had one lifetime experience, 7% had two, 19% had three or four, 19% had five or six, 4% had seven to eight, and 44% had nine or more. Palmer (1979) presents an abbreviated summary, indicating that 3% of experients had one lifetime déjà vu experience, while the majority (97%) had two or more. The frequency for Palmer (1979) is somewhat higher than for Kohr (1980), probably because Palmer's sample consisted of members of a paranormal club. To expect that respondents can give a reasonably accurate accounting of the total number of lifetime déjà vu experiences may stretch credibility, but the outcome of both investigations suggest that déjà vu is not a singular, one-time experience. If you have experienced déjà vu, it is *highly* likely that you have had more than one. In fact, nearly half of Kohr's (1980) experients estimated that they had had seven or more lifetime déjà vu experiences.

Relative Frequency

A more general way to assess déjà vu frequency among experients is by relative categories, with most such surveys using one or more of the following categories (in addition to "never"): seldom/rare, occasional, and often/frequent. In the General Social Survey (GSS) done by the NORC (1984, 1988, 1989), most respondents fell in the seldom ("once or twice") (44%) and occasional ("several times") (44%) categories, with only a few claiming frequent ("often") déjà vu (12%). The trend across these three categories was similar in each separate survey year: 39%, 47%, and 15% for 1984; 48%, 42%, and 10% for 1988; 46%, 43%, and 11% for 1989. McCready and Greeley (1976) found that these percentages (respectively) for the 1973 NORC survey were 49%, 41%, and 10%, and these figures are also close to that found by Leeds (1944): 44% seldom, 39% occasional, and 18% frequent. Averaging across all of the above outcomes yields 46% for seldom, 41% for occasional, and 13% for frequent.

Harper (1969) also defined three incidence categories of occasional (70%), moderate (more than once a year) (21%), and frequent (more than once a month) (9%). Frequent déjà vu was also claimed by 16% of respondents in Green (1966) and by 15% in Brauer et al. (1970), and both of these outcomes are within to the 10% to 18% range found above. In general, déjà vu is predominantly a seldom to occasional experience, with about one in eight experients claiming frequent episodes.

Temporal Frequency

Déjà vu frequency also has been measured by temporal evaluation, either with reference to "when was your last déjà vu experience" or "how often

TABLE 4.3. Temporal Frequency of Déjà Vu Experiences ("at least every ...")

	Day	Few Days	Week	Few Weeks	Month	Few Months	6 Months	Year	5 Years
Ardilla et al. (1993)		5	19		63				
Roberts et al. (1990, Study 1)		2	9		36				
Roberts et al. (1990, Study 2)	1	3	11		52				
Brown et al. (1994)	0	5	12	44	56	90		96	
Harper (1969)					9			30	
Chapman & Mensh (1951)					10	12	39	50	62
Neppe (1979)					19		50		
Neppe (1983e) normal							63	84	95
Neppe (1983e) neuro							77	86	86
Neppe (1983e) schizo					20		54	54	85

do you have a déjà vu experience?" For the present analysis, these two questions are considered comparable: if an individual's last déjà vu was within the past week, it is assumed that their incidence of déjà vu is weekly. Temporal evaluations are presented in Table 4.3, with the percentages of experients claiming each frequency cumulated across intervals. For example, Ardila et al. (1993), found 5% of experients claimed a déjà vu experience ("at least") every few days, 14% said they had an experience every week, and 44% stated that déjà vu occurred every month. Thus, the percentage of experients having déjà vu *at least* every week represents the sum of every few days and every week (5% + 14% = 19%), and the month category cumulates days, weeks, and months (5% + 14% + 44% = 63%).

There is a wide range of estimates on the temporal frequency of the déjà vu experience, and much of this difference is probably due to the range of response options provided. To illustrate, Roberts et al. (1990, Study 2) found déjà vu to be much more frequent than Chapman and Mensh (1951), but their response scales barely overlap: Roberts et al.'s options ranged from "more than once a day" (not tabled) to "less than once per month" (also not tabled), whereas Chapman and Mensh's (1951) categories ranged from "once a month" to "once in 10 years" (not tabled). Given these different set-points, it is not surprising that the estimate of the temporal frequency of the déjà vu experience varies considerably, and examining the six to one difference across the eight outcomes in the *once a month* category highlights this possible bias.

The higher monthly incidence in the subgroup of outcomes at the top of Table 4.3 (Ardila et al., 1993; Brown et al., 1994; Roberts et al., 1990) may result from the younger age sample in these investigations. Younger adults experience déjà vu more frequently than older adults (see Chapter 6), and these three investigations sampled either college students (Brown et al., 1994; Roberts et al., 1990) or a younger adult sample (Ardila et al., 1993; mean age = 24 years). Another factor that may partially account for the discrepancy in the incidence between those studies in the top and bottom of Table 4.3 is the cultural increase in the understanding and acceptance of déjà vu experience across decades (see Chapter 6). Outcomes at the top of the table are from the 1990s, while those in the bottom portion of the table were taken in the 1950s through the 1980s.

As an interesting footnote to the measurement of frequency, Gaynard (1992) asked his respondents to provide an open-ended, rather than scale-based, approximation of their total number of personal déjà vu experiences *after* they first admitted to having déjà vu, but

> few respondents were able to recall the number of times ... replying with vague terms such as "several" or "many." Consequently, it was not possible to analyze further the frequency ... (p. 168)

An individual's retrospective memory for a precise number of déjà vu experiences may be problematic, and a relative or approximate estimate may be sufficient. A more likely scenario is that when asked to provide a precise frequency of déjà vu experiences, an individual first makes a rough subjective estimate on an ordinal scale (rare, occasional, frequent) and then translates that into the precise number requested.

☐ Types of Déjà Vu

Some researchers have differentiated between two types of déjà vu experience (Buck, 1970; Buck & Geers, 1967; Gaynard, 1992) and the incidence reported in Table 4.2 is an average of the two. Buck and Geers (1967) inquired about both *auditory* and *visual* déjà vu in their study. They did not describe what they meant by this distinction, but presumably it refers to the eliciting trigger. They found that 96% of respondents claimed to have had visual déjà vu, and 84% admitted to auditory déjà vu. Strangely, they found only a small, but significant, correlation of 0.39 between these dimensions. Buck (1970) also differentiated between visual and auditory déjà vu but only reported the combined incidence. From a different perspective, Gaynard (1992) distinguished between déjà vu for *events* ("the sensation that an *event* had been experienced previously") and *places* ("the sensation that a *place* had been visited previously") and found a slightly higher incidence for event (42%) than place (38%) experiences. Although these two types of déjà vu may seem very similar, there was some differentiation: 31% of respondents claimed *both* event and place déjà vu, 11% claimed to have experienced *only event* déjà vu and 6% *only place* déjà vu. Zangwill (1945) differentiated reactive déjà vu (external: precipitated by the environmental stimuli) and endogenous déjà vu (internal: elicited by brain mechanisms), while Chari (1962, 1964) distinguished between normal and pathological déjà vu. However, neither Zangwill (1945) nor Chari (1962, 1964) reports differential incidences for the separate types of déjà vu.

☐ Chronic Déjà Vu

While most individuals have occasional déjà vu, some individuals report chronic or continual experiences. Pick (1903) reported a patient who suffered from chronic déjà vu for several years, and Coriat (1904) notes several instances of continual déjà vu in individuals with alcoholism, general paralysis, and senile dementia. Kinnier Wilson (1929) describes one case of general paralysis with frequent déjà vu, plus an epileptic with chronic déjà vu not confined to the preseizure aura. As discussed earlier, Leeds (1944) kept an in-depth record of his 144 déjà vu experiences over a 12-month period. These examples are clearly anomalous, but a careful examination of such unique cases could provide insight into the normal mechanisms underlying déjà vu.

☐ Summary

Subjective evaluations have consistently framed déjà vu as a very common and universal experience. Objective evaluations, however, suggest that the incidence of déjà vu is not universal. Estimates vary widely across studies, but it appears that about two thirds of respondents have had a déjà vu experience at some point in their lives. Factors that probably influence this variability in estimate are the age composition of the sample (younger samples yield higher incidence), the survey year (more recent samples yield higher incidence), and the type of questions accompanying the déjà vu item. If a person has had a déjà vu experience, it is highly likely that they have had more than one. Experients are much more likely to claim seldom or occasional déjà vu, with only a few confessing to frequent déjà vu. Although the modal response for temporal estimates vary from "at least" every month to every six months across studies, the precision of these retrospective evaluations is suspect, given the relative rarity of the experience and the possible bias caused by the different temporal scales used across such evaluations. Some have reported separate incidences of different types of déjà vu experiences, and a few instances of chronic déjà vu can be found in the literature.

CHAPTER

Nature of the Déjà Vu Experience

Surprisingly, relatively few investigations address the nature of the déjà vu experience. Some that do examine the various dimensions of the illusion fail to report summary statistics (Sno et al., 1994) or base their findings on very small samples (Neppe, 1983e). To address this empirical lacuna, we (Brown et al., 1994) constructed a survey on various subjective and objective dimensions of the déjà vu experience. This survey was given to 353 individuals in sections of Introductory Psychology, and the summary is presented in this chapter. As one would expect, the majority of respondents (80%) are in the 18 to 22 age range (mean = 20 years; median = 19 years).

Supplementing this are two additional surveys. The "Web Survey," designed by Otto MacLin at the University of Northern Iowa, was an extension of Brown et al. (1994) and designed to gather responses from a broader sample beyond the academic environment. Over 2 years, 57 individuals responded to the questionnaire, and the age composition is nearly identical to the university-based sample (mean = 22 years; median = 21 years). The second supplementary survey was open-ended, with participants instructed simply to provide a detailed description of one of their déjà vu experiences. Responses from 343 students in Introductory Psychology classes at Southern Methodist University and the University of Texas at El Paso (with the assistance of Dr. Kim MacLin, now at the University of Northern Iowa) were coded by Sandy Zoccoli, Ann Wassel, Julia Burke, and Matt Leahy (at SMU). These open-ended survey results are referred to as the "Texas Survey."

☐ Specific Triggers

Brown et al. (1994) queried respondents on the components believed to trigger a déjà vu, using two different approaches. First, participants were asked to indicate whether their *typical* déjà vu experience contained each of six different elements, listed in the left-most column of Table 5.1, using a three-point scale: "always," "sometimes," or "never." These responses are summarized in the second through fourth columns of Table 5.1. Participants also were asked to provide a short written description of their most recent déjà vu experience. These descriptions were coded for the same six elements, and these data appear in the fifth column of Table 5.1. Note that this column total is greater than 100% because each protocol could contain multiple elements.

These six dimensions show a remarkable consistency across surveys with respect to their relative importance in eliciting a déjà vu experience. Clearly, the physical setting is seen as the most likely eliciting stimulus in a déjà vu experience, for both typical and most-recent assessments. In more than half of the "typical" déjà vu experiences, the physical setting is a necessary ("always") element. In addition, the physical setting was a component in nearly half of the most-recent déjà vu experiences, and topped both the Web and Texas Surveys. Others' spoken words is the second most central element in déjà vu experiences: 83% of the typical déjà vu experiences tie in with others' words either always or sometimes and 31% of actual descriptions contain others' words as a component. Furthermore, others' spoken words is also the second-ranking response (percentage wise) in both the Web and Texas Surveys. One's own spoken words ranks third across all surveys, and actions (one's own and others) turn out to be somewhat less important than words. Finally, objects are least important in the typical déjà vu, and are rarely mentioned in the most-recent descriptions. Several other elements appeared in the Texas

TABLE 5.1. Stimulus Dimensions Which Appear to Trigger a Déjà Vu Experience

	Brown et al. (1994)				Web Survey	Texas Survey
	Typical			Most Recent		
	Always	Sometimes	Never			
Physical setting	54%	43%	3%	46%	88%	52%
Other's spoken words	10	73	17	31	56	31
Own spoken words	6	66	28	19	54	21
Other's actions	17	64	19	16	51	10
Own actions	15	62	23	18	47	17
Objects	18	57	26	5	39	9

Survey but did not comprise a significant proportion of responses (smell = 4%; taste = 3%; music = 2%; sounds = 2%).

Neppe (1983e) also surveyed participants about the dimensions that trigger a déjà vu. As with Brown et al. (1994), he found that *places* were most frequently noted (55%). The other eliciting dimensions, included meeting (44%), reading (39%), situations (36%), hearing (33%), doing (27%), thinking (23%), and passive experiencing (25%). Definitions of the déjà vu experience presented earlier, in Chapter 2 (Table 2.2), also reflect the importance of *place* in eliciting a déjà vu, with over a third (19 of 53) making reference to a physical location. Mention of words (conversation), sights, objects, or actions also occurs in some definitions but to a much lesser extent. Harper (1969) suggests that his participants reported more déjà vu "... when visiting places or when in conversations ..." (p. 70) but could not be more specific about circumstances likely to trigger a déjà vu experience.

One odd footnote concerning the déjà vu experience is the number of incidents involving castles, which occur when either confronting the exterior or entering a room in the interior:

> *Dunottar Castle* (McKellar, 1957)
> *Pevensey Castle* (Carpenter, 1874; Ellis, 1897, 1911)
> *Sussex Castle* (Gregory, 1923)
> *Stanton Harcourt* (Hawthorne, 1863)
> *Albrechtsburg at Meissen* (Smith, 1913)

Kinnier Wilson (1929) also relays a story about a friend's déjà vu experience at a castle, without mentioning a specific physical structure. Perhaps the distinctiveness of the castle, or the excitement of confronting such a grand edifice, heightens one's sense of awareness concerning any incongruous sense of familiarity. Given the importance of physical setting in triggering déjà vu experiences, perhaps a castle presents a uniquely imposing, all-encompassing, and emotionally provocative setting ideal for eliciting a déjà vu.

☐ Stress, Fatigue, Anxiety, and Illness

An unusually large number of anecdotal reports link the occurrence of déjà vu with periods of acute physical or psychological distress (Allin, 1896a; Anjel, 1878; Arlow, 1959; Bergson, 1908, cited in Neppe, 1983e; Burnham, 1889; Conklin, 1935; de Nayer, 1979; Dugas, 1894, 1908; Ellis, 1897, 1911; Freud, 1933, 1959; Gordon, 1921; Groh, 1968; Harriman, 1947; Heymans, 1904, 1906; Kraepelin, 1887, cited in Parish, 1897; Krijgers Janzen, 1958; Kuiper, 1973; Leeds, 1944; MacCurdy, 1925; Marková & Berrios,

2000; Murphy, 1951; Oberndorf, 1941; Osborn, 1884; Poetzl, 1926; Quaerens, 1870; Richardson & Winokur, 1967, 1968; Schilder, 1936; Schneck, 1962; Scott, 1890; Siomopoulos, 1972; Smith, 1913; Sno et al., 1992a; Titchener, 1924; West, 1948; Wigan, 1844; Wolf, 1940; Yager, 1989). The following are typical of such evaluations:

"... this delusion occurs only when the mind has been exhausted by excitement, or is from indigestion, or any other cause, languid ..." Allin (1896a, p. 252)

"it occurs most frequently after periods of emotional stress, or in the state of extreme mental fatigue ..." Titchener (1924, p. 187)

In his early studies, Heymans (1904, 1906) found that most déjà vu episodes occurred following "... unpleasant or confusing mental or physical exertion ..." (cf. Sno & Draaisma, 1993) and fatigue was associated with 82% of the déjà vu experiences in the second study (Heymans, 1906). Wigan (1844) provides an unusually detailed account of the contribution of sleep deprivation, hunger, grief, and physical exhaustion in a personal déjà vu experience while standing on the street, waiting to view the funeral procession for a friend.

Leeds' (1944) extensive analysis of his repeated déjà vu experiences revealed that frequency of déjà vu was directly related to his current level of stress. At one point, his monthly average for déjà vu experiences dropped by more than half (from about 12 to 5), and he attributed this to positive changes at work (more interesting) and school (fewer courses), noting that the reduction in déjà vu experiences correlated with being "... much more alert and clear-minded" (p. 29). Interestingly, Linn (1954) states that déjà vu is frequently experienced by soldiers going into battle. Marching through new terrain and into foreign towns under the heightened stress of anticipating combat may present a unique mix of high stress plus novel settings ideal for eliciting déjà vu experiences. This also may relate to the higher incidence of déjà vu in travelers (see the later section in this chapter), because a trip often involves moderate stress. Given the relationship between fatigue and déjà vu, it is not surprising that déjà vu was one of many symptoms in a case of severe self-imposed sleep deprivation experienced by a radio disc jockey (Brauchi & West, 1959).

☐ Context of the Déjà Vu Experience

Aside from what apparently triggers the déjà vu experience is the issue of where one is, and what one is doing, when the déjà vu occurs. To address this question, we coded the déjà vu experiences reported in the Texas Survey by three categories: physical setting, activity, and social setting.

TABLE 5.2. Physical Setting Within
Which the Déjà Vu Experience Occurred

	% of Response
Domicile	36
Own	22
Relative	4
Other	10
Public building	36
School	16
Restaurant	6
Office	5
Store	4
Theater	1
Motel	1
Other	4
Vehicle	16
Own	5
Other's	11
Outdoors	12

Physical Setting

Nearly two thirds of the responses in the Texas Survey (63%) provided information on the physical setting within which the déjà vu experience occurred, and these data are presented in Table 5.2, relative to those who provided such information.

Over three quarters of déjà vu experiences occur inside a building, and these are evenly split between public and private. Many fewer experiences happen outdoors or in a vehicle, and these together only account for just over a quarter of the events. Déjà vu experiences should be more likely in those locations where individuals spend most of their time (personal residence, school, vehicle), and this is confirmed by the survey results.

Activity

The general class of activity during the déjà vu experience was roughly divided into work, recreation, and commuting. Eating and shopping were classified as "maintenance" behaviors because each of these could involve activities related to either work or recreation. Note that some of this information is related to, and can be inferred from, the previous information on physical setting. That is, if you are in a vehicle, you are

TABLE 5.3. Activity Engaged in During the Déjà Vu Experience

	% of Response
Recreation	51
General	45
Watching TV/movie	6
Commuting	34
Driving	17
Walking	16
Unspecified	1
Work	10
General	7
School	3
Maintenance	6
Eating	4
Shopping	2

probably commuting. Nearly half of the responses contained this information (45%), and the percentage (out of this total) in each category is presented in Table 5.3.

These data suggest that most déjà vu experiences occur during recreational occasions, while one is relaxing or unwinding. This may be because of the greater variety of visual and social stimulation during recreation, compared to a relatively more routine and static work environment. Déjà vu experiences also seem to be strongly related to commuting, which may again relate to a greater variety of visual (and social) stimuli during these physical transitions.

Social Setting

We also coded the Texas Survey protocols for the social context within which the déjà vu experience occurred. Well over half of the written descriptions (59%) included such information, and these data appear in Table 5.4. As before, percentages are relative to those who provided this information.

These data suggest several clear trends. First, a déjà vu rarely happens when one is alone. Second, there is a strong tendency for the déjà vu experience to occur in the company of friends, rather than with relatives or undefined others. The first finding is remarkable because most individuals spend a reasonable amount of time by themselves. Thus, there may be something special about a social mix that facilitates the occurrence of déjà vu. Or alternatively, a déjà vu in the presence of others may elicit discussion of the experience, thus making it more memorable.

TABLE 5.4. Social Setting During the
Déjà Vu Experience (in Percentages)

	Relationship			
	Friend	**Relative**	**Other**	**Total**
Self only				6
One other	24	11	9	44
Two other	4	8	2	14
Group	18	8	9	35
Total	46	27	20	

About half of déjà vu experiences happen in the company of friends, but the significance of this finding is ambiguous without some additional information on how young people distribute their social time across various social configurations.

☐ Duration

Brown et al. (1994) asked respondents how long the typical déjà vu experience lasts. Most thought it lasted a few seconds (57%), while some believed it lasted half a minute (23%) to a minute (14%), and a few estimated longer than a minute (7%). Similarly, in the Web Survey, a third (34%) declared that the déjà vu experience lasted 5 seconds or less, 30% claimed between 7 and 30 seconds, with the remaining (36%) identifying the déjà vu as lasting a minute or longer. In the open-ended Texas Survey, only 13% of the protocols included a temporal duration, and three-quarters of these made reference to several seconds.

These temporal duration estimates may be especially sensitive to distortion with the passage of time. However, the Web Survey provides a unique opportunity to evaluate this possibility. Nearly half (26) of the Web Survey responses were submitted within 3 days of the respondent's actual déjà vu experience. Within this subset, the percentages were similar to the larger sample, with 29% claiming the déjà vu experience lasted 5 seconds or less, 41% estimating between 7 and 30 seconds, and 39% suggesting a minute or longer. Thus, duration does not appear to become substantially distorted with the passage of time, although there is some tendency to shorten the estimate as time since the déjà vu increases.

Both Reed (1979) and Titchener (1924) informally observe that the déjà vu experience lasts only a few seconds, and Krijgers Janzen (1958) suggests that the déjà vu experience may last "… a single moment, but generally lasts a few minutes …" (p. 106). Burnham (1889) notes that "in most cases the illusion appears suddenly and vanishes suddenly" (p.

445), and Harper's (1969) respondents claimed that most déjà vu experiences were "… of sudden onset and of brief duration …" (p. 70). Finally, Probst and Jansen (1994) found that across a series of surveys, the duration of déjà vu was typically less than a minute. The above evaluations collectively support the survey findings that the experience is very brief. A precise estimate may be difficult to obtain for two reasons. First, one's subjective evaluation of the duration of surprising or unpredictable events tends to exceed the actual duration (Boltz, 1998). Second, one's mental ruminations of the experience may extend the time frame of the illusion, given that there is no clear objective or subjective demarcation that the déjà vu is over.

☐ Time of Occurrence

There are several survey and case study reports that contain information concerning when the déjà vu experience occurs, and this information is evaluated below separately by time of day, day of the week, and month of the year.

Time of Day

Is a déjà vu experience more likely to occur at a certain time of day? When confronted with this question, Brown et al. (1994) found that about two thirds of respondents did not remember (68%). Of those who did, most said afternoon (64%), fewer said evening (30%), and morning was only rarely identified (6%). Because Brown et al.'s sample was college students, morning was probably rare because many students are not awake by then. On the Web Survey, more people designated a time of day (87%) in an open-ended question, probably because many had experienced their déjà vu relatively recently. While P.M. predominated over A.M. by about two to one, of those who designated a specific time the responses were evenly distributed across morning (32%), afternoon (33%), and evening (35%). Finally, in the Texas Survey, of the 9% of responses making reference to clock time, evening predominated (4%) over afternoon (3%) and morning (2%).

In his personal prospective evaluation, Leeds (1944) found that déjà vu experiences increase systematically across the day. He classified déjà vu experiences by hours *prior to lunch* and hours *prior to dinner*. Assuming that Leeds had lunch at 12:00 noon and dinner at 6:00 P.M., he found the following distribution for his 79 experiences: 11% in early morning,

27% in late morning, 23% in early afternoon, and 39% in late afternoon. Leeds (1944) classified déjà vu experiences by hours prior to a meal to evaluate the relationship between *fatigue* and déjà vu. He found a systematic increase in déjà vu experiences with each hour approaching a meal (collapsed over prelunch and predinner times): 11% to 15% to 15% to 27% to 32%. Leeds also claimed that the number of experiences rose again after dinner to a peak prior to bedtime, but provided no data on this. In another prospective investigation, Heymans (1904) noted that most déjà vu experiences occurred in the evening. Summarizing the data across the survey studies, plus Leeds (1944) and Heymans (1904), it appears that déjà vu experiences happen more frequently in the afternoon to evening periods.

Day of the Week

Information on the particular day when déjà vu experiences occur comes from three different sources, and all suggest a reliable difference in déjà vu frequency as a function of time of the week. Examining data from the Web Survey, the Texas Survey, and 26 in-depth personal déjà vu experiences reported by Leeds (1944), déjà vu experiences tend to occur more often during the later part of the week, Thursday through Saturday, compared to the early part of the week, Sunday through Wednesday. Combining these three sources yields the following percentages by day: Sunday = 5%, Monday = 11%, Tuesday = 13%, Wednesday = 11%, Thursday = 18%, Friday = 22%, and Saturday = 20%. Thus, 60% of déjà vu experiences (20% per day) occur Thursday through Saturday, while the rate is half that (10% per day) on Sunday through Wednesday. This early versus late week trend is reliable across each of the three individual studies (respectively): Web Survey = 13% versus 17%; Texas Survey = 7% versus 24%; Leeds (1944) = 10% versus 21%. This shift upward at the end of the week may be because of an increase in (a) fatigue or excitement as the weekend approaches, or (b) periods when one is more likely to engage in leisure activities and experience new situations.

Month of the Year

Information on the time of year when déjà vu experiences happen comes from the Web and Texas Surveys. In the Web Survey, respondents were asked to select the month of the year when they believed that the déjà vu occurred, and most respondents (84%) were able to provide this information. With 48 responses, the data were spread across all 12 months with no obvious pattern. Grouped by season, more occurred during Fall (23%) and Winter (38%) than in the Spring (21%) and Summer (19%). With the Texas Survey, specific reference was made to season by 6% of respondents, and to month by 8% of respondents. Again grouping these 46 responses by season yielded the following distribution: Fall (32%), Winter (13%), Spring (0%), and Summer (55%). Finally, Leeds (1944) logged his personal déjà vu experiences by month. Keeping in mind that this is an idiosyncratic record from an individual with frequent déjà vu experiences, the monthly average across the four seasons are as follows: Fall = 11.5, Winter = 8.3, Spring = 14.2, and Summer = 11.5. In short, no strong and consistent seasonal trend emerges across these data sets, although both surveys suggest that a déjà vu experience may be less common during Spring.

☐ Emotional Reaction

Some believe that the affective component of a déjà vu experience is its most distinctive element (MacCurdy, 1925; Stern, 1938). Reed (1979) speculates that "… what constitutes the experience of déjà vu is this perplexity, resulting from the discrepancy between objective knowledge and subjective response in a situation of heightened affect" (p. 25), and Rapaport (1959) argues that the way the person interprets the emotion creates the déjà vu response. Sno and Linszen (1991) suggest that affect is central to the experience, in that déjà vu may be a disturbance of apperception—defined as "… perception modified by one's emotions and thoughts" (p. 1419). As indicated earlier in Chapter 4, the affective (feeling) predominates over the cognitive (conviction, impression, appearance, sensation, awareness) in published descriptions of the déjà vu state.

Brown et al. (1994) asked an open-ended question about one's emotional reaction to a typical déjà vu experience and the predominant response was surprise (54%), followed by anxiety, curiosity, and confusion (12% each), and then awe (6%), fear (4%), weirdness (4%), and shock (3%). A few respondents found no emotion (8%) associated with déjà vu. In a closed-ended question on the Web Survey, employing some of these same emotional reactions discovered by Brown et al. (1994), yielded a somewhat different pattern. Curiosity (54%) predominated, followed by confusion (39%), surprise (42%), excitement (39%), anxiety (25%), frustration (21%), fear (25%), shock (19%), awe (23%), and anticipation (12%) (respondents could use more than one term).

The Texas Survey contained a much broader array of feeling responses, with approximately half of the free-form descriptions includ-

TABLE 5.5. Terms Describing the Subjective Déjà Vu Experience (Texas Survey) (Number of Responses in Parenthesis)

Disquieting

eerie (65), strange (17), confused (15), odd (11), scary (7), unnerving (5), awkward (4), overwhelming, shock, weird (3), sickly, bad feeling, frustrated, bizarre, taken aback, crazy, creepy, chill (2), discomfort, anxiety, tense, hysterical, overpowering, dread, lack of control, stunned, unusual, upset (1)

Unreal

slow motion (5), tripping, through another's eyes (3), out of place (2), in another life, disoriented, fantasy, out of body, distorted reality, acting in a movie (1)

Pleasant

cool (4), comfortable, at ease, nice, happiness (1)

Exciting

mind boggling, unbelievable (2), amazement, surprise, tingling, like a rush (1)

Other

funny (4), awareness, flashback, cloudiness, vague, falling, haze (1)

ing such information. The predominant reactions were eerie (19%) followed by strange (5%), confused (4%), odd (3%), and scary (2%). The numerous descriptive terms roughly fell into five different categories shown in Table 5.5, with the various responses (and associated frequencies) listed after them.

Both surveys suggest that respondents' emotional response to déjà vu is moderate, with no consistent evidence on whether a positive or negative response predominates. In fact, some of the "feeling" responses are more cognitive than emotional (curiosity, confusion, awe, weirdness). Some researchers argue that a pleasurable reaction predominates in a déjà vu experience (Krijgers Janzen, 1958; Pickford, 1940), whereas others suggest that negative emotion is more characteristic (Arlow, 1959; Coleman, 1944; MacCurdy, 1925). Some of the negative reactions attributed to the déjà vu experience by various writers are listed in Table 5.6.

These negative emotions do not appear to be directly attributed to the déjà vu experience, but rather to its aftermath. Burnham (1889) suggests that anxiety is caused by "… the vain attempt to comprehend clearly the obscure ideas floating before the mind" (p. 445), while Grasset (1904) suggests that "anguish" results from a struggle to match the present familiarity with the missing past memory, and likens the emotion to that experienced in dreams of a dead friend who appears to be alive! Ellis (1911) proposes that the intensity of the emotional disturbance associated with a déjà vu is directly related to the temperament of the particular individual. In a broader perspective, much of the diversity in how the déjà vu experience is described, defined, and evaluated (as detailed in

TABLE 5.6. Negative Emotional Reactions Informally Associated with Déjà Vu

anguish (Grasset, 1904)
anxiety (Burnham, 1889; Lalande, 1893; Neppe, 1983e; Sanders, 1874; Sno & Linszen, 1990; Stern, 1938)
apprehension (Lalande, 1893)
disagreeableness (Oberndorf, 1941)
discomfort (Osborn, 1884)
disquieting affect (Oberndorf, 1941)
failure (Coleman, 1944)
fear (Krijgers Jenzen, 1929)
pain (Bernard-Leroy, 1898; Grassett, 1904; MacCurdy, 1925, 1928)
perplexity (Sno & Linszen, 1990)
tension (Sno & Linszen, 1990)
uncertainty (Coleman, 1944)
uneasiness (Osborn, 1884; Sanders, 1874; Silbermann, 1963; Stern, 1938)
unpleasantness (MacCurdy, 1925; Pickford, 1942b)

Table 2.2), may be more a function of one's reaction to the experience, rather than to the illusion itself.

☐ Physical Response

Brown et al. (1994) queried respondents about any physical response associated with the déjà vu experience and discovered that the modal response was "none" (40%). "Stop" was the most common reaction (24%), followed by tense (13%), aroused (10%), weird (5%), alerting (3%), and lightheaded and relaxed (2% each). Similar to Brown et al. (1994), the Web Survey also found that many claimed to have no physical response (36%) and those who did volunteered that the déjà vu experience made them relaxed (26%), faint (21%), and tense (19%). In general, it appears that a distinctive or memorable physical response is not associated with déjà vu, and many simply "stop" what they are doing because of the surprise. Respondents may have difficulty with this question because the mental dynamics are so dominant that individuals simply fail to notice a physical reaction.

☐ Subjective Sense of Time and Space

Informal observations in the déjà vu literature suggest that one's subjective sense of time is altered during déjà vu. For example, Krijgers Janzen (1958) notes that "sometimes the event seems to take place at extraordinary speed, while at other times it is precisely as if time stood still" (p. 171). In the Brown et al. (1994) survey, most said that their sense of time was "slowed down" (61%) during a déjà vu, although a few indicated that it "speeded up" (8%), and many claimed that time was unaffected (30%). Similarly, in the Web Survey more said that time slowed down (33%) than speeded up (18%), but about half (49%) said that the time sense was unaffected during déjà vu. Thus, an alteration in the time sense is by no means universal, but when it occurs a slowing is more likely.

Because the physical setting appears to be a central component of the déjà vu experience, Brown et al. (1994) also asked respondents about their subjective sense of space during a déjà vu. Half of the respondents (50%) claimed that space was unaffected during a déjà vu, while a third (33%) said that space was "compressed" and a few (17%) claimed that space was "expanded." Clearly, an alteration of space is not an important or noteworthy aspect of the déjà vu experience.

☐ Time Since Original Experience

When a déjà vu occurs, there is the implication that this particular experience seems to have happened before. So it seems logical to ask respondents how long ago the "original" experience appears to have occurred. Brown et al. (1994) presented four choices which appear in Table 5.7, plus the option of "can't tell." Out of the 93% of the respondents who could tell, the adjusted percentages are presented in the table.

Two aspects of these data are noteworthy. First, *most* respondents considered the question germane and answerable, with only 7% abstaining. Second, there is a nearly uniform distribution of responses across all time period choices. The Texas Survey yielded a remarkably similar outcome from open-ended responses. Participants included information regarding how long ago the déjà vu experience happened in 42% of their protocols, and the distribution of these time estimates also appear in Table 5.7, relative to those who provided such information. Again, there was a uniform distribution across the four temporal categories. This uni-

TABLE 5.7. Estimate of When Prior Repeated "Experience" Occurred

	Brown et al. (1994)	Texas Survey
Day(s) ago	27%	21%
Week(s) ago	24	27
Month(s) ago	28	22
Year(s) ago	23	29

formity in both surveys could be interpreted to mean either that (a) there is a wide diversity (and uniformity) across temporal frameworks, or (b) that the respondents really can't tell and are simply distributing their responses randomly across categories. Given that the "prior" experience did not supposedly happen, this assessment may be too abstract, convoluted, or speculative for most individuals. But what is important is that almost everyone understood the general concept and was willing to provide an estimate.

☐ Literary Descriptions

Literature can often provide unique insights into the subjective dimension of psychological experiences, as viewed through the eyes of gifted and insightful writers. Numerous descriptions of déjà vu experiences can be found in fiction and poetry written over the past several centuries (Spatt, 2002), as one might expect given the high incidence reported in the general public. Although they will not be analyzed here, the interested reader is directed to several extensive summaries (Crichton-Browne, 1895; Sno et al., 1992a; White, 1973). For example, Sno et al. (1992a) provide 24 literary references to the déjà vu experience, and discuss the variety of possible etiologies represented in the descriptions, including seizure, ego defense, reincarnation, dreams, implicit memory, telepathy, and drugs. Such descriptions do not represent direct empirical evidence on the illusion, but most authors probably draw from their personal experiences (White, 1973). Farina and Verrienti (1996) also point out that reference is made to déjà vu in the works of Camus, D'Annunzio, Simeon, Bunuel, and Schnitzler, but do not provide specific citations. Kohn (1983) also notes that a number of public figures have struggled with déjà vu, including General George S. Patton, William Hone, Lord Lindsay, and John Buchan.

☐ Summary

The déjà vu experience appears to be elicited primarily by physical settings, although spoken words (own and others) also seem to be a trigger on a substantial proportion of occasions. The experience is most likely to occur indoors (home; building) while one is engaged in recreational activities and in the company of others (mainly friends). The déjà vu apparently lasts only a few seconds, and is more likely in the afternoon/evening and during the later part of the week (Thursday through Satur-

day). The emotions elicited by déjà vu tend to be neutral or slightly negative (surprise, awe), and negative affective responses may result from the
cognitive distress associated with the déjà vu. While respondents have
volunteered reactions concerning changes in their physical state, as well
as time and space, these reactions are probably overshadowed by the
cognitive response. Individual's estimates on how long ago the prior illusory experience seems to have occurred are distributed evenly across
days, weeks, months, and years. More research is needed on the physical
and psychological dimensions of the déjà vu experience, and future questionnaires (both prospective and retrospective) should include a more
detailed query on these topics.

Physical and Psychological Variables Related to Déjà Vu

Much of the research on déjà vu has been aimed at linking the experience to various forms of pathology, and this literature will be covered in Chapters 7 and 8. However, survey research also has sought to discover whether there is any systematic association between déjà vu and various physical and psychological dimensions characteristic of normal individuals.

☐ Age

One of the most pervasive findings in the déjà vu literature is that the incidence *decreases* with age (Adachi, Adachi, Kimura, Akanuma, & Kato, 2001; Adachi et al., 2003; Bernhard-Leroy, 1898; Brauer et al., 1970; Burnham, 1889; Chapman & Mensh, 1951; Dixon, 1963; Dugas, 1894; Ellis, 1911; Fox, 1992; Gallup & Newport, 1991; Gaynard, 1992; Harper, 1969; Irwin, 1996; Kohr, 1980; Kraepelin, 1887, cited in Parish, 1897; Lalande, 1893; Levin, 1993; MacCurdy, 1925; McCready & Greeley, 1976; Oberndorf, 1941; Palmer, 1979; Reed, 1979; Richardson & Winokur, 1967, 1968; Sander, 1874; Sno et al., 1994; Stanford, 1982, 1983; Zuger, 1966) (but see Neppe, 1983d, 1983e, for an exception).

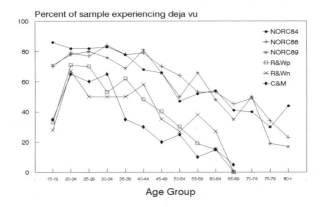

Percent of sample experiencing deja vu

Age Group

FIGURE 6.1. Lifetime déjà vu incidence in 5-year age groups.

Lifetime Incidence Changes with Age

Many of the above evaluations are based on personal observations, but there are several convincing empirical demonstrations of this trend. Three investigations have extensively evaluated changes in lifetime déjà vu experience across a broad age range. Chapman and Mensh (1951) assessed déjà vu incidence in 11 different 5-year age spans (from 15 to 19 years through 65 to 69 years). As shown in Figure 6.1, Chapman and Mensh (C&M) discovered a systematic decline in the lifetime incidence of the déjà vu with increasing age, from the early 20s through the late 60s. The only anomaly in this trend is the lower rate found with teenagers. Richardson and Winocur (1967) modeled their research after Chapman and Mensh, and queried patients admitted to a hospital for neurosurgery (R&Wn) and psychiatric (R&Wp) treatment. The age trend in both of their groups is similar to that found by Chapman and Mensh (see Figure 6.1). There was again a systematic decline in déjà vu lifetime incidence across the adult age span from the 20s through the 60s, with the exception of a lower incidence for teenagers.

The third extensive evaluation of age-related data comes from the NORC, which collects questionnaire data from large samples for the General Social Survey. The 1984, 1988, and 1989 surveys included a question on the incidence of déjà vu, and data from these surveys are available on the Web at http://www.icpsr.umich.edu:8080/GSS/homepage.htm. The results from the large sample of respondents for each year (1984 = 1,435; 1988 = 1,452; 1989 = 989) spanning ages 18 to 89 is presented in Figure 6.1 (NORC84, NORC88, NORC89) and the data pattern is remarkably reliable across the three years. The NORC incidence stays steady at around 75% to 80% from the teens to early 40s but declines systematically from there. The dramatically lower incidence among teenagers in Chapman and Mensh (1951) and Richardson and Winocur (1967) was not apparent with the NORC data, but the NORC data plotted in the 15 to 19 category include only 18-year-olds (12%) and 19-year-olds (88%). A 1973 NORC survey also included a déjà vu item, but these data are not available on the Web. McCready and Greeley (1976) analyzed these data, and also failed to find the dip in déjà vu incidence with teenagers. In fact, the déjà vu incidence was distinctly higher among teenagers (87%) than persons in their 20s (80%) and declined systematically for persons in their 30s (70%), 40s (55%), 50s (57%), 60s (38%), and 70s (38%). Adachi et al. (2003) combined teenagers (18–19) with those in their 20s, but found a similar systematic decline in déjà vu incidence across persons in their 20s (89%), 30s (82%), 40s (66%), 50s (63%), and 60s (54%).

A variety of other studies using only two or three age groupings also support the inverse relationship between age and déjà vu. Harper (1969) found an 81% lifetime incidence in persons between 15 and 25, which dropped to 60% among those 25 and older, and Zuger (1966) discovered the 72% incidence in those 25 and under declined to 61% in those over 25. Cutting his data into three age groups, Palmer (1979) found the lifetime incidence of déjà vu was 83% for those 30 and under, 69% for those 31 to 50, and 52% for those over 50. Furthermore, Gallup and Newport (1991) claim that déjà vu is "... almost twice as likely to have occurred among Americans 18 to 29 years of age as among Americans over 50" (p. 140). Finally, significant and negative correlations have been consistently found between age and déjà vu experience: –0.38 (Adachi et al., 2003), –0.22 (Sno et al., 1994), –0.23 (Chapman & Mensh, 1951), –0.32 (Kohr, 1980), –0.34 (NORC, 1984), –0.31 (NORC, 1988), –0.34 (NORC, 1989). In short, lifetime incidence of déjà vu shows a systematic and linear decline with age across numerous comparisons.

Frequency Changes with Age, Among Experients

Aside from lifetime incidence, another question is whether the frequency of déjà vu changes with age among experients. The *mean number of déjà vu experiences per year* for experients was provided by Chapman and Mensh (1951) and are displayed in Figure 6.2. These data show a systematic decline in yearly incidence with age, beginning with the teenage years, and suggest that teenage experients show a comparable yearly frequency to those in their 20s, even though a smaller percentage of teenagers supposedly experience déjà vu. Richardson and Winocur (1967) also com-

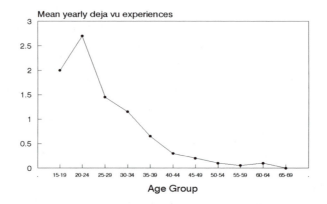

FIGURE 6.2. Yearly incidence for déjà vu experience in 10-year age groups.

pared younger (<45 yrs) and older (45+ yrs) patients on déjà vu *in the past year* and found a dramatic and consistent age-related decrease in each patient subgroup: cerebral pathology only (younger = 46%; older = 15%), psychiatric illness (younger = 45%; older = 14%) and no cerebral or psychiatric dysfunction (younger = 41%; older = 14%). Thus, the number of déjà vu experiences per year appears to drop off across the adult age span more sharply than the percentage of individuals who have had a lifetime déjà vu.

To examine this issue from another perspective, the data from the NORC surveys are plotted by three different déjà vu lifetime incidence categories: "once or twice," "several times," and "often." Although the response scale may be suspect (is there much difference between the first and second categories?), it is assumed that respondents used these categories in an ordinal fashion. These data, plotted in Figure 6.3, show that the age-related decline in estimated *frequency* of déjà vu is systematic and linear within each of the three response categories (once or twice, several times, often). Thus, the age-related decline represents a uniform reduction in the percentage of experients in each of the relative frequency categories, rather than a disproportionate shift of experients from higher to lower frequency categories with increasing age.

All the above analyses suggest that the age composition of samples used in déjà vu survey research can dramatically affect estimates of déjà vu incidence, a point that was empirically verified in Chapter 4. Setting the measurement/sampling issue aside for a moment, there are two logical paradoxes in these age-related data. The first is that teenagers have a lower percentage of experients than those in their 20s (Figure 6.1).

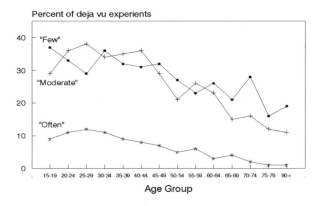

FIGURE 6.3. Frequency of déjà vu among experients.

Age at First Experience

When does a person first begin having déjà vu experiences? Does one have to reach a certain level of cognitive development before having a déjà vu illusion? No research has directly queried children about déjà vu, and retrospective estimates from adults about their earliest déjà vu experiences are suspect. Some have suggested the cognitive maturation necessary for déjà vu is not fully in place until 8 or 9 years of age (cf. Crichton-Browne, 1895; Kohn, 1983; Neppe, 1983e). White (1973) provides an account of a second grader's (8 years old?) déjà vu experience as recalled by that individual at age 37, and Ouspensky (1931) describes a personal déjà vu experience from when he was 6 years old. Neppe (1983e) proposes that from a Piagetian perspective, several components of cognitive development are necessary to experience déjà vu: object relations, spatial memory, and appreciation of the concepts of past-ness and familiarity (both appropriate and inappropriate forms). These do not become fully developed until the age of 8 or 9, an idea supported by Crichton-Browne (1895) in his informal observations (cf. Kohn, 1983).

Neppe (1983e) asked respondents when they had experienced their first déjà vu. Although it is debatable whether one could even roughly date such a fleeing initial experience, he found that the mean age was 24 in his group without paranormal experiences and 15 in his group who claimed paranormal experiences. His sample was very limited (11 persons across both groups), but it suggests that people believe that their first déjà vu occurs sometime in their mid-teens to early 20s. Despite his assertion that the minimum age for déjà vu is 8 to 9, Neppe (1983e) provides three adults' personal recollections of déjà vu experiences at ages 5 and 6. He also notes that 10 other individuals surveyed claimed déjà vu at age 7 (three participants) and 8 (seven participants) although the individuals understandably could give no specific details concerning these episodes. Fukuda (2002) asked a sample of college students when they had their first déjà vu experience, and discovered that most indicated that it was between the ages of 6 and 10 (49%) or between 11 and 15 (33%). It appears reasonable to conclude that the metacognitive awareness of inappropriate familiarity may not be fully developed until the second decade of life, and may involve hearing or reading about the experience from others in order to properly interpret such an experience.

"Cause" of the Adult Age-Related Decline in Déjà Vu

A second paradox in the age analyses is that the lifetime incidence of déjà vu drops off systematically in older adults. Individuals in their 60s were once in their 20s, so it is logically inconsistent that a much smaller percentage of 60-year-olds than 20-year-olds report *ever* having had a déjà vu. It is important to separate this issue from the frequency of déjà vu among experients, which also drops off with age (see Figure 6.3). The function relating lifetime déjà vu experience and age should either increase or remain flat with increasing age but certainly should *not* decrease. There are three possible explanations for this logical incongruity.

1. *Memory problem*: déjà vu experiences only occur during youth, and then are forgotten over time (cf. Chapman & Mensh, 1951)
2. *Response bias*: older adults feel less comfortable admitting to having a déjà vu experience. Neppe (1983e) strongly argues that there is *no* actual age difference and that the decline is strictly because of this response bias.
3. *Cohort effect*: societal awareness and acceptance of déjà vu has systematically increased across the last 50 years

Two sets of outcomes support the third explanation. Gallup and Newport (1991) found that, from 1978 to 1990, the percent of people who *believe* in the déjà vu experience nearly doubled from 30% to 55% (cf. Sobal & Emmons, 1982). In addition, the General Social Survey (NORC) shows an increase in the reported lifetime incidence of déjà vu from 59% in 1973 to 68% in 1988 (Levin, 1993). This societal increase in the belief in, and reporting of, déjà vu experiences may account for the decrease in reported déjà vu incidence with age. More specifically, older cohorts matured during an era when belief in déjà vu was not as accepted as today. In fact, it is possible that some portion of older adults may be unaware of the particular memory phenomenon referred to as a déjà vu.

Aside from the issue of lifetime incidence, a reason why older adults who *do* claim to have déjà vu have *fewer* experiences may be that they are less sensitive to the qualities of their own cognitive experiences. That is, older adults are less accurate in identifying the source of information (Brown, Jones, & Davis, 1995) and are less likely to spontaneously use source information in making memory evaluations (Multhaup, 1995). These changes may make them less sensitive to the type of source memory conflicts that potentially underlie déjà vu (see Chapter 14). Older adults also tend to be more settled in their routine physical surroundings, making them less likely to encounter new settings and experiences that could elicit déjà vu. Adachi et al. (2003) also suggest that older adults have a greater tolerance of ambiguous personal experiences, and thus are more likely to dismiss déjà vu with little note.

A reasonable conclusion is that several factors contribute to the age related decline in déjà vu. The frequency of déjà vu probably does decrease with age, as this decline occurs *within* experients (see Figure 6.3). It is also likely that a gradual increase in the awareness and acceptability of the déjà vu phenomenon has contributed to this trend. At the very least, a successful explanation of the déjà vu experience must accommodate the ubiquitous and reliable age-related decline in déjà vu frequency and future surveys using a broad age sample should require participants to evaluate the acceptability of the déjà vu experience both personally and culturally.

☐ Education

There appears to be a positive relationship between the déjà vu experience and years of education (Adachi et al., 2003; Chapman & Mensh, 1951; Crichton-Browne, 1895; Dugas, 1894; Fox, 1992; Gallup & Newport, 1991; Harper, 1969; Neppe, 1979, 1983e; Palmer, 1979; Richardson & Winokur, 1967, 1968). Even in early speculations, Crichton-Browne (1895) suggested that déjà vu experiences "... abound amongst the educated, the refined ..." (p. 2), and Dugas (1894, cited in Ellis, 1911) noted that déjà vu appears to affect "... educated people, and notably people of more than average intellect, who use their brains much, especially in artistic and emotional work ..." (Ellis, 1911, p. 240).

With respect to the empirical data on education level, Chapman and Mensh (1951) and Richardson and Winocur (1967) both found system-

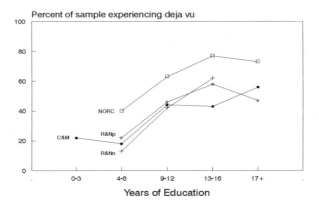

Percent of sample experiencing deja vu

Years of Education

FIGURE 6.4. Lifetime déjà vu incidence as a function of years of education.

atic increases in déjà vu incidence across years of education, and these data are presented in Figure 6.4. For Richardson and Winocur (1967), the data are presented separately for the neurological (R&Wn) and psychiatric (R&Wp) samples. Data are also presented from the NORC (1984, 1988, 1989) database in Figure 6.4. These data show a positive relationship between déjà vu incidence and years of school, and this increase is especially sharp between elementary and high school. Finally, Adachi et al. (2003) found years of education was significantly greater in those who had experienced déjà vu compared to those who had not.

The correlation between déjà vu incidence and education is positive but weak in a number of comparisons: 0.13 (Adachi et al., 2003), 0.16 (Chapman & Mensh, 1951), 0.10 (Kohr, 1980), 0.20 (NORC, 1984), 0.16 (NORC, 1988), 0.19 (NORC, 1989). Except for Kohr (1980), these correlations are all statistically significant. Comparing five levels of educational achievement, Palmer (1979) noted the lowest incidence of déjà vu (48%) at the bottom rung (grade school only) and the highest incidence (81%) among those with a graduate degree. Thus, most research shows a direct relationship between déjà vu incidence and years of schooling, although this relationship is modest (correlationally) in most instances.

Chapman and Mensh (1951) speculated that level of education may account for the age-related decline in déjà vu (see previous section) in that younger respondents may have more education, as borne out by a significant negative correlation between age and education (–0.37). Partialling the effects of education out of this correlation between age and déjà vu reduced it from –0.23 to –0.18, but it still remained significant. So while education may contribute to this age-déjà vu relationship, it does not completely account for it. Taking a different approach to the apparent confounding of age, education, and déjà vu frequency, Adachi et al. (2003) compared years of education for those who had, versus had not, experienced déjà vu with age as a covariate (ANCOVA), and found that those with déjà vu experiences still had significantly more education. Thus, age differences cannot completely account for the positive relationship between education and déjà vu.

☐ Socioeconomic Status

Déjà vu incidence has also been assessed as directly related to socioeconomic status (SES) (Chapman & Mensh, 1951; Crichton-Browne, 1895; Gallup & Newport, 1991; Harper, 1969; Palmer, 1979; Richardson & Winokur, 1967, 1968). To some extent, socioeconomic status and academic achievement are closely related and somewhat confounded in the analyses. For example, Chapman and Mensh (1951) defined six different "occupation" groups and declared that those better educated (their definition) (professional = 45%; student = 42%; clerical = 41%) had a higher déjà vu incidence than those less educated (skilled = 33%; unskilled = 28%; housewife = 31%). Richardson and Winocur (1967) used a similar system to classify their samples of psychiatric and neurosurgery patients, and found a comparable difference: a higher déjà vu incidence in the "clerical, professional, and student groups (47% to 73%)" compared to the "unemployed (retired), unskilled, housewife and skilled groups (25% to 43%)" (p. 624). Comparing a number of different occupational levels, Palmer (1979) found the highest incidence of déjà vu among professionals (80%) and the lowest incidence among blue collar workers (50%). The NORC data stand in marked contrast to the above findings. Comparing four different ordinally increasing levels of socioeconomic class (self assessed) yielded essentially no difference in the incidence of déjà vu: lower = 63%, working = 67%, middle = 66%, upper = 65%.

To separate the effects of education and socioeconomic class, the NORC data were divided into low (lower; working) and high (middle; upper) socioeconomic class *within* each of the four education levels. This yielded a higher incidence of déjà vu for low than for high class (respectively) within each of four education level categories: < 9 years = 44% versus 32%; 9–12 years = 65% versus 57%; 13–16 years = 79% versus 77%; 17+ years = 76% versus 72%. These statistics indicate that both socioeconomic status and education level are associated with déjà vu experience, but in opposite ways: (a) déjà vu is *inversely* related to socioeconomic class, being more prevalent among lower- than upper-class individuals; (b) déjà vu is *directly* related to education level, with the percentage of experients increasing with more years of school. Separate chi square tests within each education level did not reveal any significant difference in the déjà vu prevalence between lower and upper classes. However, the reliability of this difference is strong evidence for its empirical reality.

With respect to differences in déjà vu as a function of income level, Palmer (1979) found no relationship between déjà vu incidence and income in either the townspeople or college samples. NORC (1984, 1988, 1989) collected data on total family income as a dichotomous split of less than $25K versus $25K or more per year. This reveals a significant difference in déjà vu incidence between individuals with higher (71%) versus lower (64%) incomes, $X^2 (1) = 21.12, p < .001$. Separate analyses on each survey year revealed that déjà vu incidence was consistently and significantly greater for higher than lower income groups (respectively) in 1984 (71% vs. 65%; $X^2 (1) = 5.32, p < .05$), 1988 (71% vs. 65%; $X^2 (1) = 6.62, p < .01$) and 1989 (70% vs. 59%; $X^2 (1) = 11.44, p < .001$). As suggested earlier, this difference may be confounded with education level and SES.

While these trends are intriguing, it must be kept in mind that in the NORC survey, the déjà vu question was accompanied three items on paranormal experiences, making the outcome potentially biased by the complex ways in which paranormal experiences are viewed across differing educational and socioeconomic levels. At the very least, these analyses provide a caution the typical blanket statements that déjà vu "... is more likely to be reported by college graduates and those with higher incomes than the less well educated and those with lower incomes" (Gallup & Newport, 1991, p. 140).

☐ Gender

Many investigations have compared the incidence of déjà vu in males and females, but no consistent gender difference has emerged. Some suggest a higher incidence among *females* (Brown et al., 1994; Chapman & Mensh, 1951; Myers & Grant, 1972; Richardson & Winocur, 1967, psychiatric patients), others report a higher incidence among *males* (Green, 1966; National Opinion Research Center, 1984, 1988, 1989; Richardson & Winocur, 1967, neurosurgical patients) and many have declared no gender difference (Adachi et al., 2001; Bernhard-Leroy, 1898; Fox, 1992; Gaynard, 1992; Green, 1966; Harper, 1969; Kohr, 1980; Lalande, 1893; Leeds, 1944; Palmer, 1979; Probst & Jansen, 1994; Sno et al., 1994). The correlation between gender and déjà vu experience was +.02 in Kohr (1980) and −.04

TABLE 6.1. Gender Comparisons of Déjà Vu Incidence

Study	% of Participants Experiencing Déjà Vu	
	Females	Males
Adachi et al. (2003)	80	72 (ns)
Brown et al. (1994)	98	95 (sig)
Chapman & Mensh (1951)	35	31 (ns)
Gaynard (1992)	46	34 (ns)
Green (1966)	73	84 (ns)
Leeds (1944)	91	92
Myers & Grant (1972) (with depersonalization)	81	80
Myers & Grant (1972) (without depersonalization)	61	40
NORC (1984)	65	69 (ns)
NORC (1988)	67	67 (ns)
NORC (1989)	60	68 (ns)
Richardson & Winocur (1967, neurosurgical)	35	42 (ns)
Richardson & Winocur (1967, psychiatric patients)	48	40 (ns)

in the NORC (1984, 1988, 1989) data. The differences between female and male incidence rates are provided in Table 6.1, and where a statistical test was performed, the outcome is indicated in parenthesis.

Both Chapman and Mensh (1951) and Brown et al. (1994) compared males and females on reported déjà vu frequency among experients, and these data appear in Table 6.2.

Chapman and Mensh (1951) do not draw any conclusions based on their data, and Brown et al. (1994) found no statistically significant difference in the frequency distribution between the sexes. Chapman and Mensh (1951) also broke down the sex difference by age, and these data are plotted by decade in Figure 6.5 for lifetime incidence of déjà vu. It is very clear from this plot that there is no interaction of sex with age, with respect to lifetime déjà vu experience. Chapman and Mensh (1951) also present the total number of déjà vu experiences per sex/age subgroup (their Figure 2) and these data are represented in Figure 6.6. This plot shows that males have a much higher frequency per experient in the teenage years, but the average number drops substantially

TABLE 6.2. Gender Comparisons of Déjà Vu Frequency Among Experients

Déjà Vu Occurs *Once* Every ...	Chapman & Mensh (1951)		Brown et al. (1994)	
	Females	Males	Females	Males
... month	14%	6%	57%	55%
... several months	29	32	35	34
... year	34	29	5	8
... several years	23	35	3	4

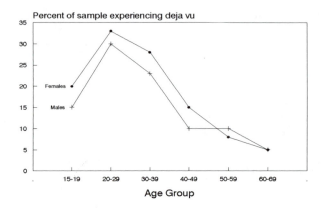

FIGURE 6.5.   Incidence of déjà vu across age, comparing males and females.

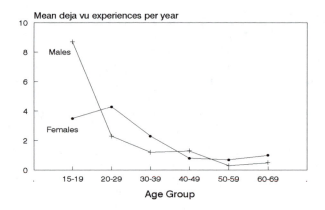

FIGURE 6.6.   Frequency of déjà vu across age, comparing male and female experients.

below females during the 20s and 30s. From age 40 on, there is no obvious sex differences.

☐ Race

There has been little effort to examine racial differences in the incidence of déjà vu. Survey samples rarely include a substantial number of minorities (if any) or evaluate these particular subgroups separately. For instance, Palmer found no racial differences in déjà vu experience, but their town sample consisted of 92% white, 7% black, and 1% Asian American, while their university sample was 98% white, 2% Asian American, and 0% black. Richardson and Winocur (1967) did note a significantly higher incidence in whites than blacks in both neurosurgery (whites = 41%; blacks = 17%) and psychiatric (whites = 45%; blacks = 21%) patients. Richardson and Winocur (1967) did eliminate both age and education as possible contributors to this racial difference, but the unusual nature of these hospital samples and the small number of blacks in both the neurosurgical (N = 18; 11%) and psychiatric (N = 14; 5%) groups does not support any strong conclusion. Using a much larger NORC (1984, 1988, 1989) database, a comparison of blacks (N = 448) and whites (N = 3287) shows no difference with 66% of individuals in *both* racial groups claiming to have had a lifetime déjà vu experience (cf. Fox, 1992).

☐ Travel Frequency

Logically, those individuals who travel should have more opportunities to experience déjà vu because they encounter new physical settings more often than those who don't travel. Several investigations support this speculation. The data from Chapman and Mensh (1951) and Richardson and Winocur (1967; two samples), presented in Figure 6.7, reveal a generally positive relationship between travel frequency and déjà vu, but the most dramatic difference exists between those who travel and those who don't. Chapman and Mensh (1951) discovered that people who don't travel have a 11% incidence of déjà vu, while those who do have a 32% incidence, and Richardson and Winocur (1967) found a similar relationship with both neurosurgery and psychiatric patients. For neurosurgery patients, there was an 11% déjà vu incidence among those who never travel, and 42% among those who do; for psychiatric patients, there was a 33% incidence in nontravelers, and a 47% incidence for those who do travel. In contrast to these findings, Adachi et al. (2003) did not find a significant correlation between travel frequency and déjà vu experience (0.10). However, it is unclear what measure they used, and whether they included *no* travel as a level of the travel variable. It also appears that this relationship may be curvilinear, and perhaps a measure of the linear association may not be appropriate.

Thus, most of the data suggest that those who travel have more déjà vu experiences than those who don't, but the amount of travel appears to make little difference. This association of déjà vu with travel is probably interrelated with educational level and income, in that those with more education and income are more likely to travel (see earlier discussion).

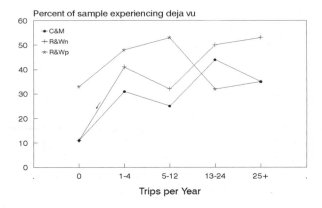

FIGURE 6.7.   Lifetime déjà vu incidence as a function of travel frequency.

☐ Religious Belief

Analyses of the NORC database (1984, 1988, 1989) for the relationship between religious preference and déjà vu incidence reveal no significant differences comparing Protestant (64%) and Catholic (69%) (Jewish was differentiated, but the sample size was very small) (cf. Fox, 1992). Palmer (1979) also found no relationship between déjà vu and religious preference in both a townsperson and college sample, although the religion was predominantly Protestant in both samples. On a related dimension, Kohr found a significant correlation between the déjà vu experience and meditation experiences ($r = .18$, $p < .05$), but Palmer (1979) failed to find such an association between déjà vu and a "formal technique of stilling the mind" (p. 238) in either his townspeople or college sample. Furthermore, McClenon (1994) found no correlation between déjà vu and religiosity.

The NORC survey also asked respondents to rate how fundamentalist their religious belief system is, regardless of religious affiliation. There was a lower déjà vu incidence among fundamental (61%) versus moderate (69%) and liberal (68%) groups, and a comparison of the difference between fundamental and nonfundamental (moderate + liberal) was statistically significant, X^2 (1) = 23.49, $p < .001$.

☐ Political Orientation

Several studies have noted a difference in the incidence of déjà vu along lines of political persuasion. Kohr (1980) reports that déjà vu is more common among liberals than conservatives, citing a significant positive correlation of .14 between déjà vu incidence and a dimension ranging from conservative to liberal political orientation. Palmer (1979) noted the same statistically significant difference in déjà vu incidence between liberals (83%) versus conservatives (61%) in a community sample, but no difference in the student sample. A similar and significant liberal (74%) versus conservative (64%) difference is also present in the combined NORC (1984, 1988, 1989) database, X^2 (1) = 25.73, $p < .01$. Looking at separate years, this liberal versus conservative difference is significant (respectively) in 1984 (75% vs. 63%; X^2 (1) = 13.23, $p < .001$) and 1988 (78% vs. 66%; X^2 (1) = 13.92, $p < .001$), but not in 1989 (69% vs. 63%; X^2 (1) = 1.41, $p > .10$). However, there was no significant difference in the incidence of déjà vu across Democrat (64%), Independent (70%), and Republican (65%) affiliation, X^2 (2) = 3.69, $p > .10$, and this lack of a difference was consistent in each survey year. Thus, while there is evidence that déjà vu incidence is higher in liberals than conservatives, there is no apparent difference as a function of political party.

☐ Dreams and Related Phenomena

Dreams can relate to the déjà vu experience in three different ways. First, some déjà vu experiences appear to duplicate events that occurred during a prior dream rather than from a waking experience (Osborn, 1884). When Brown et al. (1994) asked respondents to evaluate what the duplicated experience in their typical déjà vu seems to relate to, nearly twice as many respondents said a real event (38%) than a dream (22%), although many indicated that it could be either (40%). It is quite likely that the sense of unreality that pervades the déjà vu experience makes it resemble a dream, leading individuals to logically assume that the strange sensation of familiarity originates from this state (cf. Krijgers Janzen, 1958). A second possible connection is that elements of a remembered dream may subsequently connect to stimuli encountered while awake, resulting in a déjà vu (Baldwin, 1889; MacCurdy, 1925) (this is examined in more detail in Chapter 14). Finally, some individuals claim to have a déjà vu experience during a dream state (Burnham, 1889; Ellis, 1911; Epstein & Collie, 1976; Hodgson, 1865; Kirshner, 1973; Kraepelin, 1887; Osborn, 1884; Parish, 1923; Schneck, 1964; Silbermann, 1963). All these possible linkages have motivated several assessments of the connection between déjà vu and dream frequency, as well as related cognitive dimensions of daydreaming and childhood fantasy.

Several investigations have scrutinized the relationship between déjà vu and dream frequency (Buck & Geers, 1967; Kohr, 1980; Neppe, 1983e;

Palmer, 1979; Zuger, 1966). Zuger (1966) asked respondents whether they experience déjà vu *and* remember their dreams, and a striking relationship emerged: *all* 10 respondents who reported *no* dream memory also reported *no* déjà vu experiences, and *all* 36 respondents who reported déjà vu also reported remembering their dreams (nine reported dream memory but no déjà vu). This close association between remembering dreams and experiencing déjà vu was found for both younger (25 and younger) and older (over 25) individuals. Neppe (1983e) also examined the relationship between dream recall and déjà vu frequency. Unlike Zuger (1966), Neppe (1983e) did not find a strong relationship but did discover that the *absence* of dream recall is associated with "rare" déjà vu.

Palmer (1979) examined the relationship between déjà vu and four separate dimensions of dreams: recall, vividness, lucidity, and analysis. All four dream dimensions were significantly correlated with déjà vu in his community sample (no correlation values given) but not in his student sample. In another community sample with a broad age range, Adachi et al. (2003) did find a significant positive correlation between dream memory and déjà vu experiences (.25). Similarly, Kohr (1980) found significant (albeit modest) positive correlations in a broad community sample between déjà vu and dream recall (.22), dream vividness (.30), dream lucidity (.22), and number of lucid dreams (.28). Buck and Geers (1967) failed to find a significant correlation between déjà vu and dream memory among *college* students, replicating Palmer (1979). However, null effects for college students in both studies (Buck & Geers, 1967; Palmer, 1979) may be caused by ceiling effects: the high incidence of déjà vu among college students could mask a correlational relationship.

Related to dream experiences, four studies have examined a possible relationship between déjà vu and the occurrence of imagery during periods of altered consciousness just prior to falling asleep (hypnopompic state) and when emerging from sleep (hypnogogic state) (Buck, 1970; Buck & Geers, 1967; McKellar, 1957; McKellar & Simpson, 1954). Despite this interest, only Buck and Geers (1967) reported any empirical data. They combined hypnopompic and hypnogogic imagery into a "transition to sleep" variable, and showed moderate, significant correlations between this dimension and both auditory déjà vu (.27) and visual déjà vu (.35).

Daydreams

The relationship between daydreams and déjà vu also has been examined. In fact, Chapman and Mensh's (1951) research was designed to compare déjà vu and daydreaming (article title: "déjà vu experience and conscious fantasy in adults"). Despite this explicit intent, they never directly compared the two phenomena and only provide indirect indications of an association: both déjà vu and daydreaming (a) drop off systematically with age and (b) are unrelated to gender. Wolfradt (2000) did discover a relationship between déjà vu and daydreaming in a sample of college students, while Buck and Geers (1967) found a modest but significant correlation between déjà vu and daydreams (.25 for visual déjà vu; .39 for auditory déjà vu). Adachi et al. (2003), however, found that the correlation between déjà vu and daydreaming was nonsignificant (.15). Thus, there may be a modest relationship between déjà vu and daydreaming but the logic behind why these two experiences should be connected has not been clearly spelled out.

Childhood Fantasy

Given the strange and unreal quality of déjà vu, it is natural to assume that the experience may have some relationship to one's fantasy world. For instance, Burnham (1889) speculated, based on his personal observations, that it is more prevalent in those "gifted with vivid imagination." Myers and Austrin (1985) used the Wilson-Barber Inventory of Childhood Memories and Imaginings (Myers, 1983) and found a significant positive correlation between "fantasy proneness" and whether or not the person has experienced déjà vu ($r = .16$), as well as the frequency of déjà vu experiences ($r = .18$). However, while these correlations are significant because of the large samples, they are relatively small and thus not particularly meaningful. Furthermore, Irwin (1996) found no relationship between déjà vu and whether or not one's parents encouraged "imaginative involvement" during childhood. Thus, evidence of a relationship between childhood fantasy and déjà vu is neither strong nor convincing.

☐ Belief in Déjà Vu

Apart from the personal experience of a déjà vu, a separate issue is one's *belief* in the reality of the déjà vu state, whether or not one has experienced it. This issue has been examined by Gaynard (1992), and in Gallup Polls done in 1978 (summarized in Emmons & Sobal, 1981; Sobal & Emmons, 1982) and 1990 (summarized in Gallup & Newport, 1991).

Gaynard (1992) found that belief in déjà vu (estimated from his Figure 4 on p. 174) ranged from certain (54%) to likely (22%) to possible (18%) to unlikely (4%) to impossible (3%). Interestingly, the percent who believe in déjà vu (certain + likely + possible) is 93%, considerably *above* the 39% who reported a lifetime déjà vu experience. According to the 1978 Gallup Poll, 30% believed in déjà vu (Emmons & Sobal, 1981; Sobal & Emmons, 1982), whereas 12 years later, the 1990 Gallup Poll indicated that 55% believe in déjà vu (Gallup & Newport, 1991). Estimates of belief in déjà vu vary so much across these three studies to be almost meaningless (from 30% to 93%). However, the truth may be somewhere in the middle. Gaynard's (1992) estimate of "belief" may be inflated because respondents knew his positive bias, as the teacher of a course on paranormal phenomena, whereas the Gallup Polls may be biased low because the déjà vu item accompanies items about paranormal phenomena.

The 1978 Gallup Poll was further analyzed by both Emmons and Sobal (1981) and Sobal and Emmons (1982) concerning the relationship between belief in déjà vu and various demographic variables. The strong trend of decreasing déjà vu experience with age (earlier in this chapter) is also reflected in belief. There is a significant negative correlation between belief in déjà vu and age (–.29) (Emmons & Sobal, 1981), and the percentage of believers shows a systematic, significant decline across five age groups: 51% (18 to 29 years) to 32% (30 to 39 years) to 31% (40 to 49 years) to 24% (50 to 64 years) to 11% (65+ years).

With respect to education, belief also resembles experience as reflected in a significant positive correlation between education and belief in déjà vu ($r = .22$; Emmons & Sobal, 1981). Sobal and Emmons' (1982) data on belief in déjà vu generally increased across educational levels: 9th to 11th grade (20%), high school graduate (31%), technical/trade school (43%), some college (51%), and college graduate (35%). Sobal and Emmons (1982) only report an overall significant increase across all categories, a pattern generally consistent with the experiential data (earlier this chapter) with the exception of their highest category of college graduate where belief drops. Sobal and Emmons suggest that this dip may be attributable to greater skepticism at higher levels of educational attainment.

Earlier analyses provide no indication that gender is related to déjà vu experience, and the Gallup Poll suggests that belief in déjà vu shows a similar lack of gender difference in the mean belief for females (32%) and males (30%) (Emmons & Sobal, 1981). Gaynard (1992), however, did find a significant gender difference in belief (5-point scale; 4 = "certain" to 0 = "impossible"), with females higher (3.31) than males (3.07) (means estimated from Gaynard, 1992, Figure 5, p. 176).

With respect to race, significantly fewer blacks (18%) than whites (33%) believe in déjà vu (Sobal & Emmons, 1982), and this difference also was reflected in a significant (if small) negative correlation of –.10 (Emmons & Sobal, 1981). Emmons and Sobal (1981) found that belief in déjà vu is higher for unmarried (single = 43%; divorced = 56%) than married (29%) persons, and Gaynard (1992) found that belief in déjà vu was lower among scientists (3.07) than artists (3.24) (5-point scale), although not significantly so.

☐ Summary

One of the most consistent findings in the déjà vu literature is a negative relationship between déjà vu and age, with both lifetime incidence and frequency among experients decreasing with age. There are two anomalies in this age relationship. One is the lower rate for teenagers (than those in their 20s), which is most likely because of the late emergence of a metacognitive awareness required to appreciate the déjà vu experience. The second anomaly is the decreasing lifetime incidence of déjà vu with age, which is probably a result of a growing cultural awareness of the experience over the past 50 years. Déjà vu is positively related to education and income but negatively related to socioeconomic class. The experience is also positively associated with travel, but in a dichotomous manner: People who travel are more likely to experience déjà vu than those who don't, but the amount of travel makes no apparent difference. Déjà vu incidence is higher in liberals than conservatives, but does not appear to be related to gender or race. Those with a fundamentalist religious belief system have a lower incidence of déjà vu than those who classify themselves as moderate and liberal, although déjà vu incidence does not differ across religious denominations. Finally, déjà vu incidence is positively related to dream recall. Similar to data on déjà vu experience, belief in déjà vu also shows a negative association with age and a positive relationship to education.

7
CHAPTER

Physiopathology and Déjà Vu

Much of the early research on déjà vu emerged from a conceptual framework in which the experience reflected some form of underlying physical pathology. Since the 1800s, investigators have speculated about the relationship between déjà vu and epilepsy in general, although other neurological conditions have been evaluated for links to déjà vu and the experience has been associated with the consumption of, and withdrawal from, various prescription and nonprescription drugs.

The association between déjà vu and epilepsy has a long history reaching back more than a century. In fact, much of the early interest in déjà vu was spurred by Jackson's (1888) writings that described its appearance in the "dreamy states" associated with the psychic experiences immediately preceding an epileptic seizure (aura). This publicity motivated physicians, philosophers, and psychologists to examine the phenomenon more closely, but had the unfortunate side effect of stigmatizing déjà vu as pathological. This literature on déjà vu and epilepsy is extensive, but most has focused on whether the déjà vu experience is *diagnostic* of seizure activity. As this line of research progressed, it became apparent that the déjà vu experience was primarily associated with epileptics whose seizure activity originates in the temporal lobe (TLEs).

One problem with research on déjà vu in TLEs is that investigators sometimes group other phenomena together with déjà vu. In the original definition of the "dreamy state" preceding a seizure, Jackson (1888) suggested that it consisted of déjà vu, jamais vu, and/or vivid hallucinations (cf. Bancaud, Brunet-Bourgin, Chauvel, & Halgren, 1994; Kinnier Wilson, 1929; Penfield, 1955). Bancaud et al. (1994) identify this dreamy state as consisting of déjà vu or vivid memories, whereas Antoni (1946) proposes that this state consists of "… the déjà vu phenomenon, sense of unreality, visions and other experiences impossible to describe …" (p. 18). Hermann and Stromgren (1944) express consternation that the "… expression 'dreamy state'—which never has been very clearly defined—has assumed the character of a 'slogan' that covers a number of widely different disturbances of consciousness" (p. 175). Thus, it is unclear in some of the early literature on epilepsy whether déjà vu was synonymous with, a component of, or not a part of what is described as the dreamy state. Some of this ambiguity also pervades more recent writings on the topic (cf. Bancaud et al., 1994).

☐ Is Déjà Vu Diagnostic of Epilepsy?

The possibility that déjà vu is diagnostic of epilepsy was first suggested in a published report by a young physician. His article appeared under the pseudonym of "Quaerens" to avoid any possible personal stigma associated with his having epilepsy. He describes a history of déjà vu experiences and how they increased in frequency and intensity just prior to his first epileptic attack (Quaerens, 1870). In subsequent discussions of the association between epilepsy and déjà vu, both Jackson (1888) and Crichton-Browne (1895) suggest that déjà vu is neither a cause of, nor result of, the seizure. Rather, déjà vu stems from the heightened neurological activity level preceding the seizure (cf. Harper, 1969). Early speculation was that the mere presence of déjà vu might signal a potential for the later development of epilepsy (Chichton-Browne, 1895; Quaerens, 1870), but Jackson and Colman (1898) and Jackson (1888) proposed a different perspective where occasional déjà vu experiences are not indicative of epilepsy, but repeated incidences are. Thus, the debate subsequently evolved into whether the quantity and/or quality of the déjà vu experience potentially differentiates persons with TLE from the rest of the population (Allin, 1896a; Bernard-Leroy, 1898; Crichton-Browne, 1895; Ellis, 1911; Harper, 1969; Hill, 1956; Maudsley, 1889; Neppe, 1983e; Richardson & Winocur, 1967; Silberman et al., 1985; Sno et al., 1994).

One simple approach to this question is to evaluate survey data as to whether the incidence of déjà vu is higher in epileptic compared to non-epileptic individuals (Cole & Zangwill, 1963; Harper & Roth, 1962; Maudsley, 1889; Weinand, Hermann, Wyler, Carter, Oommen, Labiner, Ahern, & Herring, 1994). Four studies in Table 4.2 provide such data (Harper & Roth, 1962; Neppe, 1983e; Silberman et al., 1985; van Paesschen et al., 2001). Averaged across all four studies, the incidence of déjà vu is 49%, which is actually *below* the overall mean incidence of 72% in nonclinical samples (see Chapter 4). Two of these four studies have a sample of non-TLEs for comparison. Silberman et al. (1985) found no significant difference in the lifetime incidence of déjà vu between TLEs (54%) and controls (63%), whereas Neppe (1983e) noted a higher incidence among TLEs (86%) than controls (68%) but did not statistically evaluate this difference. Overall, there is no compelling evidence in survey data that the déjà vu experience is more common in TLEs.

To tackle this issue from a different angle, Harper (1969) screened 91 individuals who were *not* epileptic for the presence of epileptic indicators. The small number of people in his sample who reported signs of epilepsy (epileptic fits, syncopal attacks, mastoiditis or middle ear disease, and migraine) were equally distributed among those reporting déjà vu and not reporting déjà vu.

Considering all the research on the subject, it is difficult to completely rule out the possibility that déjà vu is indicative of epilepsy. However, most researchers now accept that it is *not* and the weight of evidence argues against déjà vu as more common in epileptics, or as diagnostic of seizure pathology (Harper, 1969; Richardson & Winocur, 1967).

☐ Association with Preseizure Aura

Déjà vu is part of the aura immediately preceding the seizure in some TLEs, and this phenomenon has been described in both personal experiential reports (Jackson, 1888; Leeds, 1944; Wohlgemuth, 1924) and retrospective anecdotal reports (Cole & Zangwill, 1963; Crichton-Browne, 1895; Epstein & Freeman, 1981; Fish, Gloor, Quesney, & Oliver, 1993; Gil-Nagel & Risinger, 1997; Gloor, 1990; Gloor, Olivier, Quesney, Andermann, & Horowitz, 1982; Gupta, Jeavons, Hughes, & Covanis, 1983; Halgren Walter, Cherlow, & Crandall, 1978; Harper & Roth, 1962; Hennessy & Binnie, 2000; Keschner, Bender, & Strauss, 1936; Krijgers Janzen, 1958; Lennox & Cobb, 1933; Mullan & Penfield, 1959; Neppe, 1981, 1983c; Pacia, Devinsky, Perrine, Ravdin, Luciano, Vazquez, & Doyle, 1996; Palmini & Gloor, 1992; Sengoku, Toichi, & Murai, 1997; Silberman et al., 1985; van Paesschen et al., 2001; Weinand et al., 1994). This preseizure aura has recently been referred to as a simple partial seizure (SPS) to differentiate it from the more serious seizure activity (complex partial seizure, or secondary generalized seizure) that follows the SPS (van Paesschen et al., 2001).

Estimates of the percentage of TLEs with déjà vu as part of their aura is actually quite low: 0% in Keschner et al. (1936); < 1% in Lennox and Cobb

(1933); 1% in Weinand et al. (1994); 2% in Sengoku et al. (1997); 5% in Mullan and Penfield (1959); 6% in Gupta et al. (1983); 6% in Palmini and Gloor (1992) (Hennessy and Binnie, 2000, found a 2% rate in a nondifferentiated group of epileptics). Some studies report a higher incidence of déjà vu in the aura of TLEs, such as 9% in Gil-Nagel and Risinger (1997), 11% in Gloor et al. (1982), 14% in Halgren et al. (1978), 29% in Pacia et al. (1996), 34% in van Paesschen et al. (2001), 48% in Cole and Zangwill (1963). However, this latter group of studies generally sample TLEs with intractable seizures who are undergoing medical procedures to correct this problem. Interestingly, Silberman et al. (1985) found that for epileptics (mixture of temporal and nontemporal), déjà vu was more likely to occur during the interval *between* episodes than during preseizure auras.

Complicating any attempt to evaluate the frequency of déjà vu in the preseizure aura is the fact that the onset of the seizure often interferes with the encoding processes (Palmini & Gloor, 1992). Thus, déjà vu experienced immediately prior to the epileptic seizure "... is often dulled by slight clouding of consciousness, impaired by apprehension and recalled only with difficulty on close questioning" (Harper, 1969, p. 70). For this reason, both Antoni (1946) and Crichton-Browne (1895) speculate that the actual incidence of déjà vu in preseizure auras may be much higher than reported.

But aside from the incidence, is the nature of the déjà vu experience in the preseizure aura of TLEs different from déjà vu not associated with an aura? Neppe (1983e) argues that these differ in several ways. First, preseizure déjà vu in TLEs lasts longer, in the range of minutes rather than seconds. In addition, the déjà vu experience in TLEs' auras is often duplicated, with the same déjà vu on repeated occasions. There also may be substantial changes in thinking and emotions accompanying aura-based déjà vu in TLEs, whereas such changes are brief and transient in nonepileptics, and there often is a heightened sense of awareness of body and environment during preseizure déjà vu, while there is little alteration in these dimensions for non-TLEs (see Chapter 5). Neppe (1983e) also makes a very cogent point that déjà vu in a TLE's aura may not fit the technical definition of a déjà vu experience. The sensations preceding a seizure should be *familiar* to the TLE, cued by the same endogenous physiological sensations that the individual has repeatedly experienced, so the requisite objective evaluation of a particular situation as being unfamiliar should be lacking.

As a curious footnote in the research on TLEs, Stevens (1990) conducted a 20- to 30-year follow-up of 14 patients who underwent surgical procedures to correct their intractable seizures. Among those six patients whose psychiatric status worsened after surgery, several had experienced déjà vu as part of their preseizure aura prior to the surgery. In contrast, none of those whose psychiatric status improved or remained the same had experienced déjà vu as part of their previous aura. On the basis of this highly selective and limited data, Stevens (1990) concluded that the presence of déjà vu was part of a set of negative indicators for postsurgical mental health among epileptics. However, any strong conclusion on this topic must clearly await further investigation.

☐ Eliciting and Recording Déjà Vu Experiences

When seizure activity in TLEs cannot be controlled through medication, surgical removal of brain tissue may be required. Prior to this procedure, efforts are made to identify the tissue that is focal to the seizure and to avoid surgery on areas important to language function. These presurgical procedures allow a unique opportunity potentially to identify, through electrical stimulation and recording, those areas of the brain associated with déjà vu experiences. The two procedures that have been used for this purpose are cortical surface stimulation and deep electrode stimulation/recording.

Penfield (1955), one of the first researchers to keep records on this topic, reports that in surface stimulation of the cortex preceding the operation for focal epilepsy in 190 successive cases, he occasionally produced an experience similar to Jackson's (1888) "dreamy state." All parts of the cortex were tested, but instances of déjà vu-like experiences were found only with temporal lobe stimulation.

> … he was apt to have a strange feeling that all of this had happened before. It was, he said, as though he were in the "future listening to the past." (Penfield, 1955, p. 458)

Mullan and Penfield (1959) also reported that cortical surface stimulation duplicated the pre-seizure aura in 10 of 217 TLEs, and déjà vu occurred in 6 of these 10 patients in the temporal area.

> I had a feeling of repetition … . It is a feeling that comes over me, as thought the whole set-up had occurred before. (p. 276)

> … a feeling that I knew everything that was going to happen … as though I had been through all this before, and I thought I knew exactly what you were going to do next. (p. 277)

There are also a number of investigations that use deep electrode implantation in TLEs for both electrical stimulation and recording procedures (Bancaud et al., 1994; Fish et al., 1993; Gloor, 1990; Gloor et al., 1982; Halgren et al., 1978). Halgren et al. (1978) used deep electrode stimulation with 36 TLEs and found that five individuals experienced a total of 19 déjà vu experiences: three patients reported one déjà vu each, one patient reported six experiences, and one patient had 10 déjà vu experiences. Fish et al. (1993) also used deep electrode stimulation on TLEs and discovered that a déjà vu could be elicited in 6 of 75 of these patients. Gloor et al. (1982) noted that 4 of his 35 TLEs experienced déjà vu (a total of 23 episodes) as a result of such stimulation. Finally, Bancaud et al. (1994) examined seizures elicited by deep electrode implant or chemical activation in 16 TLEs, and discovered that three had a déjà vu accompany an induced seizure (electrical or chemical).

While these deep electrode studies verify that a déjà vu experience can be elicited electrically (or chemically), there are several cautions to such a procedure. Halgren et al. (1978) point out that stimulation induced in one area often spreads to other regions, as verified by recordings from other implanted electrodes. For example, Fish et al. (1994) noted that while one TLE had a déjà vu from direct stimulation only, there were four TLEs who experienced déjà vu *both* from direct stimulation and from indirect spreading afterdischarge, and one TLE who had a déjà vu only as a result of indirect discharge. Also, nearly all of the TLEs experiencing a déjà vu in response to stimulation also have déjà vu as part of their aura (e.g., four of five in Halgren et al., 1978; all three in Fish et al., 1994). Thus, these individuals may have become accustomed to automatically identify déjà vu as a component of such experiential electrical brain activity. Finally, there is no published confirmation that déjà vu can be elicited in nonepileptic individuals, so it is difficult to know whether such experiences resemble those found with non-TLEs.

Whereas most investigators studying the role of déjà vu in the preseizure aura assume that it reflects the beginning of a seizure, Harper (1969) has a different interpretation. He suggests that déjà vu actually triggers a seizure rather than being a byproduct of it.

> … a vivid déjà vu experience and the strange emotions associated with it may in combination with the appropriate structural and electrical vulnerability in an area of the temporal cortex, itself act as a trigger for an abnormal discharge. (p. 71)

☐ Hemispheric Origin of Seizure in TLEs with Déjà Vu

TLEs who experience déjà vu have received special scrutiny as to whether the hemisphere of their seizure focus differs from TLEs without déjà vu. Depending on one's orientation, the search for this relationship is diagnostic or cognitive. From a diagnostic perspective, is déjà vu an indicator of a subset of TLEs who are physiologically differentiated from other TLEs with respect to the hemispheric location of their cerebral pathology? From a cognitive perspective, are the brain mechanisms associated with the déjà vu experience localized in one particular hemisphere?

Early observations by Jackson (1888) and Crichton-Browne (1895) suggest that the seizures in TLEs with déjà vu originate predominantly in the right hemisphere, and this early conclusion has been supported by most subsequent research (Adachi et al., 1999; Cole & Zangwill, 1963; Cutting & Silzer, 1990; Fish et al., 1993; Gloor, 1991; Gupta et al., 1983; Mullan & Penfield, 1959; Palmini & Gloor, 1992; Penfield & Mathieson, 1974; Penfield & Perot, 1963; Sengoku et al., 1997; Weinand et al., 1994). For TLEs reporting déjà vu as part of their aura, the ratio of right versus left hemisphere origin (respectively) of the seizure was nine to one in Mullan and Penfield (1959), nine to four in Cole and Zangwill (1963), five to one in Weinand et al. (1994), four to zero in Palmini and Gloor (1992), eleven to two in Gupta et al. (1983), six to eight in Adachi et al. (1999), and one to one in Sengoku et al. (1997) (cf. Scheyer, Spencer, & Spencer, 1995).

Across these seven studies, 73% (45 of 62) of TLEs *with* déjà vu in their aura have seizures originating in their right hemisphere. This distribution is significantly different from a chance, or even, split, $X^2(1) = 12.64$, $p < .01$. Among TLEs *without* déjà vu in their aura, the right/left division of hemispheric seizure origin (respectively) is more even at 23 to 16 in Palmini and Gloor (1992), eight to six in Cole and Zangwill (1963), and ten to seven in Adachi et al. (1999). Across these three investigations, 59% of TLEs (41 out of 70) without déjà vu in their aura have seizures originating in the right hemisphere, a distribution that does not differ from chance, $X^2(1) = 2.06$, $p > .05$. Fish et al. (1993) did not report on the origin of the seizure, but describe five TLEs who had déjà vu experiences in response to deep brain stimulation, and in four of them it was in response to right-side stimulation.

Gloor et al. (1982) implanted deep electrodes in 35 TLEs who were suffering from intractable seizures, and found evidence that most déjà vu experiences were connected to the right hemisphere. In fact, one patient provided a unique within-subject verification of this hypothesis. This individual had two seizures, one originating in the left and one in the right temporal lobe. The one in the right temporal lobe had an associated déjà vu experience, while the one in the left did not. The spontaneous déjà vu experience was later duplicated through electrode stimulation to the right temporal lobe, but no déjà vu resulted from similar stimulation of the left temporal lobe.

Ide, Mizukami, Suzuki, and Shiraishi (2000) present a case study of a TLE with an unusually high frequency of déjà vu experiences (several per day) unrelated to the aura. A SPECT analysis revealed a reduced blood flow, or hypoperfusion, in the right temporal (and frontal) lobes. Subsequent drug treatment increased the blood flow to the right hemisphere and eventually eliminated the déjà vu (and seizure) experiences.

The bulk of the evidence presented in this section strongly indicates that the majority of TLEs with déjà vu experiences in their aura have their seizure origin in the right hemisphere, and that TLEs without déjà vu do not exhibit such a clear hemispheric laterality of seizure. Although it may be tempting to conclude that the déjà vu experience also originates in the right hemisphere, as does the seizure, there is a possibility that the déjà vu results from the spread of electrical activation originating in the opposite hemisphere (cf. Halgren et al., 1978).

☐ Hemispheric Laterality and Déjà Vu

In addition to the issue of the hemisphere of origin of the seizure, another related question addressed in investigations on TLEs is the possible difference in language localization (and handedness) in TLEs with and without déjà vu. Interestingly, there is a higher than normal percentage of left-handed individuals among TLEs who experience déjà vu in their pre-seizure aura: 15% (2 of 13) in Cole and Zangwill (1963); 21% (3 of 14) in Adachi et al. (1999); 25% (2 of 8) in Weinand et al. (1994); 20% (2 of 10) in Mullan and Penfield (1959). Across these four investigations, the incidence of left-handedness among TLEs with déjà vu (20%) is about double the incidence in the general population. Using an estimate of a populaton incidence of 10% left-handedness, this deviation is significant, $X^2(1) = 5.00$, $p < .05$.

Most suggest that déjà vu occurs in the hemisphere nondominant for language (Gloor, 1991; Mullan & Penfield, 1959; Palmini & Gloor, 1992; Penfield & Perot, 1963; van Paesschen et al., 2001; Weinand et al., 1994) or speech (Cole & Zangwill, 1963; Gupta et al., 1983; Scheyer et al., 1995). For example, Cole and Zangwill (1963) found 3 of 13 (23%) TLEs *with* déjà vu had the seizure focus in the hemisphere dominant for speech, a split significantly less than chance (50%). In marked contrast, there was an even split (7 of 14, or 50%) in seizure focus between the speech dominant and nondominant hemispheres in TLEs *without* déjà vu.

In contrast to the above, Weinand et al. (1994) propose that déjà vu occurs in the hemisphere nondominant for handedness rather than language. In eight TLEs with déjà vu, all had language localized in the left hemisphere (verified by sodium amytal testing). However, the six right-handers in this group had a right-hemisphere seizure focus, whereas two left-handers in this group had a left-hemisphere seizure. Thus, Weinand et al. (1994) concluded that localization was in the hemisphere nondominant for handedness, rather than language (but see Inoue, Mihara, Matsuda, Tottori, Otsubo, & Yagi, 2000, and Scheyer et al., 1995, for exceptions).

☐ Brain Structures Associated with Déjà Vu

Investigations evaluating the seizure localization in epileptics have provided some evidence on brain structures possibly associated with the déjà vu experience. Several different approaches have been used to gather such data. For instance, researchers have evaluated the site where the epileptic seizure originates in TLEs with déjà vu in their aura, and it appears that the majority have the focus of their seizure in the anterior portion of the temporal lobe (Gibbs, Gibbs, & Lennox, 1937; Jasper, 1936). Although one interpretation of this outcome is that déjà vu is associated with the anterior temporal lobe, it is also possible that other structures are involved with déjà vu, and are activated *indirectly* by the spread of the electrical discharge (Halgren et al., 1978).

Using a different approach, Gil-Nagel and Risinger (1997) divided 35 postsurgical TLEs into two groups: those with hippocampal versus extrahippocampal temporal lobe seizures. Of 16 hippocampal patients, none had déjà vu associated with their aura, while 3 of 19 parahippocampal patients did. Similarly, Ardila, Montañes, Bernal, Serpa, and Ruiz (1986) evaluated the presence of "paroxysmal psychic phenomena" in patients who had clear evidence of both epileptic symptoms *and* circumscribed brain damage, and the subgroup of six patients with déjà vu in their preseizure aura had the anatomical focus of brain damage in the parahippocampal area of the limbic structures. Thus, there is some evidence that déjà vu may be related to brain structures outside of, but adjacent to, the hippocampus.

A second approach is to evaluate the association of the déjà vu experience with brain activity using deep electrode implantation (Bancaud et al., 1994; Fish et al., 1993; Gloor, 1990; Gloor et al., 1982; Halgren et al., 1978). This research with TLEs is, needless to say, restricted primarily to the temporal lobes. But given this qualification, there appear to be a wide variety of structures apparently associated with déjà vu experiences through such procedures: amygdala (Bancaud et al., 1994; Fish et al., 1993; Gloor, 1990; Gloor et al., 1982), hippocampus (Bancaud et al., 1994; Fish et al., 1993), parahippocampal gyrus (Gloor et al., 1982), medial temporal lobe (Bancaud et al., 1994; Halgren et al., 1978), lateral temporal lobe (Bancaud et al., 1994) and temporal isocortex (Fish et al., 1993, but see Gloor, 1990, for an exception). Fish et al. (1993) provided a more specific accounting of the 21 déjà vu experiences derived from six TLEs: 10 occurences via stimulation of the hippocampus, eight associated with the amygdala, and three from the temporal isocortex.

Extending this electrode procedure, Gloor et al. (1982) implanted deep electrodes in TLEs and performed both electrode stimulation (in one session), as well as continuous recording from each electrode for two to five weeks. Unfortunately they did not clearly identify whether each of the 23 déjà vu responses experienced by 4 of 35 TLEs were part of a natural seizure or in response to electrical stimulation. In one patient, two seizures with déjà vu both originated in the right temporal lobe, and in another patient, stimulation of the right parahippocampal gyrus and right amygdala yielded déjà vu experiences. Gloor et al. (1982) identified the medial temporal lobe as the seat of déjà vu, and noted that stimulation of the lateral temporal lobe did not produce these experiences.

Aside from the selectivity of electrode location used in such explorations, there is also an interpretative problem because of the spread of electrical activity to other areas of the brain, so one can't necessarily identify the stimulation site as the point of origin of the déjà vu (Fish et al., 1994; Halgren et al., 1978). Déjà vu experiences also result from stimulating the nondiseased hemisphere, suggesting that the déjà vu may not even be specific to the tissue where the seizure originates (Halgren et al., 1978). Complicating the interpretation of these data even further, Halgren et al. (1978) found that the elicitation of déjà vu through electrical stimulation may not be reliable. They stimulated several dozen brain locations on each of two different sessions, two weeks apart, and found a number of sites that elicited a déjà vu in one session but not the other. For example, one patient had three stimulation sites elicit a déjà vu experience in session one (left middle hippocampus, left posterior hippocampal gyrus, right anterior hippocampal gyrus) but stimulation of these same sites did *not* elicit a déjà vu in session two. Furthermore, four stimulation sites that *failed* to elicit déjà vu in session one did so in session two (left anterior hippocampus, right amygdala, right anterior hippocampus, right medial hippocampal gyrus). Neppe (1983e) suggests that the déjà vu in session two may actually be a result of prior familiarity with the stimulation experienced during session one (cf. Penfield, 1955). By implication, a prior endogenous electrical discharge may be the source of the experiential familiarity in all déjà vu experiences (not just those associated with TLEs' auras), and have little to do with the concurrent environmental stimulus circumstances.

In summary, this research using deep electrode implantation has shown that déjà vu is elicited primarily via stimulation of the amygdala, hippocampus, and structures adjacent to the hippocampus (parahippocampal), and that they are more likely to occur in TLEs who experience déjà vu as part of their routine preseizure aura. Although such research has the potential to help identify specific brain areas possibly associated with déjà vu, those areas identified are logically in or around the temporal lobe as a consequence of studying TLEs. Also, because some of those individuals are accustomed to déjà vu experiences as part of their aura, they may be biased to interpret some sensations from brain stimulation as déjà vu, whereas TLEs without déjà vu in their aura and nonepileptics may interpret such stimulation differently. Finally, electrodes are not implanted in a manner to systematically and scientifically investigate a variety of cortical locations. Rather, the background of the individual patient, and discretion of the surgeon, are more likely to dictate site selection (cf. Bancaud et al., 1994). In short, these data are fraught with some serious interpretive problems and should be evaluated with caution.

☐ Other Neuropathology

Most research relating déjà vu to physical pathology has focused on persons with TLE, but several investigations have addressed the question of whether déjà vu is differentially associated with other types of neurological disorders. For example, Hermann and Strömgren (1944) sorted through the records of a large number of patients (644) admitted to a neurosurgical department across a 7-year period and found eight instances of déjà vu among 68 patients with organic brain problems, three of which were associated with temporal lobe pathology. However, it is difficult to interpret the significance of these data given the amorphous definition of déjà vu ("disturbance of consciousness" and "increase of recognition") used by Hermann and Strömgren (1944), and their vaguely defined sampling procedures.

Keschner et al. (1936) examined 110 patients with temporal lobe tumors and found no instances of déjà vu. In contrast to this, Cole and Zangwill (1963) found a higher incidence of tumors in TLEs with déjà vu (10 of 13, or 77%) compared to TLEs without déjà vu (4 of 14, or 29%), and suggest that this relationship of tumor to déjà vu may be of some diagnostic significance. Brickner and Stein (1942) also report a patient with *déjà pensée* (see Chapter 2), a type of déjà vu in which a thought that is original feels like it has been thought before. During a subsequent autopsy, this patient was found to have a temporal lobe lesion.

Richardson and Winocur (1968) compared seven different neurosurgical patient categories on the incidence of déjà vu, and these data appear in Table 7.1.

TABLE 7.1. Déjà Vu Incidence in Various Neurological Conditions (Richardson & Winocur, 1968)

	Déjà Vu	
Diagnostic Group	No. of Cases	Incidence
General (Parkinsonism, MS, seizure)	25	54%
Brain (concussion, subdural, tumor)	44	45
Spinal cord/nerve roots (HNP)	39	33
Peripheral nerves (carpal tunnel, tic)	23	22
Meninges	4	0
Cerebral vessels	16	31
Neurosurgical disease	10	60

Richardson and Winocur (1968) found no important differences across the groups with sufficient sample sizes, but did note that those groups with brain dysfunctions (the first two listed above) show a higher incidence of déjà vu. Richardson and Winocur (1968) recombined their neurosurgery and psychiatric patients into three different groups, and found a relatively comparable déjà vu incidence across those with cerebral pathology only (42%; N = 47), psychiatric illness only (48%; N = 289), and no cerebral or psychiatric illness (39%; N = 73).

Weinstein, Marvin and Keller (1962) examined a large number (200) of head trauma patients who had been admitted to a hospital, and discovered déjà vu in some of those who had amnesia, but they did not provide specific percentages or extensive analyses of their findings. Harper (1969) found that déjà vu is more common in head injury patients who have suffered loss of consciousness, compared to those who have not, but this difference was not statistically significant. Finally, Weinstein (1969) noted that déjà vu may occur in a transient fashion during the recovery phase following brain trauma with disturbances of consciousness (i.e., closed head injury). This small group of studies suggests that it may be informative to more closely search for the occurrence of déjà vu in individuals who experience some brain trauma with accompanying disturbance or loss of consciousness. However, the rest of the literature on various neurological disorders does not point to a clear association of déjà vu with any particular neurological dysfunction.

☐ Drugs

In the only survey inquiry into the connection between drug use and déjà vu, Palmer (1979) failed to find a significant relationship in either a college or townsperson sample. However, a number of different case study reports have implicated various prescription and nonprescription drugs in eliciting déjà vu experiences either during administration or withdrawal. For example, Ellinwood (1968) found déjà vu experiences to be connected with amphetamine psychosis, which presumably is a result of the hyperexcitability of the limbic system associated with the drug. Déjà vu also has been noted as a side effect related to abuse of toluene-based solvents (Takaoka, Ikawa, & Niwa, 2001), and withdrawal from medications prescribed for bipolar disorder (carbamazepine; clonazepam) (Garbutt & Gillette, 1988).

There is also a report of a medication *reducing* the incidence of déjà vu experiences. Ide et al. (2000) present a case study of an individual with occasional psychomotor seizures (twice a week) who experienced frequent déjà vu unrelated to the seizure activity at the rate of several per day. Although the patient had been on carbamazepine to control the seizures, on a hospital readmission she was started on clonazepam (1.5 mg/day), along with sodium valproate. This new treatment eliminated the seizures, and decreased the déjà vu experiences. After two weeks, the dosage of clonazepam was increased (2.5 mg/day) and the déjà vu experiences stopped. Ide et al. (2000) attribute the disappearance of the déjà vu symptoms to increased cerebral blood flow to the temporal (and frontal) lobes because of the administration of clonazepam. Whereas the disappearance of déjà vu may have been a result of the elimination of seizure activity, it is possible that these two symptoms were independent of each other because the initial dose of medication eliminated the seizures but only reduced the déjà vu experiences.

A particularly interesting case study of an association of déjà vu with medication was reported by Taiminen and Jääskeläinen (2001). A 39-year-old man became ill with viral (type A) influenza and began taking both amantadine hydrochloride (100 mg) and phenylpropanolamine hydrochloride (25 mg) twice a day for 10 days. The day after the medication was started, the patient began having several déjà vu experiences every hour. These experiences stopped immediately after the medications were discontinued, and he did not have any déjà vu experiences between ceasing medication and a follow-up clinic visit four weeks later. While on medication, each déjà vu episode lasted between several seconds and several minutes, and he also experienced several episodes of déjà vu while dreaming. Taiminen and Jääskeläinen (2001) concluded that the experiences were *not* caused by the flu, because the patient had experienced prior infections without déjà vu. Rather, the déjà vu experiences were probably a result of excessive dopamine in the mesial temporal structures, because both amantadine hydrochloride and phenylpropanolamide hydrochloride facilitate the dopaminergic neurotransmission in these areas.

Turning to the relationship between alcohol and déjà vu, Turner (1910) claims that there is a high prevalence of pseudoreminiscence (including déjà vu) in alcoholics (60%), a figure that corresponds to Ascherson's (1907) estimate of 70%. Although both percentages differ little from the overall average incidence of déjà vu presented in Chapter 4, these are higher than the typical figures from surveys conducted during their era (Bernhard-Leroy, 1898; Heymans, 1904; Osborn, 1884). In the NORC surveys, a strong relationship appears to exists between alcohol consumption and déjà vu. Among individuals who drink, the incidence of déjà vu is significantly higher (71%) than among those who don't drink (53%), X^2 (1) = 91.06, $p < .01$. This finding of higher déjà vu among drinkers than non-drinkers (respectively) is reliable across the surveys taken in 1984 (72% vs. 54%; X^2 (1) = 47.52, $p < .01$), 1988 (71% vs. 56% X^2 (1) = 21.08, $p < .01$), and 1989 (70% vs. 47%; X^2 (1) = 23.01, $p < .01$). As a final note, one anecdotal report relates déjà vu to the use of "soft drugs." More specifically, David Crosby wrote the song "Déjà vu" about a personal déjà vu experience while under the influence of street drugs (Crosby & Gottlieb, 1988).

☐ Summary

The studies on the presence of déjà vu in TLEs lead to several conclusions. First, there is a small percentage of TLEs who have a déjà vu experience as part of their aura. These individuals seem to have the focus of their seizure activity in the right hemisphere, one that is consistently minor for speech/language function. The nature of the déjà vu for TLEs may differ from those experienced by nonepileptics in that it is slightly protracted, and the same déjà vu may repeatedly occur. Although a déjà vu experience can be recreated in these individuals through surface and deep electrical stimulation, the experience is difficult to reproduce from the same brain sites in the same people. Three sites where seizures associated with déjà vu have been shown to originate are the mesial temporal lobe (Jackson, 1888; Halgren et al., 1978; Weinand et al., 1994), the superior lateral temporal cortex (Penfield & Perot, 1963), and a network involving both lateral and medial aspects of the temporal lobe (Bancaud et al., 1994; Gloor, 1990) (cf. Adachi et al., 1999). In general, physiological research with TLEs provides considerable potential for understanding déjà vu, but the comparability of déjà vu experiences in TLEs and nonepileptics needs to be more clearly established, as well as whether déjà vu experiences produced through electrical stimulation of cortical and deeper structures of the brain in TLEs also can be elicited in non-TLEs. Reports of various prescription and nonprescription drugs triggering déjà vu deserve further exploration as an avenue for the controlled elicitation of déjà vu. Also, an apparent positive relationship between déjà vu and alcohol use should be investigated in more detail.

Psychopathology and Déjà Vu

As noted previously, much of the earliest research on déjà vu was conducted under the assumption that the experience may be diagnostic of psychological pathology. Some include the déjà vu experience in their defining set of psychotic symptoms (cf. Harriman, 1947). For example, Calkins (1916) suggests that déjà vu "... is paralleled by experiences characteristic of many forms of insanity ..." (p. 260), and Pickford (1944) claims that "... there is no doubt that déjà vu can occur as an incidental symptom in a variety of psychotic conditions ..." (p. 155). Although this orientation has skewed the manner in which déjà vu was examined in many research projects, it has yielded an extensive literature on the link between déjà vu and various forms of psychopathology.

☐ Schizophrenia

Attempts have been made to determine if the déjà vu experience is a symptom of schizophrenia (Cutting & Silzer, 1990; Kirshner, 1973; Sno, Linszen, & De Jonghe, 1992b), or a transient embodiment of that particular psychopathology (Arnaud, 1896; Carrington, 1931; Kraepelin, 1887, cited in Neppe, 1983e). It is difficult, however, to know whether the nature of a déjà vu experienced by schizophrenics is similar to that experienced by individuals lacking such pathology. In a more general sense, does the *nature* of the déjà vu experience differ between individuals with and without serious psychiatric impairment? Some argue that there is a *qualitative* difference (Berndt-Larsson, 1931; Chari, 1964; Harper, 1969), whereas others suggest that the difference is more quantitative than qualitative (Arnaud, 1896; Sno & Linszen, 1990; Sno et al., 1992b).

Crichton-Browne (1895), in one of the earliest scientific discussions of the topic, proposes that déjà vu experiences "... involve disorder of mind, trifling and transitory no doubt, like cramp in a few fibres of a muscle, but disorder nevertheless ..." (p. 2). While Burnham (1889) claims that most instances are experienced by "normal" individuals, he insists that déjà vu has an important connection to psychopathology. What differentiates déjà vu in normal versus pathological cases is that in the former, the illusion is immediately corrected but in the latter it remains uncorrected (cf. Hill, 1956). Sno et al. (1992b; 1992c) also argue for a distinction between pathological and nonpathological varieties of déjà vu, based not on any qualitative aspects but, rather, on the quantitative dimensions of duration, intensity, and frequency (Neppe, 1983e). They suggest that the "minor" form of déjà vu is sudden but transient, with reality testing intact and a sense that the entire situation (event) is being repeated (cf. Sno, 2000). In contrast, the "major" form is prolonged, with impaired reality testing (cf. Kirshner, 1973; Neppe, 1983e) and a sense that the present situation is a partial (but not complete) duplication of a prior experience. Similarly, Arnaud (1896) differentiated between the mild and severe forms of déjà vu. The mild form, which occurs in normal individuals, ends abruptly and is rectifiable. In contrast, the severe form is characteristic of pathological individuals, and this variety is long lasting and not easily dismissed. Sno et al. (1994) further argue that the major forms of déjà vu experience may be useful in predicting psychotic relapses, thought disorders, cognitive impairment, and complex partial seizures (cf. Sno & Linszen, 1990; Sno et al., 1992c). Zangwill (1945) argues for distinguishing between endogenous (organic, neuropathological) and reactive (environmentally triggered) déjà vu experiences, while Chari (1964) proposes a distinction between abnormal (associated with alcoholic psychosis, migraine, schizophrenia, epilepsy, general paresis, psychoneurosis) and normal (environmentally triggered) déjà vu.

Given this historical interest, there is surprisingly little documentation of déjà vu among schizophrenics. In fact, Neppe (1983e) could identify only one article (Kirshner, 1973) presenting case studies confirming the presence of déjà vu in schizophrenia. However, it is difficult to determine whether the déjà vu experience in schizophrenics is similar to that experienced by nonschizophrenics since schizophrenics exhibit a variety of cognitive distortions (Cutting & Silzer, 1990; Harper, 1969), and something as subtle as déjà vu may pale against this background. Considering how difficult it has been for nonclinical individuals to introspect and clearly define the personal experience of déjà vu, it is no wonder that there is a paucity of personal reports from schizophrenics.

Some suggest that the incidence of déjà vu is more common among schizophrenics than the population in general, and that these extended déjà vu experiences in schizophrenics occur repeatedly, pervading their everyday lives (Cutting & Silzer, 1990; Kirshner, 1973). Greyson (1977) did find a higher incidence in schizophrenics (65%) versus a group of nonschizophrenic psychiatric hospital patients (51%) (see Table 4.2). However, Richardson and Winocur (1968) failed to find a difference between schizophrenic and normal controls: the incidence among schizophrenics (54%) was not substantially higher than in other psychiatric patient subgroups (44%) and close to that found in their nonpsychiatric controls (41%). Similarly, Neppe (1983e) found little difference in déjà vu incidence between schizophrenic (65%) and normal (69%) samples (see Table 4.2). In general, these three studies do not support a higher incidence of déjà vu among schizophrenics: the average déjà vu incidence across the three studies is 61%, which is below the average incidence of 72% in nonclinical samples (see Chapter 4).

Other Recognition Disorders Associated with Schizophrenia

Schizophrenics experience other recognition dysfunctions that have a superficial relationship with déjà vu.

- abnormal tempo of events, in which present experience is speeded up or slowed down (as in time-lapse photography) (Brown, 1988).
- disordered sense of the beginning or duration of past events (Davidson, 1941).
- reduplication of time, in which an individual exists simultaneously in the present and the past (Weinstein, Kahn, & Sugarman, 1952).
- incorrect event sequencing, in which simultaneous events appear sequential or sequential events appear simultaneous (Head, 1920).
- disordered sense of the passage of present, ongoing time (Fraisse, 1964).

Cutting and Silzer (1990) argue that these time distortions (including déjà vu), are predominantly related to right-hemisphere dysfunction in brain damaged individuals, and by implication, these distortions in schizophrenics also may have a right-hemisphere origin.

- *micropsia*, a distortion of space, in which the present environment appears to become distant or far away, and space shrinks in size (Myers, 1977).
- *chronophrenia*, a feeling that one's entire life has been lived through before, putting the person in a perpetual state of déjà vu. A patient described by Pethö (1985) had the experience for more than a decade.
- *reduplicative paramnesia*, a belief that the present situation is one that has been duplicated from the past (Ellis, Luauté, & Retterstøl, 1994; Hakim, Verma, & Greiffenstein, 1988; Langdon & Coltheart, 2000; Marková & Berrios, 2000; Pick, 1903). A prototypical episode of reduplicative paramnesia involves a patient who mistakenly thinks that their present hospital is the same one they have been in earlier but in a different geographical location. The person's subjective evaluation remains unaltered in the face of clear evidence contradicting their impression (Langdon & Coltheart, 2000).

☐ Neurotic Conditions

The déjà vu experience has also been associated with more moderate forms of psychological maladjustment. For example, Crichton-Browne (1895) suggested that déjà vu is more common in the "neurotic classes," although one of his contemporaries, Bernhard-Leroy (1898, cited in Sno et al., 1992c), concluded that the incidence of déjà vu was no different in "neuropathic" compared to normal individuals.

A higher incidence of déjà vu has been supposedly linked to a variety of different moderate to severe psychological disturbances, including unstable mood fluctuations (Heymans, 1904, 1906), psychasthenia (Gordon, 1921; Kinnier Wilson, 1929), and bipolar mood (manic-depressive) disorder (Lewis, Feldman, Greene, & Martinez-Mustardo, 1984; MacCurdy, 1924). In addition to such informal speculation and rare case reports, some have conducted a more systematic comparison of déjà vu incidence in various diagnostic groups (Harper, 1969; Richardson & Winocur, 1968; Silberman et al., 1985). Richardson and Winocur (1968) analyzed data on 301 psychiatric patients to evaluate whether déjà vu incidence varied across subtypes of psychopathology. Déjà vu incidence in six of these groups is presented in Table 8.1 (three groups with five or fewer patients are not presented: acute brain syndrome; miscellaneous; no psychiatric diagnosis).

Comparing of the four psychiatric groups with a substantial sample size (first four listed in Table 8.1) reveals little difference in déjà vu inci-

TABLE 8.1. Déjà Vu Incidence in
Psychiatric Categories (From Richardson &
Winocur, 1968)

Diagnostic Group	No. of Cases	Incidence
Depression	127	42%
Psychoneurosis	51	47
Alcoholism and addiction	41	46
Undiagnosed	25	48
Chronic brain syndrome	11	0
Personality disorder	11	81

dence. Richardson and Winocur (1968) break down the psychoneurotic group into three subgroups, and report that hysterics (57%) and anxiety neurotics (58%) have a higher déjà vu incidence than depressive reaction (38%). However, with no information on the size of each subgroup, it is difficult to interpret these percentages. Richardson and Winocur (1968) point out the high incidence of déjà vu in personality disorder (see above) and suggest that déjà vu may be helpful in clarifying the nature of this particular disorder. But with such a small sample, this conclusion does not warrant serious consideration.

In contrast to Richardson and Winocur (1968), Harper (1969) found no relationship between déjà vu frequency and specific neurotic traits (and phobias) or general psychiatric health. In fact, déjà vu appeared to be *less* common in neurotic individuals. A subgroup with "borderline psychiatric health" (19% of the sample) was no different from a group defined as "psychiatrically healthy" in déjà vu incidence (although no statistics were supplied). Harper (1969) also noted a lower déjà vu incidence in a subsample with "marked neurotic traits" but individuals experiencing déjà vu actually tended to be *less* emotionally sensitive than those not experiencing déjà vu. Finally, Silberman et al. (1985) compared individuals with major depressive disorders and controls (hypertensive out-patients) but found no significant difference in déjà vu between the groups (73% and 63% incidence, respectively). Interestingly, they discovered that a déjà vu experience was less likely during a depressive episode than in the interval between episodes.

In summary, at this time there is no strong or compelling evidence that the incidence of déjà vu differs across various psychiatric categories. Clearly, more systematic research using broader samples with more reliable instruments and diagnostic procedures might be informative. However, such an approach necessarily implies an assumption that is probably false: that déjà vu is reflective of pathological, rather than normal, cognitive processes. And the same cautionary note brought up with schizophrenics applies here: Given the subtle nature of the déjà vu experience, it may not show up as clearly against a background of the type of cognitive difficulties experienced by individuals with moderate to severe psychological disturbances.

☐ Depersonalization

The experience of depersonalization is characterized by feelings of unreality or strangeness about the environment or the self (or both) and has also been referred to as estrangement and alienation. This experience tends to be associated with schizotypal personality disorder or schizophrenia, and may occur in those experiencing intense anxiety, stress, or fatigue. When this sense of unreality focuses outward, rather than inward, it is referred to as derealization and appears to be similar to déjà vu (Bird, 1957; Federn, 1952). Thus, a number of researchers have been intrigued by a possible connection between depersonalization and déjà vu (Adachi et al., 2003; Arlow, 1959; Barton, 1979; Bernhard-Leroy, 1898; Brauer et al., 1970; Buck, 1970; Buck & Geers, 1967; Dixon, 1963; Federn, 1952; Freud, 1936; Harper, 1969; Hartocollis, 1975; Heymans, 1904, 1906; Janet, 1903; Kuiper, 1973; Levitan, 1969; McKellar, 1978; Myers & Grant, 1972; Nemiah, 1989; Oberndorf, 1941; Pickford, 1942a, 1942b, 1944; Poetzl, 1926; Roth, 1959; Schilder, 1936; Shapiro, 1978; Siomopoulos, 1972; Sno & Linszen, 1990; Wilmer Brakel, 1989).

Some suggest that depersonalization, derealization, and déjà vu are interchangeable and refer to the same phenomenon (Brauer et al., 1970; McKellar, 1978), but this is clearly an imprecise and inaccurate use of the terms (Barton, 1979). Both depersonalization and derealization represent disturbances in the sense of reality, whereas with déjà vu both the environment and self appear normal. It is simply one's interpretation of their familiarity that is altered. Taking a slightly different perspective, both Freud (1936) and Nemiah (1989) suggest that déjà vu may represent a positive counterpart of depersonalization (and derealization), in that one has an inappropriate sense of familiarity rather than unfamiliarity.

Several investigations have found a direct empirical relationship between depersonalization and déjà vu experiences. Heymans (1904, 1906) discovered that 82% of those experiencing depersonalization also had déjà vu, whereas only 48% of those *not* experiencing depersonalization had déjà vu. Based on these data, Heymans (1904, 1906) suggests that déjà vu is simply a milder form of depersonalization. Similarly, Myers and Grant (1972) found a higher déjà vu incidence in those with, versus without, depersonalization experiences but that this difference was statistically significant only for the males (80% vs. 40% déjà vu incidence, respectively) but not the females (80% vs. 61% déjà vu incidence, respectively). Roth (1959) also noted that a substantial percentage (37%) of phobic anxiety patients *with* depersonalization had either déjà vu or related disturbances of time, whereas none of the patients *without* depersonalization had any such experience (cf. Harper & Roth, 1962). Buck and Geers (1967) found that four varieties of depersonalization (self image, body image, physical environment, other people) were positively related to déjà vu with the relationship stronger for auditory than visual forms. Finally, Harper (1969) discovered that depersonalization was reported significantly more often among those individuals experiencing déjà vu than among those not experiencing déjà vu.

In contrast with the above, several studies fail to support a relationship between déjà vu and depersonalization. Dixon (1963) used a depersonalization questionnaire and found that 12 items formed a factor identified as self-alienation (sample item: "As I was talking, my voice sounded strange to me. It was as if someone else were talking and I was just listening"; p. 372). The déjà vu items did not show an appreciable loading on this factor. In another investigation, Brauer et al. (1970) did find that déjà vu was significantly correlated with depersonalization (0.32), but not with derealization (0.18). In general, however, Brauer et al. (1970) noted that déjà vu "... correlated with very few of the variables that depersonalization and derealization did, and thus most likely represents a different type of symptom or experiential state" (p. 513). Finally, Adachi et al. (2003) found a nonsignificant correlation between déjà vu and depersonalization (0.13), and that that they loaded on different factors in a factor analysis of the Inventory for Déjà Vu Experiences Assessment (IDEA).

Although equivocal, the evidence shows a possible but moderate relationship between derealization and déjà vu, and this topic certainly deserves further empirical exploration.

☐ Dissociation

Dissociation, in which an individual withdraws from present reality into a different cognitive state, also has been connected to déjà vu. Irwin (1996) tried to establish a relationship between déjà vu and two measures related to dissociative tendencies: parents' encouragement of imaginative activities in children, as measured by the Parents and Imagination Scale (PAIS), and childhood trauma, as measured by the Survey of Traumatic Childhood Events (STCE; Council & Edwards, 1987). The PAIS was unrelated to déjà vu experiences, and the only item on the childhood trauma scale related to déjà vu was intrafamilial physical abuse during child-hood ($r = 0.30$). Thus, these two aspects of dissociative experience showed little relationship to déjà vu.

A questionnaire specifically designed to measure dissociation, the Questionnaire of Experiences of Dissociation (or QED; Riley, 1988), includes a déjà vu item: "I have never had periods of déjà vu, that is, found myself in a new position with a distinct sense that I had been there or experienced it before" (p. 449). Out of 26 items, this déjà vu item has the lowest item-to-total correlation (.08) which strongly suggests that déjà vu may be dissociated from dissociation. Although a déjà vu item is *not* included on the Dissociative Experiences Scale (or DES; Bernstein & Putnam, 1986), Sno et al. (1994) found a significant positive relationship between reported déjà vu incidence and DES score. Although evidence does not suggest a close relationship between dissociation and déjà vu, some clinicians still assume that déjà vu may be part of, or related to, dissociative experiences (Riley, 1988).

☐ Summary

Early researchers tried to establish a link between déjà vu and serious psychopathology with hopes of finding the experience of some diagnostic value. However, there does not seem to be any special association between déjà vu and schizophrenia or other neurotic conditions. Other cognitive disturbances related to déjà vu are unique to schizophrenia (and brain damage), such as reduplicative paramnesia. There is also some indication of a relationship between déjà vu and depersonalization, but little to link déjà vu and dissociative experiences. More systematic exploration is needed on how déjà vu does, or does not, relate to a variety of psychopathological conditions. There are those who argue *for* (Sno & Linszen, 1990; Sno et al., 1992b) and *against* (Pagliaro, 1991) including déjà vu as a pathology in the Diagnostic and Statistical Manual (DSM) of the American Psychiatric Association (APA). Sno et al. (1992b) suggest that prior to such a time, déjà vu can be subsumed under "dissociation" in *DSM-IV-R* because it is defined as "disturbances or alterations in the normally integrative functions of identity, memory, perception or attention" (Sno et al., 1992b, p. 565).

Jamais Vu

Whereas déjà vu involves an experience of inappropriate familiarity, one can also experience the opposite illusion of recognition: inappropriate *un*familiarity, or jamais vu. More specifically, a jamais vu experience involves an objectively familiar situation that feels unfamiliar, such as walking into your bedroom and momentarily having no sense of familiarity associated with this setting. Whereas the translation of déjà vu means "already seen," jamais vu means "never seen."

Many have described the jamais vu experience and commented on its relationship to déjà vu (Adachi et al., 2003; Ardila et al., 1993; Bancaud et al., 1994; Breese, 1921; Burnham, 1903; Chari, 1964; Conklin, 1935; Cotard, 1880, 1882; Critchley, 1989; Cutting & Silzer, 1990; Devereux, 1967; Ey, Bernard, & Brisset, 1978, cited in Sno, 2000; Gloor et al., 1982; Harper & Roth, 1962; Heymans, 1904, 1906; Hunter, 1957; Irwin, 1993, 1996; Jackson, 1888; Krijgers Janzen, 1958; Morgan, 1936; Myers & Grant, 1972; Neppe, 1983e; Oberndorf, 1941; O'Connor, 1948; Penfield, 1955; Reed, 1974, 1979; Roberts et al., 1990; Searleman & Herrmann, 1994; Silbermann, 1963; Silberman et al., 1985; Siomopoulos, 1972; Sno, 1994, 2000; Sno & Draaisma, 1993; Sno & Linszen, 1990; Stern, 1938; Taylor, 1979; Wolfradt, 2000; Woodworth, 1948; Yager & Gitlin, 1995). The jamais vu experience has been referred to as "illusion of the never seen" (Conklin, 1935; Gordon, 1921), "alienation" (Stern, 1938; Hunter, 1957), and "feeling of strangeness" (Morgan, 1936; Woodworth, 1948; Tiffin et al., 1946). A sampling of jamais vu definitions appear below:

"... a circumstance seems totally unfamiliar despite the experient's knowledge that it has been encountered on numerous previous occasions" (Irwin, 1993, p. 159).

"... objects with which he knows he is familiar appear unfamiliar as if he were seeing them for the first time" (Oberndorf, 1941, p. 316).

"familiar places or people are somehow not familiar or the way they should be" (Ardila et al., 1993, p. 138) (cf. Roberts et al., 1990, p. 83).

☐ Incidence of Jamais Vu

A few individuals have suggested that everyone has experienced jamais vu (Silbermann, 1963) and that jamais vu is as common as déjà vu (Taylor, 1979), but most agree that jamais vu is much rarer than déjà vu (Ardila et al., 1993; Cutting & Silzer, 1990; Findler, 1998; Harper & Roth, 1962; Reed, 1974, 1979; Morgan, 1936; Neppe, 1983e; Roberts et al., 1990; Silberman et al., 1985; Sno, 2000; Tiffin et al., 1946; Wolfradt, 2000). Investigations comparing the incidence of déjà vu and jamais vu (see Table 9.1) bear this out. In every comparison the incidence of jamais vu considerably lower than déjà vu.

A comparison of the frequency of experiences among experients, as presented in Table 9.2, clearly suggests that déjà vu is more common than jamais vu across all frequency categories. Note that Roberts et al. (1990) combined the "never" and "less than one per month" categories, so one cannot derive a lifetime incidence from these data.

TABLE 9.1. Lifetime Incidence of Déjà Vu Versus Jamais Vu

	Sample N	Déjà Vu	Jamais Vu
Silberman et al. (1985)			
Affective disorder	44	73%	5%
Epileptic	37	54	5
Control	30	63	3
Harper & Roth (1962)			
TLEs	30	23	3
Phobic anxiety depersonalization	30	40	30
Ardila et al. (1993)	2500	91	52
Neppe (1983e)			
Normal	28	68	0
TLEs	14	86	58
Schizophrenics	20	65	0

TABLE 9.2. Frequency of Déjà Vu (DV) Versus Jamais Vu (JV) Experiences Among Experients

	Never	< Once/ Month	Once/ Month	Once/ Week	Several/ Week
Ardila et al. (1993)					
Déjà vu	9	34	40	13	4
Jamais vu	48	29	16	5	2
Roberts et al. (1990, Study 1)					
Déjà vu		68	23	6	2
Jamais vu		89	9	2	0
Roberts et al. (1990, Study 2)					
Déjà vu		69	36	7	2
Jamais vu		91	8	1	0

The data presented in both Tables 9.1 and 9.2 clearly show that the incidence and frequency of jamais vu is consistently, and substantially, lower than déjà vu. The variability across surveys on jamais vu incidence is quite striking (Table 9.1), but may be due to the difficulty in presenting a precise definition of the experience.

☐ Jamais Vu and Temporal Lobe Epilepsy

Because of the superficial relationship between déjà vu and jamais vu, and the fact that jamais vu is occasionally reported by TLEs, some investigations have examined the presence of jamais vu in the preseizure auras of TLEs (cf. Penfield, 1955).

> In another patient, who called his attacks 'losses of understanding,' there was clearly both 'word-deafness' and 'word-blindness,' with retention of ordinary sight and hearing. (Jackson, 1888, p. 191)

Neppe (1983e) discovered that none in his nonclinical sample who had déjà vu had experienced jamais vu, but half of his TLEs who had déjà vu also had experienced jamais vu. Based on these data, Neppe (1983e) suggests that jamais vu (rather than déjà vu) might be an important indicator of TLE, but this conclusion seems unwarranted given the small samples in both TLE and nonclinical groups.

Kinnier Wilson (1929) classified two types of recognition dysfunction in the TLE preseizure aura: Type I (déjà vu, or familiarity) and Type II (strangeness, unreality, or unfamiliarity). Both Jackson (1888) and Kinnier Wilson (1929) report cases where jamais vu rather than déjà vu was present in the preseizure aura of TLEs, and Sengoku et al. (1997) found that among patients with "dreamy states" in their preseizure auras, jamais vu (six patients) was actually more common than déjà vu (two patients). However, Pacia et al. (1996) found the opposite: of 21 TLEs, six had déjà vu as part of their aura, but only one experienced jamais vu.

Whereas it is clear that both déjà vu and jamais vu can occur in the preseizure aura of TLEs, the data are too limited to draw any conclusion about its incidence, significance, or association with déjà vu.

☐ Relationship Between Déjà Vu and Jamais Vu

The superficial resemblance between déjà vu and jamais vu has led many researchers to characterize the two phenomena as representing opposite ends of a familiarity dysfunction (Cotard, 1880, 1882; Cutting & Silzer, 1990; Ellis et al., 1994; Gordon, 1921; Heymans, 1904, 1906; Hoch, 1947; Irwin, 1993; Mullan & Penfield, 1959; Neppe, 1983e; Penfield, 1955; Reed, 1974, 1979; Silbermann, 1963; Sno, 1994, 2000; Sno & Linszen, 1990; Stern, 1938; Taylor, 1979; Woodworth, 1940). Déjà vu and jamais vu have been viewed as polar opposites in various ways. Kinnier Wilson (1929) contrasts the two phenomena as hyperfamiliarity versus hypofamiliarity, Taylor (1979) suggests that a brain mechanism exists for "tagging" all information as familiar or unfamiliar and that jamais vu and déjà vu represent different failures (respectively) of each labeling function, while Ey et al. (1978, cited in Sno, 2000) argue that both déjà vu and jamais vu reflect pathological connections between the present reality and the past: with déjà vu, it is a pathological association; with jamais vu, it is a pathological dissociation.

Another group of investigators does not draw the specific distinction, but describe the general dysfunction connecting the two phenomena. Critchley (1989) speculates that déjà vu and jamais vu are both temporary malfunctions of the familiarity response, both involving the temporal lobe, whereas Myers and Grant (1972) propose that both are forms of depersonalization. Penfield (1955) refers to these two experiences as both "interpretive" illusions of opposite nature, and Ellinwood (1968) suggests that both reflect disturbances of assimilating present and past experiences. Many have also noted that jamais vu, like déjà vu, is more likely to occur under conditions of stress or fatigue (Burnham, 1903; Conklin, 1935; Reed, 1979; Tiffin et al., 1946).

In contrast to the above perspective, some consider jamais vu distinct from déjà vu (Reed, 1974). Wolfradt (2000) claims that déjà vu is related to daydreaming, whereas jamais vu is connected to depersonalization

(Myers & Grant, 1972). Adachi et al. (2003) found a nonsignificant correlation between déjà vu and jamais vu experience (.13), and in a factor analysis of the IDEA (Adachi et al., 2001; Sno et al., 1994), déjà vu and jamais vu loaded on different factors. Others have noted a distinct contrast in the affect associated with déjà vu and jamais vu. Sengoku et al. (1997) found that TLEs with déjà vu in their aura describe it as familiar and pleasant, whereas TLEs with jamais vu in their aura describe it as fearful and unpleasant. Similarly, Critchley (1989), suggests that "with déjà vu there may be an accompanying feeling of warmth and with jamais vu a feeling of coldness as well as strangeness" (p. 196).

Bernstein and Putnam (1986) argue that jamais vu is a dissociative experience and déjà vu is not. In fact, the DES (cf. Carlson & Putman, 1993; Carlson, Putnam, Ross, Anderson, Clark, Torem, Coons, Bowman, Chu, Dill, Lowenstein, & Braun, 1991) has a jamais vu item ("some people have the experience of being in a familiar place but finding it strange and unfamiliar") but no déjà vu item. In contrast, the QED has a déjà vu item ("I have never had periods of déjà vu, that is, found myself in a new position with a distinct sense that I had been there or experienced it before") but no jamais vu item (Riley, 1988, p. 449). Thus, those designing clinical questionnaires differ in their views concerning whether both déjà vu and jamais vu are related to dissociative experience.

Hoch (1947) suggests that during the recovery from electroconvulsive therapy (ECT), an individual may experience jamais vu, or a loss of familiarity, even though they typically do not experience déjà vu. However, it is unclear whether Hoch is defining jamais vu correctly because from his description, the patient does not appear to be surprised that the present objectively familiar situation momentarily feels unfamiliar. Despite this issue, the possible presence of déjà vu and jamais vu during post-ECT recovery should be explored further, as a disturbance of recognition appears to be a typical side-effect of such treatment (Cahill & Frith, 1995; Squire, Chace, & Slater, 1976).

☐ Explanations of Jamais Vu

There exists an abundance of explanations for déjà vu (see Chapters 12 through 15) but little speculation on the etiology of jamais vu. One cannot simply reverse an explanation for déjà vu because déjà vu reflects the presence of an unanticipated response (familiarity), whereas jamais vu represents the absence of an expected response. Or, can unfamiliarity be considered a response? Hunter (1957) has offered one of the few explanations for the déjà vu experience:

We may return to a room we know well: all seems familiar yet strangely unfamiliar—until at last we specify the cause. Some piece of furniture has been changed since we saw the room last. We had vaguely recognized some change but, without being able to characterize the nature of the change more closely, we were left with the puzzlement of unaccountable unfamiliarity. (p. 41)

Findler (1998), Morgan (1936), and Hunter (1957) similarly believe that one slight, and undetected, alteration in a familiar environment may trigger a sense of unfamiliarity that overgeneralizes to the entire setting. The logical problem with this particular interpretation, however, is that the preponderance of familiar elements in an accustomed setting should override the sense of unfamiliarity engendered by *one* changed or missing element. When we bump into an old acquaintance who had changed one aspect of their physical appearance (dyed hair; shaved moustache) we are not overwhelmed by a sense of unfamiliarity. Rather, the cues to the individual's identity are sufficiently strong that we have only a modest sense of memorial discord rather than an attention-grabbing absence of familiarity characteristic of jamais vu. In a more complex and less familiar setting, such as the lounge at the university student center, we may be struck by a similar sense of unfamiliarity but be less able to attribute it to a minor change in the elements comprising the scene.

Searleman and Herrmann (1994) propose that jamais vu occurs when encountering familiar persons in a different context (cf. Read, Vokey, & Davidson, 1991). When you seen your mail delivery person in an ice cream parlor, you may fail to recognize her because of the changed context. However, Searleman and Herrmann's (1994) analogy is not technically appropriate because one does not experience the feeling of unfamiliarity unless that individual gives you some indication that they should be familiar (e.g., says "Hello" to you). If they don't do so, then you may not even be cognizant of your recognition failure. More specifically, you routinely and repeatedly fail to recognize people as you walk past them at the mall. If you brush pass your priest at the grocery store and fail to recognize him in this particular context, it does not necessarily lead to a jamais vu experience. For a jamais vu to occur, one needs the *expectation* of familiarity to be violated by the momentary impression of unfamiliarity.

Another possible mechanism underlying jamais vu could be memory distortion resulting from repeated retrievals or mental rumination. To illustrate this interpretation, Reed (1974) points to a study conducted by Belbin (1950). Her experimental participants sat in a waiting room for several minutes prior to her "study," with a poster on the wall facing them a dozen feet away. When taken to another room for the experiment, some participants were asked to recall the details of the poster (experimental group), while others did an unrelated task (control group). On a subsequent recognition test on the same poster, 88% of control but only 25% of experimental participants selected the correct poster from among a set of related alternatives. Belbin (1950) concluded that retrieval distorts memory of the original stimulus through the generation of erroneous material to "fill the gaps" in the description.

Dywan (1984) performed a similar study. A set of simple line-drawings of common objects were presented one at a time. Participants then recalled the list items a varying number of times prior to a subsequent recognition test. Even one recall reduced subsequent recognition performance by one third, compared to a control group with no interpolated recalls efforts, and additional recall trials further eroded recognition performance (cf. Jacoby, Kelley, & Dywan, 1989). Apparently, the act of recall creates an elaboration of the original memory, such that the memory no longer matches the original stimulus (cf. Reed, 1974), causing a reduction in familiarity similar to that experienced with jamais vu. This type of memory distortion may also be related to the Aussage effect, in which "… in describing a picture immediately after it has been seen, objects not contained in the picture are given, the position and number of objects are altered and colors are falsely named." (Smith, 1913, p. 55)

The jamais vu experience is also similar to "word alienation," "word blindness," or "loss of meaning of words" (Reed, 1974) where an ordinary word suddenly looks or sounds unfamiliar (Heymans, 1904, cited in Sno and Draaisma, 1993; Jackson, 1888; Sno & Draaisma, 1993). Heymans (1904, 1906) found word alienation to be quite common (77% incidence) and the association between déjà vu and word alienation supported his speculation that déjà vu and jamais vu may be related. Reed (1974) suggests that one can induce word alienation by simply staring at a particular word for about a minute.

> The word will no longer suggest any meaning … and may in fact no longer seem like a word. This effect … may be a humble parallel to one of the techniques used to induce a state of mystical contemplation in oriental religions … (Reed, 1974, p. 108)

While loss of meaning of words is visually based, an auditory parallel to this experience is semantic satiation (Breese, 1921), in which the repeated oral pronunciation of a word causes it to suddenly lose its connotative meaning (Amster, 1964; Kounios, Kotz, & Holcomb, 2000; Reed, 1974).

Roediger (1996) proposes that jamais vu is related to cue-dependent forgetting (Thompson & Tulving, 1970; Tulving & Thompson, 1973). When context is changed from encoding to test, an individual may fail to recognize a word as old. For example, the word "blue" is first studied in the pair "chair-BLUE" during a paired associate learning task. Following this, the participant is given a supposedly unrelated free association task and provided with stimuli ("sky-____") highly likely to elicit response words from the preceding paired associate list ("blue"). When subsequently asked to identify whether any generated responses in this free association task had appeared earlier on the paired associate list, there is a low likelihood of identifying these. Such recollection failure of generated words is presumably because of the changed context. That is, the word "blue" learned originally with "chair" is experienced in a different context when generated to "sky," and thus the lack of a connection. However, what's missing in the cue-dependent forgetting analogy of jamais vu is the participant's awareness of this unfamiliarity. They are not *struck* by the unfamiliarity of the generated word in the free-association task but simply overlook it. To have a jamais vu, one must experience surprising unfamiliarity in the face of expected familiarity.

Another phenomenon related to jamais vu is cryptomnesia. Jamais vu entails *recognition* unaccompanied by an expected sense of familiarity, whereas cryptomnesia involves *recall* (or generation) unaccompanied by familiarity (Dunlap, 1922). More specifically, with cryptomnesia one generates a supposedly novel or creative response that is, in fact, inadvertently copied (or plagiarized) from some prior experience or person (Brown & Halliday, 1991; Brown & Murphy, 1989; Marsh & Bower, 1993). This phenomenon is a form of source amnesia (Schacter, Harbluk, & McLachlan, 1984), in which an individual is amnestic regarding the source of a prior experience. Thus, cryptomnesia and jamais vu reflect the effects of source amnesia in retrieval and recognition, respectively (Humphrey, 1923; Neppe, 1983b; Reed, 1974, 1979). With cryptomnesia, one is not "struck" by the unfamiliarity, whereas with jamais vu one is jarred by the subjective sense that this should be familiar.

☐ Capgras' Syndrome

In the clinical realm, the Capgras' syndrome is closely related to jamais vu (Capgras & Réboul-Lachaux, 1923). In Capgras' syndrome, an individual believes that someone familiar, such as a friend or close relative, has been replaced by an imposter. This is one of the most thoroughly studied of the delusional misidentification syndromes, and does not occur in normal adults. It is experienced almost exclusively by schizophrenics or persons with organic brain damage (Critchley, 1989) involving the right hemisphere (Förstl, Almeida, Owen, Burns, & Howard, 1991). Berson (1983) speculated that a failure of the *affective* component of familiarity might underlie the Capgras' syndrome. More specifically, a momentary absence of the affective response routinely felt when encountering someone very familiar is interpreted to suggest that this person is not who they appear to be, and is actually a double or an impostor. Benson and Stuss (1990) propose that this difficulty ties in with the prefrontal lobe function. Thus, whereas the TLE literature implies temporal lobe involvement in recognition dysfunction of déjà vu, the prefrontal cortex may contribute to familiarity dysfunctions related to jamais vu. Two other rare misidentification syndromes are often connected with the Capgras' syndrome: Frégoli syndrome (Courbon & Fail, 1927), in which an *unfamiliar* person has been replaced by a friend or relative, and inter-metamorphosis (Courbon & Tusques, 1932), in which a *familiar* individual has been replaced by a familiar friend or relative.

☐ Summary

The jamais vu ("never seen") experience is a recognition illusion that involves the loss of the feeling of familiarity for an objectively familiar stimulus or setting. Jamais vu is considerably less common than déjà vu, and while the experience has been described by many scholars, relatively little research has been done on it. Some claim that déjà vu and jamais vu have similar underlying mechanisms and are at the opposite extremes of familiarity dysfunction, but others suggest that these two experiences have different etiologies. In contrast to the plethora of explanations for déjà vu, there has been scant speculation on the cause of jamais vu. A number of other recognition dysfunctions resemble jamais vu, including loss of meaning of words, semantic satiation, the Aussage effect, and Capgras' syndrome.

Parapsychological Interpretations of Déjà Vu

For more than a century, researchers have proposed numerous interpretations for the déjà vu experience. In fact, Neppe (1983b) suggests that 44 different causes for déjà vu have been put forth and that "... one single explanation for déjà vu is probably as untrue as one single cause for headache" (Neppe, 1983a, p. 33). Other researchers similarly believe that déjà vu may have multiple causes depending on the person and situation, and there may even be different causes for different déjà vu experiences by the same person (Angell, 1908; Ellis, 1911; Schneck, 1962; Smith, 1913; Sno & Linszen, 1990, 1991; Sno et al., 1992b; White, 1973). In fact, the incredible variety of interpretations is further testament to the enigmatic and complex nature of the experience.

The main purpose of this book is to emphasize the many plausible and potentially testable scientific explanations of déjà vu presented over the past 150 years (Chapters 12 through 15). Nonscientific interpretations of déjà vu from parapsychological and psychodynamic perspectives are covered in the next two chapters. It should be strongly emphasized that such explanations are not useful for the goal of gaining an understanding of déjà vu. Rather, these interpretations are presented for completeness and to provide a historical account of the various ways we have viewed the experience. Also, some famous and otherwise credible authors—such as Aristotle, Plato, Jung, and Pythagoras—discuss the déjà vu experience from a parapsychological perspective, and a formidable body of litera-ture (over 50 articles) exists in this domain. An unfortunate side-effect of such explanations is that they create an impediment to empirical research on the phenomenon, causing serious scientists to keep their distance from the phenomenon (cf. Funkhouser, 1983a). The interested reader should consult Neppe (1983e) and Sno and Linszen (1990) for a more complete coverage of these explanations.

The degree to which the déjà vu experience has engaged the parapsy-chological community is reflected in over two dozen articles on the topic in parapsychological journals: *Journal of Parapsychology* (three articles), *Parapsychological Journal of South Africa* (seven articles), *Proceedings of the Society for Psychical Research* (five articles), and *Journal of the American Society of Psychical Research* (10 articles).

The very existence of parapsychological interpretations of déjà vu may have been "forced" by the strange nature of the experience. For instance, a predominant (if not logical) reaction to the strong sense of familiarity to an ostensibly new experience is that one actually *has* expe-rienced this situation before in another life. Carmichael (1957) even sug-gests that "it may be that the idea of reincarnation so common in Eastern religions may be based in part on the *déjà vu* experience" (p. 123), and Stern (1938) similarly asserts that déjà vu embodies one of the psycholog-ical experiences from which "the doctrines of pre-existence, transmigra-tion of souls, and reincarnation drew their inspiration" (p. 210). Walter (1960) vividly alludes to the power of the illusion to lead one to believe in the supernatural:

> ... the déjà vu phenomenon, the feeling that "all this has happened before"—a sensation vivid enough to convince some people of the transcendental nature of personality by demonstrating how to side-step the inexorable flood of time. (p. 7)

☐ Relationship Between Déjà Vu and Belief in the Paranormal

The déjà vu experience has been implicitly (and unfortunately) character-ized as paranormal in surveys that embed déjà vu items with ones on paranormal phenomena (Gallup & Newport, 1991; Gaynard, 1992; Gree-ley, 1975; Green, 1966; Greyson, 1977; Irwin, 1993; Kohr, 1980; McClenon, 1988, 1994; NORC, 1984, 1988, 1989; Palmer, 1979; Ross & Joshi, 1992; Ross et al., 1989). But what do the data say about such an association? Several outcomes suggest that déjà vu is separate from the realm of the paranormal. Gaynard (1992) found the percent overlap between experiencing déjà vu and various paranormal phenomena in his sample to be relatively low: ghosts (19%), poltergeists (7%), precognition (38%), OBE (7%), telepathy (14%), psychokinesis (6%), UFOs (6%), and apparition of living person (3%). Furthermore, Gaynard (1992) found an asymmetry between déjà vu and the paranormal phenomena: 74% of those experiencing precognition also experience déjà vu, but only 38% of those with déjà vu also had precognitive experiences; 65% of those experiencing ghosts had déjà vu, but 19% of déjà vu experients have seen a ghost. If paranormal phenomena are closely related to déjà vu, these percentages logically should be more symmetrical.

Fox (1992) examined the relationship between déjà vu and four paranormal items in the NORC (1984, 1988, 1989) survey data. While the four paranormal dimensions (ESP, clairvoyance, contact with the dead, and mysticism) were strongly interrelated with each other, déjà vu was unrelated to any of them. In fact, a factor analysis yields a single factor solution for these variables when déjà vu is *excluded*, but not when it is included. Simply put, Fox's (1992) analyses strongly suggest that déjà vu is clearly differentiated from the paranormal experiences. Gallagher et al. (1994) found that the correlation between the déjà vu item from their Anomalous Experiences Inventory (AEI) and total scores from three other paranormal inventories was relatively low, ranging from .10 to .20, and the item-to-total correlation of déjà vu with the "anomalous/paranormal" experience scale on the AEI (29 items) was only .23. Finally, Palmer (1979) uses an indirect, exclusionary criterion to argue that déjà vu should be considered separate from paranormal phenomena: whereas age and déjà vu are strongly correlated, age is unrelated to any of the parapsychological dimensions evaluated (e.g., ESP, OBE, poltergeists).

In contrast to the above, McClenon (1994) did find that déjà vu was positively correlated with ESP, out-of-body experiences, contact with dead, and night paralysis in "most" of his six different samples of respondents. Sobal and Emmons (1982) discovered that most correlations between belief in déjà vu and belief in "unexplained phenomena" were statistically significant: ESP (.41), precognition (.47), clairvoyance (.37), Loch Ness monster (.29), Sasquatch (.30), ghosts (.31), witches (.24), and astrology (.17). In a factor analysis, déjà vu belief loaded high on the factor that also included precognition, ESP, and clairvoyance. It needs to be emphasized, again, that these data used by Sobal and Emmons (1982) were derived from a 1978 Gallup Poll, which may be biased by the déjà vu item's inclusion with "unexplained or paranormal phenomena." Kohr (1980) also suggests that there is a moderate relationship between déjà vu and paranormal phenomena, and found that déjà vu loaded moderately (.53) on a factor that also included past-life memory and apparitions, and significantly correlated (.01 level) with all phenomena (e.g., ESP, haunting, mystical experience, etc.).

In general, the empirical connection between the déjà vu experience and paranormal phenomena appears to be weak, at best. One must keep in mind that those investigations showing a positive association used data derived from survey instruments mixing déjà vu and paranormal items (Kohr, 1980; Palmer, 1979; McClenon, 1994). Thus, a built-in positive bias can't be ruled out in these findings.

☐ Precognition

Personal descriptions of déjà vu often include a feeling of being able to predict what will happen next (Burnham, 1889; Chari, 1964; Dugas, 1894; Holmes, 1891; Jensen, 1868, cited in Marková & Berrios, 2000; Kraepelin, 1887; McKellar, 1957; Osborn, 1884; Reed, 1979; Sander, 1874, cited in Marková & Berrios, 2000; Sno & Linszen, 1990; Titchener, 1924; Ward, 1918). Typically, one has the impression that they know what someone will say before they say it, or know what events will unfold before they do. Some even incorporate this dimension into their definition of déjà vu (Carrington, 1931; Dugas, 1894; Jensen, 1868; Krijgers Janzen, 1958; Lalande, 1893; Myers, 1895; Sno, 2000; Titchener, 1924; Ward, 1918) (see Table 2.2), including statements such as déjà vu is "... sometimes connected with a 'feeling that we know exactly what is coming' ..." (Titchener (1924, p. 187) and the person "... can almost tell just what is about to happen next" (Carrington (1931, p. 301). Krijgers Janzen (1958) termed this phenomenon "anticipative" intuition, and Dugas (1894) suggests that it would be useful to differentiate between déjà vu with and without premonition (cf. Marková & Berrios, 2000). In the open-ended Texas Survey, 11% of the déjà vu descriptions contained some indication that individual felt as if they could predict what would happen next.

The sense of precognition may be manifest in two different forms: the present events (a) were foretold in earlier experience, or (b) presage events to come. With the former interpretations, the foretelling is often in the form of a dream (Carrington, 1931; Chari, 1964; Funkhouser, 1983b; Hodgson, 1865; Marcovitz, 1952; Rhine, 1961; Shelley, 1880; West, 1948). With respect to the second form, the foreshadowing of future events can be in either a proximal (next moment) or distal frame of time (cf. Chari, 1962).

It is possible to reinterpret déjà vu explanations involving telepathy or clairvoyance in a more mundane and straightforward fashion by a delay in neural transmission involving the two perceptual pathways. As outlined in more detail in Chapter 13, assume that two copies of incoming information are received, one from the primary and another via the secondary perceptual track. When this secondary pathway is occasionally slowed, an individual may get the impression that the information has happened before (déjà vu) if focusing on the second, slightly delayed message. However, if their focus shifts to the first message, that momentarily precedes the second message by a separation sufficiently long to make it seem like a separate perception, then one may get a sense of clairvoyance or an ability to anticipate what will happen in the next moment (Efron, 1963; Kohn, 1983).

☐ Telepathy

A second parapsychological interpretation is that an individual is tapping into someone else's experience of the present situation in the past or future time (de Lamartine, 1835; Lalande, 1893), or even through oneself from an out-of-the-body experience, with the normal self receiving impressions from this disembodied state in either the present moment or some other point in time (Carrington, 1931; Shirley, 1936). Chari (1962) proposes that cases of apparent reincarnation (see later) can be explained as telepathic paramnesia. More specifically, children are likely to pick up information telepathically from their parents from proximal and repeated subconscious exposure. This experience then emerges into conscious awareness, as if it crosses a certain threshold (cf. Bendit, 1944). This parapsychological interpretation also connects to a reasonable scientific explanation. As detailed in Chapter 13, the information that children experience may not be completely encoded with respect to contextual tags and may, instead, get incorporated into their imagination. When this stored experience later matches present reality, this correspondence may elicit a déjà vu. Lalande (1893) proposed an even more complex explanation of déjà vu that involves both precognition and telepathy. A déjà vu results when you telepathically pick up what the person you are with is thinking about saying next, and when the statement is produced, it evokes a sensation of familiarity that is misplaced to a more distant past. A bizarre extension of the telepathy position is that déjà vu is the work of spirits. Myers (1895) remarks that "… I ascribe some precognitions to the reasoned foresight of disembodied spirits, just as I ascribe some retrocognitions to their surviving memory" (p. 340). St. Augustine proposed that his spirits were malignant and deceitful, whose purpose it is to "… sow some false belief …" (Funkhouser, 1983a, p. 13).

□ Reincarnation

The last class of parapsychological interpretations assumes that the current impression of familiarity derives from a prior life or some form of collective consciousness (Chari, 1964; Claparède, 1951; Crichton-Browne, 1895; Maeterlinck, 1919; Myers, 1895; Ouspensky, 1931; Stevenson, 1960). Plato used the déjà vu experience to justify his theory of the transmigration of souls (Platonic reminiscence; Funkhouser, 1983a), while Aristotle held it up as evidence for previous lifetimes (Neppe, 1983a; Pillsbury, 1915). Freud (1914, 1955) suggests that the idea of déjà vu as evidence of an individual having a former life originated with Pythagoras (cf. Funkhouser, 1983a), and some even refer to déjà vu as preexistence (Chari, 1964), the sentiment of preexistence (Berrios, 1995), and prenatal reminiscences (Maeterlinck, 1919). Feuchtersleben (1845, translated by Funkhouser, 1983a) suggests that the reincarnation explanation of déjà vu strains credibility because the change in fashion and customs would make it highly unlikely to find oneself in a circumstance identical to one from a former life (cf. Holmes, 1891):

> ... when one has the feeling that a situation in which one finds oneself has already once existed just as it is now ... then scarcely were we in a previous life in coattails, lace clothes, kid gloves, sitting with each other in salons at tea and crumpets. (Funkhouser, 1983a, p. 255–256)

Hereditary Transmission

A variation on the reincarnation position is that memories acquired during one's lifetime can be transmitted genetically to one's heirs (Crichton-Browne, 1895), a phenomenon referred to as racial memory (Pickford, 1940) and the law of hereditary transmission (Sully, 1887). Sully (1887) calls such a proposal "too fanciful" (p. 281), but does propose an empirical test: take a child descended from a "line of seafaring ancestors" and determine whether they show a sense of recognition when first encountering the ocean.

Two other interpretations are related to hereditary transmission. The experience of déjà vu was a central factor in motivating Carl Jung (1963) to develop his theory of *synchronicity*, that psychological forces extend through time and space and interconnect individuals with each other through certain symbols and themes. Rosen (1991) further suggests that the Jungian concept of the *collective unconscious* underlies the déjà vu phenomenon. He presents this speculation in a brief comment (cf. Sno & Linszen, 1991) and refers the reader to another article where he provides empirical support for the collective unconscious (Rosen, Smith, Huston, & Gonzales, 1991).

☐ Summary

The strange and mystical nature of the déjà vu experience has encouraged considerable parapsychological speculation. The sense of familiarity has been attributed to a precognitive experience, predicting what will happen next, or the present familiarity as foreshadowed in the past (e.g., dream). Déjà vu also has been interpreted as a telepathic awareness from another's experience, from oneself in the form of an out-of-body experience or prior lifetime (reincarnation), through the experiences of ancestors (heredity transmission), or via a generalized cultural awareness of the information (synchronicity; collective unconscious). Such interpretations have value in communicating the rich subjective experience of déjà vu (similar to good fiction), but have little value in an empirical understanding of the phenomenon.

CHAPTER

Psychodynamic Interpretations of Déjà Vu

The psychodynamic umbrella subsumes a broad diversity of interpretations of the déjà vu experience (see Arlow, 1959, for a thorough summary). As with the parapsychological interpretations, the amorphous nature of déjà vu encourages a wide range of creative interpretations based on a variety of models. Most psychodynamic interpretations assume that the déjà vu experience is an effort to relieve the anxiety resulting from the sudden and unexpected confrontation of an emotionally arousing situation (ego defense). Others interpret déjà vu as reflecting a wish that has been unfulfilled, or the dissolving of boundaries between self and environment or between parts of the psyche. As with the parapsychological interpretations, the psychodynamic perspectives are provided not as an effort toward causal clarity, but mainly for historical completeness, acknowledging the large amount of literature within this domain.

☐ Ego Defense

The predominant psychodynamic perspective is that déjà vu reflects the mind's effort to quickly block the emotional distress aroused by the present experience by shifting into a distorted state of consciousness and forcing an artificial "familiar" interpretation of the present new experience. The anxiety-provoking stimulus is blocked (Boesky, 1969; MacCurdy, 1924, 1928) or displaced into the past (Arlow, 1992) so that it does not need to be confronted. In addition, the déjà vu reduces anxiety through bit of self deception: If I have already experienced the present situation, I must have successfully coped with it before and emerged intact (Arlow, 1986, 1992; Neppe, 1983a). Thus, there is no need to be anxious. Within this framework, Myers and Grant (1972) have suggest that déjà vu is especially common in agoraphobics as a coping strategy to ameliorate the continual confrontation with anxiety provoking stimuli.

Aside from the reassurance of surviving this situation before, there supposedly are several additional, and more subtle, ways that déjà vu reduces anxiety. First, by making the experience seem dreamlike or unreal, the threat is lessened. Second, placing the focus on what is happening in the external environment diverts attention from the psychological (internal) response that is more threatening to deal with. Furthermore, substituting the current situation for the prior, anxiety-evoking experience cued by some aspect of the present setting maintains a bulwark against the psychologically charged memory popping back into one's mind. When déjà vu is accompanied by a sense of precognition, this illusion of foreknowledge provides an additional buffer against anxiety (Arlow, 1959).

Repressed Memories

Many view repressed memory as the source of anxiety related to the present situation (Banister & Zangwill, 1941a; Coleman, 1944; Fenichel, 1945; Freud, 1936; Kirshner, 1973; MacCurdy, 1924; Pickford, 1940, 1942a; Schneck, 1962, 1964; Silbermann, 1963; Zeidenberg, 1973). "The ego does not want to be reminded of something that has been repressed, and the feeling of déjà vu consists of its being reminded of it against its will" (Fenichel, 1945, p. 146). Exactly why this failure in a defense mechanism takes the form of a déjà vu experience is not clearly explained by Fenichel (Arlow, 1959). Bird (1957) suggests that the ego defends itself from threatening sensations by treating the situation as unreal (derealization), treating the self as unreal (depersonalization), or shifting the sense of time (déjà vu). These repressed memories are dealt with by the id by rationalizing that we have experienced the memory before (Pickford, 1944), successfully drawing attention away from the emotionally charged material and leaving a residual "feeling of perplexity."

A number of writers suggest the anxiety emanating from the present experience and deflected by déjà vu stems from castration fears related to

Oedipal conflicts (Boesky, 1969; Freud, 1914; Pacella, 1975; Schneck, 1961, 1962). Zangwill (1945) conducts an extensive analysis of a personal déjà vu experience published by Hawthorne (1863) and even though Hawthorne's own evaluation points to source memory failure (see Chapter 14), Zangwill concludes that it resulted from an Oedipal complex and repressed sexual desires for his mother (Pickford, 1940; Schneck, 1962). Freud (1936) attributes his own déjà vu experience while visiting the Acropolis to the same sort of repressed desire (Slochower, 1970).

A different spin on failure of repression is that the ego substitutes another (fabricated) memory during the present experience to deflect the anxiety, much like a magician misdirects one's attention. This screen memory or screen reconstruction (Good, 1998) allows the ego to momentarily sidestep the emotionally charged memory (Arlow, 1959; Boesky, 1973). Several refer to déjà vu as a *rationalizing paramnesia* that occurs when some aspect of the present experience is uncomfortable but not actually repressed, with the eliciting stimulus not as intensely emotional (Kohn, 1983; MacCurdy, 1925, 1928; Pickford, 1940).

Intrapsychic Conflict

Another psychodynamic interpretation is that déjà vu is a response to anxiety caused by an ego assault from within, rather than triggered by some external stimulus (Bergler, 1942). This ego attack can come from either the id (Arlow, 1992; Ferenczi, 1955; Freud, 1936; Myers, 1977) or superego (Bergler, 1942). When the id is involved, the ego is warding off either a libidinal (Ferenczi, 1955) or aggressive (Freud, 1936) impulse. With the superego, a déjà vu represents the ego's attempt to fend off a reproach of conscience. More specifically, if the current experience is reminiscent of a previous situation in which one acted immorally, the déjà vu reflects the ego's effort to divert the attention of the superego away from this implication. Bergler (1942) illustrates this with a case of a patient who had embezzled money and felt guilty about it. When confronted with a similar situation, a déjà vu occurred in an effort to ward off "an unconscious pang of conscience" (p. 170). Oberndorf (1941) also proposes that a déjà vu experience reflects vacillations of ego integration as it attempts to accommodate to the ego ideals and superego strivings.

One serious flaw with ego defense interpretations of déjà vu is that the experience should be consistently associated with negative feelings. Arlow (1959) incorrectly asserts that "the affective component of déjà vu is usually unpleasant ... a perplexing feeling that something is not right, a feeling that frequently merges into the sensation of anxiety" (p. 629). This evaluation simply does not correspond with the survey data presented earlier in Chapter 5. The predominant affective association with a déjà vu is positive or neutral, rather than negative.

☐ Wish Fulfillment

A different category of psychodynamic interpretations of déjà vu is that it reflects a positive effort to fulfill an unconscious desire (Arlow, 1986; Freud, 1901, 1914; Pickford, 1942a; Wilmer Brakel, 1989). As Freud eloquently stated:

> I believe that it is wrong to designate the feeling of having experienced something before as an illusion. On the contrary, in such moments something is really touched that we have already experienced, only we cannot consciously recall the latter because it never was conscious. In short, the feeling of déjà vu corresponds to the memory of an unconscious fantasy. (Freud, 1914, p. 320, in Kinnier Wilson, 1929)

Some element in the current situation reinstates a prior episode in one's life, and by experiencing the present as a repetition, the individual convinces himself that there are second chances. From this perspective, the déjà vu experience represents the illusory fulfillment of this desire for a second chance and a desire to make the outcome better this time (Markovitz, 1952; Schneck, 1964). Another perspective on wish fulfillment is that the déjà vu experience represents an individual's regressive desire (Levitan, 1967; Pacella, 1975). As the ultimate embodiment of regression, Freud (1914) suggests that a déjà vu represents a desire to return to the womb—the one place where everyone can state, with absolute certainty, that they have been before but for which they have no memory.

☐ Dissolution of Boundaries

The third general psychoanalytic perspective is that déjà vu occurs where the separation between self and environment becomes momentarily blurred. For example, Myers and Grant (1972) propose that a déjà vu could arise through a breakdown in the barriers between two domains of familiarity, one pertaining to the personal self (one's body and psyche) and the other focused on the external environment and surroundings.

could a *déjà vu* be the outcome of a fault of recognition that results in the whole of current experience suddenly becoming imbued with the sense of belonging normally accorded only to the body? ... However, the cortex may resolve the ambiguity ... not as "everything around me is part of my body" but as "everything around me is part of my personal experience," thus giving rise to the illusion of *déjà vu* (p. 64).

A second way in which dissolving boundaries could precipitate a déjà vu experience is suggested by Federn (1952). Rather than an erosion of the separation between the self and the outside world, a déjà vu involves the dissolution of one or more ego boundaries.

☐ Freud and Déjà Vu

The evolution of Sigmund Freud's views on the déjà vu experience exemplifies the challenge of nailing down a reasonable explanation of the phenomenon. Freud first speculated that déjà vu represented a recollection of an unconscious fantasy coupled with a desire to improve the present situation (Freud, 1901). He subsequently proposed that déjà vu reflected castration fantasies and the accompanying anxiety associated with this unpleasant perception (Freud, 1914). Still later, Freud suggested that déjà vu is associated with depersonalization and derealization, and reflects a positive counterpart of these phenomena (Freud, 1936). Most interesting is Freud's final assessment of the déjà vu experience—that it is just too complex and confusing a topic to pursue any further (cf. Pacella, 1975).

☐ Comment

Psychoanalytic perspectives on the déjà vu experience have spawned a number of complicated and jargon infested interpretations which discourage further discussion because of their technical density. Below is an example of one such interpretation of déjà vu that verges on parody:

> The déjà vu thus involves a controlled regression in the service of the ego as a consequence of the defensive and frantic search of the ego for the symbiotic and nonsymbiotic good, omnipotent mother, rapidly scanning the phases of life in a descent historically to the composite primal-preobject-early libidinal object-representations of mother. (Pacella, 1975, p. 312)

As noted earlier, the amorphous nature of the déjà vu experience accommodates interpretive complexity. It provides a cognitive projective test, like an intellectual petri dish for theoretical speculation. With the emerging interface among cognitive, clinical and neurobiology domains, simpler and more testable clinical perspectives have begun to emerge (Mayer & Merckelbach, 1999).

☐ Summary

A large literature has enfolded the déjà vu experience under the umbrella of psychodynamic processes. The predominant interpretation is that some aspect of the present situation causes anxiety, and the ego attempts to eliminate this by imbuing a sense of familiarity on the current experience. This anxiety may result from an aspect of the environment seen as threatening, a repressed memory, or intrapsychic strife among the id, ego, and superego. Others see the déjà vu as a desire for wish fulfillment, or reflecting the dissolution of boundaries between external versus internal worlds, or between various segments of the ego. Phenomena derived from experimental paradigms are finding their way into the clinical literature, and this cross-fertilization may lead to scientifically plausible interpretations of the déjà vu experience. For instance, Mayer and Merckelbach (1999) suggest that the first second of information processing involves a "quick and dirty" unconscious evaluation that effects our subsequent reaction. This rapid, initial emotional assessment biases how we subsequently react to such stimuli. Although they relate this specifically to anxiety disorders, their speculation can also connect to cognitive explanations of déjà vu (see Chapter 14).

CHAPTER 12

Dual Process Explanations of Déjà Vu

Attempts to explain the déjà vu experience from a scientific perspective will be presented in the next four chapters. The plethora of scientifically plausible explanations is probably a function of both the amorphous nature of the experience and the brilliant minds that have addressed the puzzle for over a hundred years. Scientific explanations for déjà vu can be grouped into four basic categories: dual processing, neurological, memory, and double perception. The dual processing explanations assume that two cognitive processes that normally operate in synchrony become momentarily uncoordinated or out of phase. From the neurological perspective, déjà vu represents a brief dysfunction in the brain involving either a small seizure or slight alteration (acceleration/retardation) in the normal time course of neural transmission. Memory interpretations assume that some dimension(s) of the present setting is actually objectively familiar, but the source of familiarity is not explicitly recollected. Finally, the double perception basis of déjà vu assumes that an initial perception under distracted or degraded conditions is immediately followed by a second perception under full attention.

Turning first to the dual processing explanations of déjà vu, these are all grounded in the existence of two separate cognitive processes that normally operate in a parallel, interactive, or closely sequential manner. The déjà vu experience is a byproduct of the disruption of the normal operation of these two processes. Four different types of disruption have been suggested: (a) the spontaneous activation of one memory function in the absence of the other, (b) the merging of two usually separable mnemonic functions, (c) an atypically long separation of two functions that are normally immediately contiguous, and (d) the emergence to the fore of a usually subservient or unobtrusive memory function.

☐ Spontaneous Activation

There are two different positions that suggest that the false sense of familiarity, so central to the déjà vu experience, can be traced to the spurious activation of a mnemonic function related to a sense of pastness.

Retrieval and Familiarity

Gloor (1990) suggests that retrieval and familiarity are two independent memory functions. Retrieving information and the assessment of its familiarity may be routinely correlated, but they originate from independent cognitive processing systems. The two usually function in a coordinated manner, with recall accompanied by a sense familiarity concerning that particular information, but these two processes may occasionally operate independently of each other. On the one hand, retrieval can be activated in the absence of familiarity, with an ostensibly familiar setting seeming to be momentarily unfamiliar, resulting in jamais vu (see Chapter 9). On the other hand, familiarity may become activated in the absence of retrieval, which leads to a déjà vu experience.

Gloor (1997) later clarified this familiarity feeling as "recognition affect," and suggests that it normally precedes the semantic information by a second or so, and is associated with the activity of the amygdala. The separation between these two processes is most obvious when we encounter a casual acquaintance in an unexpected setting. Seeing your barber at the post office is first accompanied by a rush of affective familiarity, an autonomic or viscerosensory response. The semantic identification then lags moments behind because of the lack those contextual cues usually available to facilitate name retrieval. Gloor's (1990) speculation is also related to a large literature concerning the possible independence of recall and familiarity (Gardiner, 1988; Gardiner & Parkin, 1990; Tulving, 1985). More specifically, Gardiner and his colleagues have suggested that one has a general familiarity (knowing response) concerning a particular stimulus, as well as a contextual association (remembering response) connected with the episodic experience of the prior encounter with a stimulus, and that these two processes are independent of each other. Alternatively, some argue that remember and know responses are simply two end point of a single continuum, rather than separate cognitive operations (Donaldson, 1996; Hirshman & Henzler, 1998).

Retrieval and Temporal Tags

A second version of spontaneous activation is that a temporal tag becomes activated in the absence of an appropriate experiential referent. Individual memories are usually marked, or tagged, with a variety of attributes concerning the context within which the experience occurs. These "attributes" of memory can include such information as the time when and place where the memory was formed, one's affective response to the event, and the sensory mode(s) involved (Underwood, 1969, 1983). These elements of contextual information, including the temporal tag, can be independent of the actual episodic memory in the sense that they may be forgotten while the content of the memory remains (see Chapter 14). A temporal tag may occasionally be spontaneously and incorrectly activated during a new experience. This could lead to a false sense of "oldness" to a new stimulus, thus eliciting a déjà vu.

Claparède's (1951) interpretation of déjà vu involves a similar perspective. He assumes that there exists a separate, and independent, mechanism for the temporal information that is incorporated into our encoding and recollection processes. When this temporal dating mechanism becomes defective and accompanies an essentially new experience, a déjà vu is the byproduct. This erroneous activation could also explain the feeling of premonition that occasionally accompanies déjà vu (see Chapter 5). Under those conditions in which the temporal tagging mechanism goes awry and is spontaneously activated, it is conceivable that both types of temporal errors could occur at the same time. Perhaps inappropriate sensations of both past-ness (déjà vu) and future-ness (precognition) could accompany the present experience (cf. Weinstein et al., 1962).

☐ Merged Processes

A second category of dual process perspectives is that the déjà vu experience results when two cognitive functions that are normally separate or sequential become simultaneously activated.

Encoding and Retrieval

Information input and output, or encoding and retrieval processes, are generally thought to be distinct and separable. While retrieval sometimes informs encoding, in the sense that information from semantic memory can be used to clarify new experiences and construct a usable memory code, the processes remain clearly differentiated from each other. Imagine, however, that on a rare occasion both encoding and retrieval occur simultaneously, leading to the impression that the new experience is also being retrieved from memory. The new experience would then be interpreted as old, leading to a déjà vu.

De Nayer (1979) proposes a tape-recorder metaphor of memory to illustrate this possibility. Under normal conditions, memory encoding and retrieval operate in a manner similar to the record and play heads on a tape recorder. *Either* the record ("engrammic") *or* play ("read") head is functional when the tape recorder is on, but not both at once. When processing a new experience, only the record function normally operates. However, imagine the possibility that one's memory "tape machine" has both the record and play heads active simultaneously, and the retrieval function (play button) is on during encoding (record button). This forces a false sense of familiarity, resulting in the déjà vu experience.

While this interpretation is intriguing, it is not well developed and remains at the nascent metaphoric level. In addition, it appears to be at odds with Pashler's (1994) research on the bottleneck model of attention, where a single, central processor is required for memory encoding, memory retrieval and response selection. From this perspective, encoding, and retrieval can never occur simultaneously. Furthermore, a number of models suggest that memory is simply the outcome of whatever processing occurred during input (Johnson, 1983; Kohlers & Roediger, 1984) rather than postulating separate encoding and retrieval operations.

Perception and Encoding

Another dual process interpretation of déjà vu, proposed by Bergson (1911, cited in Carrington, 1931), is similar to de Nayer's (earlier) but focuses on two processes that are both on the front end of the information processing sequence. Bergson (1911) suggests that perception and encoding are very closely associated in temporal sequence, but that the two can occasionally collapse on each other to elicit a déjà vu experience. In the following description, Bergson's (1911) term "memory" is synonymous with encoding.

> ... memory is never posterior to the formation of perception; it is contemporaneous with it. Step by step, as perception is created, the memory of it is projected beside it, as the shadow falls beside the body.... Suppose now the impulse suddenly to stop; memory rejoins perception, the present is cognized and recognized at the same time ... (Carrington, 1931, p. 303–304)

Our cognitive resources are generally focused on the perception of an ongoing event, but when we become distracted, inattentive, or fatigued, memory and perception momentarily enfold on each other. Bergson likens this to two soldiers marching in tight formation: if the first one pauses for a moment, the two will bump into each other. The idea that perception and encoding (learning) are essentially simultaneous processes also has been suggested by Tulving (1968), with the storage of information occurring the moment it is perceived. Under such conditions, these two processes could occasionally become confused, giving rise to an inappropriate false positive recognition or déjà vu.

Sensation and Recollection

Dugas (1908, translated by Ellis, 1911) proposes that we have three different "psychic" states along a continuum of intensity or quality of contextual detail from strong to weak (respectively): sensation, recollection, and image.

> The mind seizes a sensation with a stronger grasp than a recollection, and a recollection with a stronger grasp than an image. When attention is relaxed the line of demarcation between these psychic states tends to be effaced; the sensation becomes vague and floating like the recollection and the image, while the recollection and the image, on the contrary, become objective and acquire something of the brilliance and relief of the sensation. (Ellis, 1911, p. 254)

In essence, there is a leveling of these three cognitive dimensions when attention is diminished by reduced energy, making the sensation connected with the present experience lose some of its contextual detail and resemble a memory or recollection. This contrast leads to an incorrect evaluation that the present sensation has happened before, eliciting a déjà vu (cf. Anjel, 1878, cited in Ellis, 1911).

Ellis (1911) agrees with Dugas' position that temporary (or chronic) fatigue is central to the etiology of the déjà vu experience, and provides a more colorful description of how diminished energy alters the manner in which perception and memory merge:

> The mind has for the moment become flaccid and enfeebled; its loosened texture has, as it were, abnormally enlarged the meshes in which sensations are caught and sifted, so that they run through too easily.... It is as though we poured water into a sieve. The impressions of the world that are actual sensations as they strike the relaxed psychic meshwork are instantaneously passed through to become memories, and we see them in both forms at the same moment, and are unable to distinguish one from the other. (Ellis, 1911, p. 259)

In a perspective quite similar to the one above, Léon-Kindberg (1903, translated by Ellis, 1911) suggests that experience recorded while inattentive (because of distraction) takes on a different character than perception under full attention. This degraded experience is more like an unprocessed sensation than a perceptual experience, and resembles a memory more than a routine perception. Thus, one interprets it as a memory instead of sensory input, causing a déjà vu.

☐ Separated Processes

Another way in which a dysfunction involving two cognitive processes can lead to a déjà vu experience is when a predictably brief interval between the two becomes slightly extended. There is a traditional distinction between sensation and perception, where sensation involves the initial unprocessed sensory information, and perception, by contrast, refers to the information as processed, decoded, or interpreted by the brain. Perception usually follows immediately after sensation in tight sequence. It is possible, however, that this segue of raw sensory experience into a perceptible, meaningful form, may be temporarily delayed, slightly increasing the usually brief transition interval between the two. As Parish (1897) suggests, an "abnormal widening" between sensation and perception leads to the impression that the present perception connects with an event experienced long ago rather than one processed moments before (cf. Grasset, 1904). Similarly, Anjel (1878, cited in Burnham, 1889) proposes that the sequential stages of sensation and perception usually overlap, but when they become separated (because of fatigue) so that a noticeable gap occurs between them, the mind is "... unable to distinguish this fading sensation from a reproduced impression" (Burnham, 1889, p. 446).

This particular interpretation is similar to two others presented later: a neurological explanation based on an extension of the usually brief interval between information from the primary and secondary sensory pathways reaching the cortical processing centers (see Chapter 13), and a double perception position that an initial unattended glance is followed immediately by a perception under full awareness (see Chapter 15). Whereas these other explanations involve the splitting of a unitary process, the present, separated-processes explanation is based on an extended gap between two different but tightly sequential processes.

☐ Background Processing Comes to the Fore

This final category of dual processing explanations for déjà vu postulates that we have two separate cognitive monitoring systems. Each functions in the role of a global control system, but one is usually subordinate to the other. Occasionally, this secondary system comes to the forefront, and the double impression resulting from both systems operating at the full level of awareness elicits a déjà vu experience.

Dual Consciousness

Jackson (1888) suggests that we have two varieties of consciousness: *normal*, that processes information from the outside world, and *parasitic*, that monitors the thoughts and reflections of the inner, mental world. A déjà vu may occur when the activity of the normal consciousness is diminished by distraction, fatigue, or seizure. Under these circumstances, the ability to assess the familiarity of incoming sensory experiences is degraded and one must then rely on the more primitive, internal consciousness that operates primarily from mentally generated images rather than immediate sensory reality. This shift in function can result in a momentary misreading of a new experience as old.

A similar interpretation was suggested by Wigan (1844). Rather than dominant and recessive consciousnesses, he proposes two more equal and coordinated states that switch off in a tag-team approach for the primary information processing responsibility in any particular situation. Occasionally, one consciousness is not fully connected with the present experience because of fatigue or stress. After the brief "disconnect," it suddenly becomes reoriented to the present reality and then reprocesses information that has just been experienced by the other consciousness.

... only one brain has been used in the immediate preceding part of the scene—the other brain has been asleep, or in an analogous state nearly approaching it. When the attention of both brains is roused to the topic, there is the same vague consciousness that the ideas have passed through the mind before, which takes place on re-perusing the page we had read while thinking on some other subject.... We have no means of knowing the length of time that had elapsed between the faint impression received by the single brain, and the distinct impression received by the double brain. It may seem to have been many years. (Wigan, 1844, p. 85)

This interpretation of déjà vu connects with speculation stemming from research with split-brain patients on the possibility of separate states of conscious awareness associated with the right and left hemisphere (Gazzanaga, 1985).

Supraliminal and Subliminal Awareness

A concept similar to dual consciousnesses was proposed by Myers (1895), who suggests that we constantly monitor our environmental events through two parallel, yet qualitatively different, processing systems. The supraliminal self is the one of which we are consciously aware. The subliminal self is also in continuous operation but from a qualitatively different system. The two selves are differentiated in the following manner. The supraliminal self is less precise in recording the details of experience, often lagging slightly behind the actual event, distracted by conscious evaluation of the incoming information or constructing details about the information before it is actually received. Thus, the supraliminal self is subject to expectations, biases, distractions, and lingering reflections on what is experienced. It does not always stay perfectly on track with the momentary sensory experience, but often shifts a bit into the past or drifts slightly into the future. The subliminal self, in contrast, is always in the present moment, like a continuous video camera recording moment to moment. Whereas the supraliminal self is fraught with selectivity and information gaps, the subliminal self absorbs and permanently stores all details at a level below our awareness.

This division of cognition into parallel but qualitatively different tracks is made credible a century later by findings concerning explicit versus implicit memory (Roediger & McDermott, 1993; Schacter, 1987), and the reality of subconscious perceptual processes (see Chapters 14 and 15). Myers (1895) eloquently describes the particular logic in this view of déjà vu:

A horse leaps a fence, and goes through attitudes A B C D E.... Now most of the details of this moving scene ... lie beyond my sensation altogether. What I do perceive is a general effect, irregularly retarded. When the horse is at E I hear him at A and see him mainly at C; but a trail of vision persisting from A and B gives me ... a confused dissolving view of A B C, modified by a dim but irresistible foresight of D.

Now suppose ... that when the horse is at E the self that views the first prospect becomes partially aware of the self that views the second.... When the horse is actually at E I shall ... see him at C; but I shall have also an impression that I have seen him at C already ... up to the point at that the subliminal self has already registered the pictures.

Now this exactly corresponds to the promnesic sensation, that ... contains the impression that the immediate future has been lived through also, and is already known. At any given moment, of course, the subliminal perception would be only a fraction of a second in advance of the supraliminal ... (pp. 343–344)

In this particular analogy, Myers not only explains a possible cognitive mechanism for the déjà vu experience but also provides a way to demystify the feeling of precognition that is often reported as part of the déjà vu experience.

☐ Summary

One class of explanations for déjà vu assumes that two cognitive processes that are normally coordinated with each other become momentarily disjointed, unconnected, or independently activated. There are four different varieties of this interpretation. One is that a cognitive process becomes active when it should not. For instance, while retrieval and familiarity are usually activated in conjunction with each other, a déjà vu occurs when familiarity occurs in the absence of retrieval. In addition, a temporal tag may be spuriously generated during a new experience, imbuing it with an inappropriate sense of oldness. A second class of explanation is that two usually separate memorial systems become simultaneously active or merge with each other, such as encoding and retrieval, perception and encoding, and sensation and recollection. From a third perspective, two closely associated and sequential cognitive processes become slightly separated in time, creating the impression of two independent experiences. Sensation then perception usually occur in a tight and seamless fashion, but an occasional gap between the two can lead to a déjà vu. Finally, a cognitive function that is usually hidden or in the background can come to the forefront. For example, we may have two separate domains of consciousness that usually alternate with each other, but when both are active at once, this gives the sense of repetition leading to a déjà vu state. Also, there may exist both subliminal and supraliminal states of awareness, and when we occasionally become consciously aware of the subliminal domain, it makes the present experience seem to have happened before.

CHAPTER

Neurological Explanations of Déjà Vu

A second way of scientifically explaining the déjà vu experience is that it is a byproduct of momentary biological dysfunction in the brain, which can take one of two forms. At the global level, a déjà vu may occur as a result of a spontaneous electrical discharge, or seizure. At the micro level, a déjà vu might result from a slight alteration in the normal speed of the neural message, involving either slowed or increased synaptic transmission along one specific pathway. Interestingly, some of these proposals trace back to speculation over a hundred years old that corresponds remarkably well to modern interpretations based on a more sophisticated understanding of the human nervous system.

☐ Spontaneous Brain Activity

This first set of neurological explanations concerning déjà vu is that there is spontaneous electrical firing in the brain that is unrelated to the present sensory input. When this endogenously triggered cortical activity affects those cognitive centers involved with memory processing, especially those tied in with an assessment of familiarity, it can elicit a false feeling of familiarity interpreted as a déjà vu.

General Seizure Activity

One hypothesis about the etiology of déjà vu is derived from research on epileptics. Because déjà vu is part of the preseizure aura in some TLEs, a logical extension is that déjà vu in nonepileptic individuals may be the result of a small temporal lobe seizure (Penfield, 1955, 1958; Stevens, 1990). This speculation is strengthened by the fact that stimulation of the amygdala and hippocampus in TLE patients can cause a déjà vu experience (Bancaud et al., 1994; Gloor et al., 1982; Halgren et al., 1978), and it is a reasonable (although untested) assumption that similar stimulation in nonepileptics could also elicit the illusion. One could further conjecture that a right hemisphere dysfunction produces a déjà vu (Cutting & Silzer, 1990; Epstein & Collie, 1976; Epstein & Freeman, 1981; Mullan & Penfield, 1959) because research on TLEs with déjà vu consistently points to a right hemisphere origin of the seizure, compared to a relatively equal division of right and left hemisphere seizure origination in TLEs without déjà vu (see Chapter 7).

Halgren et al. (1978) propose that the increased electrical activity induced by their brain stimulation procedures is also present during a natural seizure, and this greatly increases the electrical "outflow" from the hippocampal gyrus. An increased electrical activity in an area so intimately involved in encoding and retrieval may be occasionally misinterpreted as a sensation of familiarity, causing déjà vu. Bancaud et al. (1994) support such speculation, and add that because the lateral temporal lobe receives major inputs from the visual and auditory cortices, the nonspecific seizure activity in the temporal lobe combined with current sensory input results in an inappropriate feeling of familiarity. Interestingly, Halgren et al. (1978) found that a déjà vu could be evoked by stimulation of the temporal lobe in both the diseased and *non*diseased cerebral hemisphere in TLEs. Related to this interpretation is an interesting case study report by Epstein and Collie (1976) of two sisters who had difficulties with disturbing dreams. Both reported consistent déjà vu experiences in their dreams, and both had abnormal electrical activity in the temporal lobes while asleep, suggesting that déjà vu is not connected to the physiopathology but to the electivity associated with it.

Inappropriate Parahippocampal Firing

Presenting a more precise physiological theory on déjà vu, Spatt (2002) suggests that the function of the hippocampus and prefrontal cortex is to assist in the perception of ongoing experiences, as well as encode new information and retrieve prior experiences. The parahippocampal system usually works in coordination with these structures in assessing the familiarity (or lack thereof) of the present experience. On rare occasion, the parahippocampal system, operating independently of the hippocampal/prefrontal system, will mistakenly assess an unfamiliar experience as familiar, giving rise to déjà vu. This does not imply that the hippocampus and prefrontal cortex are disengaged, because this complex necessarily recognizes the déjà vu experience as illusory and remembers it. This resembles the dual process explanation (see Chapter 12) involving retrieval and familiarity as separable processes, and a déjà vu resulting from the independent activation of a familiarity response in the absence of retrieval.

Spatt (2002) draws support for his speculation from several sources. First, Bancaud et al. (1994) found ictal activity in the parahippocampal gyrus in four of six TLE patients (67%) with déjà vu, but in only 2 of 10 TLEs (20%) without déjà vu. In addition, Weinand et al. (1994) noted consistent activity in the parahippocampal gyrus in patients with spontaneously occurring epileptic déjà vu experiences. Finally, Ardila et al. (1986) also discovered that when individuals with epileptic symptoms (not just TLEs) were evaluated for brain pathology, if déjà vu experiences were associated with the seizure then there was clear and consistent damage in the parahippocampal region.

Spatt (2002) further proposes that the déjà vu experience is tied in with the same mechanisms that support memory consolidation (cf. Brown, 2002). During sleep, consolidation occurs by a change in the pattern of brain activity such that the normal (waking) associations among neocortical structures are weakened simultaneously with an increase in the functional connectivity between the mesiotemporal and neocortical structures, to establish new memories. A reduction in intracortical activity would make one more susceptible to déjà vu, and is why déjà vu is (a) often likened to a duplicated dream experience, (b) sometimes experienced in dreams, and (c) frequently associated with fatigue states (see Chapter 5).

☐ Alteration of Neural Transmission Speed

Another class of neurological interpretations of déjà vu is based on a specific disruption in the speed of incoming information transmission along specific neural tracks. These interpretations assume that a slight alteration in the timing of the information flow can lead to a spurious interpretation that the present situation has been experienced before.

Single Pathway

One possibility is that déjà vu results from a momentary change in speed of neural transmission from the perceptual organ to the subcortical and cortical processing centers of the brain. There are two different versions of this interpretation, one in which there is an increase, and the other a decrease, in transmission speed.

Slowed Transmission

From one perspective, there is a slight increase in the normal time taken to transmit the message because of a synaptic dysfunction at some point in the series of neurons. Although this increase may be very brief (a few milliseconds), it is misinterpreted as representing that the information is old (Grasset, 1904). The logic behind this position is somewhat vague and unspecified, but it is generally assumed that this slight slowing may bring the experience under a more intense evaluation. Similarly, we are unaware of the way we walk until a pulled muscle brings this to our conscious level of attention. But one problem with this slow-transmission perspective is that it appears to be superficially at odds with research on perceptual fluency (see Chapter 15), which suggests that individuals interpret easier or faster processing of information as an indication that it has been experienced before (Jacoby, 1988; Jacoby, Allan, Collins, & Larwill, 1988). Thus, this slower processing of information should logically imply that it is new, rather than old.

Speeded Transmission

If one turns the above interpretation around and assumes that the neural transmission is spuriously speeded up rather than retarded, this neuronal facilitation could result in an impression of fallacious familiarity and correspond with Jacoby's findings on perceptual fluency.

> I have endeavored to study carefully every instance in my own experience of this feeling of strange familiarity often displayed in recognition, and I find in the majority of cases this peculiar acceleration as the chief characteristic ... (Allin, 1896a, p. 265)

Burnham (1889) proposes that an individual's level of energy can influence the speed and ease of perception in the absence of prior experience, leading to the déjà vu experience.

> The process of becoming acquainted with a thing consists in making the act of apperception easy. Hence, when the brain centers are over-rested, the apperception of a strange scene may be so easy that the aspect of the scene will be familiar. (p. 447)

Burnham (1889) argues that fatigue ironically may have the same effect as rest. A "hyperaesthesia" induced by fatigue will make perception more fluid and less effortful, and his speculation connects with the consistent observation (see Chapter 5) that déjà vu is more likely when in a fatigued state. Schacter (2001) suggests that a sudden surge of adrenaline may increase one's arousal level, and the resulting temporary acceleration in mental activity may create the subjective impression of enhanced perceptual processing. The individual then misinterprets the speeded processing as familiarity, resulting a déjà vu illusion (cf. Jacoby et al., 1989).

Ellis (1911) doubts whether such a subjective experience actually maps onto an objective increase in the speed of perceptual processing. Rather, the individual may under some circumstances misinterpret normal perceptual processes as faster than usual, leading to the strong feeling of familiarity. Thus, this perceptual/neural processing speed-up has been related to diminished energy, enhanced energy, or simply to one's subjective impression in the absence of any actual change in processing speed.

Two Pathways

A second version of this transmission speed interpretation involves *two* neural pathways rather than one, and has more logical explanatory appeal than the single-pathway proposals. Normally, incoming perceptual information is transmitted to the higher order perceptual processing centers through several different pathways. As these messages converge on the cortical areas, they do not arrive at precisely the same moment but our brain automatically merges these multiple copies of the same experience into a singular subjective event. However, any interruption of this precisely coordinated sequence of neural messages could result in an impression that the experience has been duplicated. This is a popular interpretation of déjà vu, and several variations of this position have been proposed.

Secondary Pathway Delay

The earliest version of this position assumed that information is received by both hemispheres simultaneously (Kraepelin, 1887, cited in Parish, 1897):

> ... under ordinary circumstances, every perception of each hemisphere takes place separately, and ... because of the complete simultaneity of all processes, every pathological or physiological disturbance of this harmony must lead to a temporary disintegration of the act of perception. (Parish, 1897, p. 281)

Thus, when there is a slight delay in the information to one of the hemispheres, a déjà vu results (Humphrey, 1923; Jensen, 1868; Myers, 1895; Wigan, 1844). Jensen (1868, cited in Marková & Berrios, 2000) suggests that the experience is similar to the double images produced by squinting the eyes, except that the double hemispheric perceptions are displaced in time rather than space. Holmes (1891) has a particularly colorful description of this occasional delay and its consequences:

> One of the hemispheres hangs fire ... and the small interval between the perceptions of the nimble and the sluggish half seems an indefinitely long period, and therefore the second perception appears to be the copy of another, ever so old. (p. 74)

Another version of this two-pathway speculation assumes that the primary perceptual pathway goes directly to the dominant hemisphere, while the secondary pathway, transmitting the same information, routes first through the nondominant and *then* to the dominant hemisphere (Humphrey, 1923). Thus, the information is received twice in a row with a very brief interval between the direct (dominant hemisphere) and indirect (via the nondominant hemisphere) copies. When the delay from the nondominant to the dominant hemispheres is slightly extended because of a slowing of the secondary pathway, this results in the impression that the second message duplicates one from a much earlier experience (Efron, 1963; Maudsley, 1889; Osborn, 1884; Weinand et al., 1994). In an early and more primitive version of the slowed interhemispheric transfer position, Osborn (1884), suggested that a déjà vu was caused by

> ... the supposed uneven action of the nerves supplying the eyes, one side of the brain thus receiving the image before the other, and causing the second image to appear as a familiar repetition of the first, in this way giving rise to a deception. (p. 479–480)

Weinand et al. (1994) and Efron (1963) propose that, because most seizures of TLEs with déjà vu originate in the right or usually nondominant hemisphere, the preseizure electrical disturbance may cause this slight temporal delay of the secondary pathway routing through the right hemisphere, resulting in a déjà vu. Efron (1963) also speculates that a lesion in the nondominant hemisphere could possibly slow the information transmission, and suggests that a scientific test of slowed interhemispheric transfer could be conducted during presurgical neurosurgical evaluation using a local anesthetization of the corpus callosum.

Ellinwood (1968) suggests another possibility for slowing of the information through the right hemisphere. The main cerebral disturbance caused by an amphetamine psychosis is a "… tendency toward hyperactivity of minor hemisphere functions" (p. 52) and "with stimulation by amphetamine in large amounts, any disturbance in the mutual regulations of right and left attention systems may result in a shift in the gradient of attention of the minor hemisphere" (p. 53). A hyperexcitability of an endogenous (rather than drug induced) variety may result in a similar disturbance, causing the temporal delay through the right hemisphere resulting in déjà vu.

Another version of the multiple pathway interpretation of déjà vu does not involve interhemispheric transfer of information. It has been clearly documented that in the visual system, sensory information traverses two separate pathways between the sensory organ and the higher cortical centers (Goodale & Milner, 1992; Milner & Goodale, 1995; Schneider, 1969). In most instances, the information is received in the occipital lobe first from the primary and then from the secondary pathway. The message from the secondary pathway takes slightly longer to reach the final destination, having passed through several other cortical regions (e.g., parietal cortex) (Weizkrantz, 1986). Thus, the identical perceptual information from the secondary visual pathway typically arrives moments after that received through the primary pathway. Comfort (1977) speculates that when the brief difference in processing time between the two tracks becomes slightly lengthened, the usually seamless integration of the two messages into a single perception becomes disrupted and is experienced as two separate messages. The brain interprets the second version of the information received through the slowed secondary track as a separate perceptual experience and an inappropriate feeling of "oldness" derives from the match with the first input moments earlier.

This delay in the transmission of the second neuronal message may explain the sense of precognition that sometimes accompanies the déjà vu experience (see Chapters 5 and 10). If one attends to the second, or delayed message, it may appear that this new experience is old due to the match with the earlier information received moments before. However, if one focuses on the first message, one can literally predict what will happen next, because the primary pathway foreshadows the information received moments later from the secondary pathway. In short, when a processing gap emerges and the brain differentiates two inputs, it could logically switch between comparing the second message to the first (déjà vu) or the first message to the second (precognition) and do this rapidly and repeatedly over the few seconds that a déjà vu typically lasts (cf. Efron, 1963). This could potentially explain the high co-occurrence of déjà vu and precognition in some clinical patients (Efron, 1956), if one assumes that this type of brain irregularity was chronic, rather than acute, in some individuals.

Primary Pathway Delay

Another neurological interpretation of déjà vu also involves two perceptual pathways and slowed transmission, but it reverses the above speculation. That is, a déjà vu occurs when the *primary* rather than the secondary neural path is delayed, causing the information from the secondary pathway to arrive slightly *before* the information from the primary pathway. Our initial perception is usually based on information received from the primary pathway, so when this information arrives following the secondary pathway it feels familiar because a "memory" match already exists only milliseconds old (Comfort, 1977; Efron, 1963).

These interpretations of the déjà vu experience based on slowed neural transmission seem logically reasonable, although the specific details have not been thought out. For instance, what are the possible neural mechanisms for this slowing? What specific neurotransmitters may be involved? Does it relate to any specific biochemical or behavioral (fatigue) specifics? How much does neural transmission need to be slowed down before we can detect a change (3 ms; 10 ms; 50 ms)? One might predict a higher incidence of déjà vu among older adults (Salthouse, 1998) as synaptic efficiency becomes more compromised with age, but this does not correspond to the negative relationship between déjà vu and age (see Chapter 6). Also, shouldn't individuals with various neurologically degenerative conditions (Alzheimer's, Parkinson's, Huntington's, Pick's) exhibit higher rates of déjà vu, especially those who experience a marked slowing of cognitive functioning (Parkinson's)? There is scant research on déjà vu in neurodegenerative patients, and this would appear to be an important direction for further exploration.

☐ Summary

Neurological explanations of déjà vu assume a momentary alteration in the normal neural transmission process in the brain. This can take a more global form of a small seizure, with such speculation stemming from the supposed relationship between déjà vu and epileptic seizure (TLE). It is also possible that a slight delay or acceleration in the neural transmission speed elicits an erroneous impression of familiarity. This delayed (or speeded) processing can be in a single pathway, violating the normal temporal expectations for the message transmission. The change in transmission speed also can involve one pathway of a dual pathway system. A slowing in the secondary pathway could lengthen the usual slight delay between the sequential messages, while delayed processing along the primary pathway could reverse the usual order in which the two messages are received in the cortex. Both disparities could create a sense of two independent copies of the same information and an accompanying sense that the present experience had happened before (déjà vu).

Memory Explanations of Déjà Vu

The most striking aspect of the déjà vu experience is the strong sense of familiarity in the absence of objective evidence to justify this impression. This chapter considers the possibility that there really exists some form of memory representation for some aspect or dimension of the present experience, but that this information is momentarily (or permanently) inaccessible by the individual. The first set of memory explanations under "episodic forgetting" assume that the present experience, in its entirety, has actually been experienced before but that the individual has lost access to this information. A more likely set of interpretations of déjà vu are based on the assumption that some circumscribed aspect of the present setting is stored in long-term memory, and that the individual's sense of familiarity is implicitly tied to this fragmentary information. The connection is opaque to the individual in the moment, and this ambiguous sense of familiarity is mistakenly ascribed to the entire experience.

Underlying all of these memory explanations is the concept that although the present experience does not consciously match any prior explicit memory, it does connect with implicit memory (Richardson-Klaven & Bjork, 1988; Roediger & McDermott, 1993; Schacter, 1987). Because implicit memory by definition operates outside of the realm of conscious awareness, the challenge of dissecting the déjà vu experience is to identify what feature of the prior experience elicits an inordinately strong sense of familiarity when cued by the current situation. This may be the most intractable aspect of memory interpretations of the déjà vu experience: Why is the implicit response so strong that it grabs hold of one's conscious awareness with no shred of evidence from explicit memory to support this reaction?

☐ Episodic Forgetting

The simplest explanation for the déjà vu experience is that it represents a failure of episodic memory, or "obliviscence" (Banister & Zangwill, 1941b; MacCurdy, 1924). As Chapman and Mensh (1951) note, "the individual actually has experienced the situation, or a very similar one, and now he recalls only inexactly the precise earlier experience" (p. 174). Myers (1895) further suggests that

> ... a confused recollection of actual past events gave rise to the feeling that I knew what was going to happen. This view was supported by the triviality of the occasions when I had the feeling, as in the course of some familiar game or talk. (p. 341)

Myers (1895) feels that mundane activities are typically associated with déjà vu because it is in those very settings that we are likely to have had a similar, or nearly identical, experience.

While parsimonious, the episodic forgetting explanation can handle a déjà vu during familiar activities (walking into the grocery store, doing a load of wash) but fails to account for the experience in novel situations: You have never been to Seattle, yet have a déjà vu experience as you enter the airport terminal after your plane lands.

On the surface, episodic memory failure is also at odds with the negative age-related trend in the déjà vu experience (noted earlier). Older adults are particularly vulnerable to a loss of contextual aspects of memory, and experience more source forgetting (Brown et al., 1995; Burke & Light, 1981) that should lead to a higher incidence of déjà vu under the episodic memory interpretation. In addition, individuals with chronic anterograde amnesia resulting from Korsakoff's disease, Huntington's disease, cerebral infarct, or injury, should also show a higher incidence of déjà vu, but this does not appear to be the case (Weinstein et al., 1962).

Early Childhood Experience

There are special circumstances under which an episodic forgetting interpretation could make sense. Abercrombie (1836) presents a description of a déjà vu experience where the present setting had actually been visited before, but as a small child:

> A lady, in the last stage of a chronic disease, was carried from London to a lodging in the country; there her infant daughter was taken to visit her.... The lady died a few days after, and the daughter grew

up without any recollection of her mother, till she was of mature age. At this time, she happened to be taken into the room in which her mother died, without knowing it to have been so; she started on entering it, and when a friend who was along with her asked the cause of her agitation, replied, "I have a distinct impression of having been in this room before ..." (Abercrombie, 1836, p. 105–106)

This woman only found out later that she had been in this room as a small child. Osborn (1884) describes two similar stories. In one, a man experienced a déjà vu when approaching a gateway to Pevensey Castle (Carpenter, 1874; Gregory, 1923). Later, this individual learned from his mother that he had been taken to this very spot when he was 18 months old. In a second story, the person experienced a déjà vu when visiting a Civil War battleground and discovered afterward that he and his parents had visited there when he was a very small child. The first three or four years of life are filled with many different experiences that may remain inaccessible because of childhood amnesia (Nelson, 1990), yet retain the capacity to match current experience, producing a déjà vu.

A similar process may underlie instances of unconscious plagiarism, or cryptomnesia, although the familiarity response is quite different. The following story by Bowers and Hilgard (1988) illustrates this point. At age 11, Helen Keller wrote an "original" story, "The Frost King," to give to a friend. He was so impressed that he submitted the story to a magazine. When published, an astute reader noticed a close resemblance to "The Frost Fairies" written much earlier by Margaret Canby. While this incident caused quite a stir, including a formal court of inquiry at Helen's institution, she protested throughout that she had not intentionally plagiarized the story. It was later discovered that the story was read to her by a family friend (Mrs. Hopkins) who spent time with Helen many years earlier. The information had lost its source tag and become part of Helen's creative imagination (cf. Smith, 1913). This incident illustrates that a considerable amount of information both real and fictitious can become absorbed into a young child's mind (Sully, 1887). If the familiarity remains, a déjà vu results (cf. Ellis, 1897, 1911). If the familiarity is lost, cryptomnesia could occur (Brown & Murphy, 1989).

Literature

A great writer can construct an exquisitely detailed mental picture in the mind of the reader. If the reader happens later to actually encounter a scene or situation described in the book, it could elicit a déjà vu experience. Such a scenario is presented by Knight (1895) in his book "Where

Three Empires Meet." He describes being bothered by a feeling of unto-ward familiarity in a foreign land (Tibet) and finally realized that:

> ... when a small boy I had read Gulliver's Travels, and that the voy-age to the flying island of Laputa had made a great impression on my imagination. I had conjured up that kingdom to my mind just such a perspectiveless, artificial, unreal-looking land as this; and just such a people as these queer Ladakis had those no more queer peo-ple, the Laputans, appeared to my fancy. (Knight, 1895, p. 126)

Hawthorne (1863) in "Our Old Home" presents another example of a piece of literature painting a memorial picture so vivid and clear that it evoked a déjà vu when the subsequently encountered actual scene matched the description. His déjà vu at the castle Stanton Harcourt, stemmed from a passage by Pope:

> Now—the place being without a parallel in England, and therefore necessarily beyond the experience of an American—it is somewhat remarkable that, while we stood gazing at this kitchen, I was haunted and perplexed by an idea that somewhere or other I had seen just this strange spectacle before.... In a letter of Pope's, addressed to the Duke of Buckingham, there is an account of Stan-ton Harcourt.... It is one of the most admirable pieces of description in the language, playful and picturesque ... and conveys as perfect a picture as was ever drawn of a decayed English country-house.... This letter, and other relative to his abode here, were very familiar to my earlier reading, and remaining still fresh at the bottom of my memory, caused the weird and ghostly sensation that came over me on beholding the real spectacle that had formerly been made so vivid to my imagination. (Hawthorne, 1863, p. 27–29)

This particular description has been repeatedly referred to in the déjà vu literature (Burnham, 1889; Osborn, 1884; Smith, 1913) and is the focus of an entire article by Zangwill (1925) (see Chapter 11).

Media

In addition to an episodic memory embedded in the mind of a young child or created by a literary work, it is also possible that an individual has experienced a particular situation or setting through some form of media but simply forgot the source tag for that encounter (Johnson, Hashtroudi, & Lindsay, 1993). Referring back to the prior example of a déjà vu experience when entering the airport terminal in Seattle after your plane lands, perhaps you saw this airport setting in a movie, television documentary on PBS, or picture spread in *Newsweek* magazine. Your in vivo experience activates a feeling of familiarity which you mistakenly attempt to connect to a prior actual experience rather than a vicarious one (Pickford, 1940). Ellis (1911, 1897) describes a déjà vu on visiting the ruins of Pevensey Castle, and later determined that "… the view was included among a series of coloured stereoscopic pictures with which I was familiar as a child …" (p. 243).

The possibility that source amnesia could underlie the déjà vu experience is supported by evidence that source and item information are independent (dissociable) in memory (Bayen, Murnane, & Erdfelder, 1996; Lindsay & Johnson, 1991). If source amnesia underlies déjà vu, one would expect that amnesics would experience the phenomenon more often than nonamnesics because implicit memory function remains relatively intact in amnesics, allowing prior experience to influence subsequent performance in the absence of explicit awareness (Graf, Squire, & Mandler, 1984; Warrington & Weiskrantz, 1968, 1970). Given that these circumstances should be ideal for eliciting déjà vu experiences, there is a curious lack of evidence in amnesics. Weinstein et al. (1962) extensively evaluated memory performance in several hundred amnesics but found little evidence of déjà vu.

It is possible that déjà vu may be too subtle or trivial for amnesics to notice against the context of more serious and chronic cognitive dysfunctions with which they must cope on a daily basis. It is also possible that the type of familiarity response required for déjà vu is diminished in amnesics. Knowlton and Squire (1995) demonstrate that both remember and know responses are reduced in amnesics. If the familiarity in a déjà vu experience represents an exceedingly strong know response in the absence of remembering, perhaps amnesics are unlikely to experience déjà vu because both remember and know responses are similarly compromised.

Hypnotic Analogue

Banister and Zangwill (1941a, 1941b) attempted to model the episodic forgetting interpretation of déjà vu using hypnotic suggestion to "eliminate" one's explicit memory for a prior experience. On the first day of their study, during a normal waking state, participants studied six paintings (small picture cards) for 30 seconds each, and then smelled three odors during a 2 to 3 minute period. On day 2, participants were hypnotized and presented with six additional picture cards and three additional odors, and a "forget" instruction followed the presentation of *each* individual picture ("you will have forgotten all about this card, and you will *not* be able to recognize it if it is shown to you to-morrow;" Banister & Zangwill, 1941b, p. 34) and odor ("after you wake up, you will have forgotten all about having smelt this odour, and if you should smell it to-morrow you will be unable to say what it is"; Banister & Zangwill, 1941a, p. 157).

On day 3, participants evaluated a mixture of day-1, day-2, and new pictures/odors. Rather than being presented as a memory test, participants were asked to comment on each odor/picture:

> ... tell me anything that comes into your mind in connection with each card: what it is like, what it suggests to you, whether you have seen it before, whether it appeals to you or not, and so forth. (Banister & Zangwill, 1941b, p. 35)

> ... tell me everything that comes into your mind in connection with each odour. Tell me any names, or past scenes, that the odour may call up, whether you have smelt it before or not, whether it reminds you of anything or not, or in general how you would describe it. (Banister & Zangwill, 1941a, p. 157)

For pictures, the day-2 hypnotic suggestion to forget was not completely successful. Two of five participants had full recall and one had a vague recall of some pictures being presented. The two "amnesic" participants each recognized five of the six day-2 pictures as familiar. Verbal responses for these participants are presented in detail, and none of the "restricted paramnesias" for day-2 cards were attributed to day-1 exposure but rather to some preexperimental experience. One fully amnesic participant provided a response similar to a déjà vu: "this card ... reminds me of a phrase people sometimes say: 'I am sure you said that before' or 'I am sure I have heard it before' or 'I knew you were going to say that'" (Banister & Zangwill, 1941b, p. 41).

For the odors, three of five participants showed restricted paramnesias, or familiarity with day-2 odors that they attributed to preexperimental experience. However, the recognition performance for odors was abysmal, with a hit rate of 22% for odors presented to participants when fully aware on day 1 (two participants had a 0% hit rate for day-1 odors). Thus, Bannister and Zangwill (1941a) suggest that their odor results were problematic and their control condition "inadequate."

Banister and Zangwill (1941a, 1941b) emphasize that their study supports the possibility of paramnesias, but note that the relationship between their study and the déjà vu phenomenon is "conjectural" and that the results "... throw little light on the origin of déjà vu" (Banister & Zangwill, 1941b, p. 51). This experimental outcome is occasionally cited as an induced déjà vu experience (e.g., Neppe, 1983a, 1983c, 1983e), but it is flawed in several respects. Participants may have been preexperimentally familiar with the artwork used, and the authors admit this. Also problematic is the way déjà vu was operationalized: day-2 pictures and odors misrecognized as being presented on day 1. This "error" could either be because of an ineffective posthypnotic suggestion, or a false alarm. With only pictures and odors used as stimuli, a successfully hypnotized participant could logically assume that any familiar pictures or odors must be assigned to session 1. Only three of five participants exhibited the source confusion reflective of déjà vu, and the other two were simply excluded from the analyses in both reports. Finally, a defining feature of déjà vu—"subjectively inappropriate impression of familiarity"—was not likely because the two types of stimuli could logically have been experienced earlier within that particular context.

Despite these difficulties, Banister and Zangwill's (1941a, 1941b) hypnotic procedure holds promise for eliciting déjà vu in the lab if accompanied by a sufficiently unique context within which to experience the subsequently "forgotten" stimuli. Such an investigation will require greater control over the materials, source confusions and hypnotic suggestion, as well as a larger sample of participants. In addition, the hypnotic session should precede, rather than follow, the fully aware session to better model the logical sequence of events for a forgotten episodic experience to spuriously match the present situation.

Rather than using hypnosis as an independent manipulation to induce déjà vu, Marcuse, Hill, and Keegan (1945) evaluated whether a hypnotized individual interprets their response to a posthypnotic suggestion as reflective of a déjà vu. A single participant was hypnotized on each of nine successive evenings. On seven occasions, she was instructed to provide a specific response (rub her chin) when given a particular *signal* ("please pass me a bowl of soup"). She was given the standard forget instructions after each hypnosis session, and posthypnotic suggestion was given on only seven of the nine evenings (two control days). Marcuse et al. (1945) found that the hypnotized student recognized six of seven posthypnotic suggestions as connected to the prior hypnotic session. More interestingly, half of these correct recognitions (three) were identified based on a feeling of déjà vu connected with the signal.

While Marcuse et al. (1945) speculate that the "… 'déjà vu' character of the signals resulted from failure to obtain sufficient depth of hypnosis" (p. 165), this experimental demonstration still points to the possibility of hypnotically induced déjà vu. Also, absorbing information during a hypnotic state may resemble processes that occur during various states of diminished attention (distracted; daydreaming) with such degraded input providing the mnemonic substance from which a subsequent déjà vu experience emanates.

☐ Duplication of Processing

Osborn (1884) suggests that it may not be the duplication of physical details of the present experience that elicits a déjà vu experience. Rather, it is the particular form of cognitive processing that replicates one that occurred on a prior occasion, and this correspondence leads to a déjà vu.

> ... if at any time in our past lives we passed in actual experience or in imagination over a mental track, say a b c d e, and if to-day this track is again traversed, although the former experience itself may have been long forgotten, we have a sense that it has been through the mind before ... if the mind passes over only part of the former track, say b c d, we sometimes, in the dim recognition that arises, believe we have been over the whole before ... (p. 481)

Such an interpretation can account for why the familiarity experience so essential to déjà vu can occur in a completely novel setting. This model is similar to transfer appropriate processing, first suggested by Kolers (1973) and later elaborated on by Morris, Bransford, and Franks (1977), Kolers and Roediger (1984), and Roediger, Weldon, and Challis (1989). The success of effortful retrieval depends on the degree of correspondence between the way the information is processed during input and during conscious retrieval. Similar mental procedures lead to strong recollection, and dissimilar mental processes reduce the likelihood of remembering and familiarity.

A modest extension of transfer appropriate processing could make it apply to nonconscious or inadvertent retrieval. More specifically, if one can assume that we are continually processing our present experiences at some subliminal level, then such processing matches may occur outside of our conscious awareness and elicit the hyperfamiliarity reflective of a déjà vu. Thus, the déjà vu may result even if the actual stimulus elements of the two situations are different, and if one is not paying full attention to the processing of the present experience. The key dimension is a sufficient overlap in the manner in which the two experiences are processed.

☐ Single Element Familiarity

A déjà vu experience may be triggered when a lone element of the present setting is objectively familiar but not consciously recognized because it is experienced in a changed context. The feeling of familiarity elicited by the unrecognized object is misinterpreted as a response to the entire setting, and this overgeneralized familiarity results in déjà vu. Suppose that you visit a friend's home for the first time and experience a déjà vu on walking into her living room. The grandfather clock in the corner is identical to one in your aunt's home. You experience a strong and immediate familiarity reaction to this object but are unable to make this specific connection. Instead, you misattribute this familiarity to the entire new setting.

This is similar, in part, to encountering someone you know casually (your barber) in an unfamiliar setting (the grocery store) and experiencing a strong sense of familiarity without being able to identify where you know that person from (Reed, 1974, 1979; Zangwill, 1945). Holmes (1891) also suggests that overgeneralizing the familiarity of the whole from a part is similar to how we occasionally interpret a partial resemblance (e.g., distinctive nose; unique smile) for identity in another person and "accost a stranger, mistaking him for a friend" (p. 75). With déjà vu, you are gripped by a similar familiarity experience but the particular eliciting object/person remains elusive causing you to overgeneralize the familiarity to the entire setting. As Chari (1962) colorfully suggests, "... a memory-content that figures as *part* or *aspect* of an experience infects *other* parts and aspects with an illusory 'familiarity'" (p. 268).

A large body of literature documents that a response to a particular stimulus can be altered by a prior encounter without an explicit (episodic) recollection of that previous experience (cf. Schacter, 1987; Roediger & McDermott, 1993). Thus, implicit familiarity may be the foundation for a déjà vu. Anticipating the literature on implicit memory over a century earlier, Osborn (1884) suggested that individuals process a considerable amount of information without paying full conscious attention to it, and that the processing of new information in a similar manner or form may give rise to a sensation of subjective familiarity. Thus, a prior unaware exposure to some particular stimulus might later elicit familiarity without conscious recognition, and hence déjà vu (Schacter, 1996).

Single element familiarity is one of the more popular interpretations of déjà vu. It can be found repeatedly in early writings (Banister & Zangwill, 1941b; Boirac, 1876; Boring et al., 1935; Bourdon, 1893; Breese, 1921; Burnham, 1889; Conklin, 1935; Crichton-Browne, 1895; Ellis, 1911; Grasset, 1904, cited in Ellis, 1911; Gregory, 1923; Holmes, 1891; Humphrey, 1923; Hunter, 1957; James, 1890; Jessen, 1855; Lapie, 1894; Leeds, 1944; La Lorrain, 1894; MacCurdy, 1925; Morgan, 1936; Murphy, 1933; Oberndorf, 1941; Pillsbury, 1915; Scott, 1890), as well as in more recent speculation (Chari, 1964; Findler, 1998; Jordan, 1986; Levitan, 1969; Meurs & Hes, 1993; Reed, 1979; Schacter, 1996; Sno & Linszen, 1990; Zeidenberg, 1973). Humphrey (1923) provides a lucid description of this interpretation:

Suppose ... that after I have visited the picture gallery I go to the next city where there is another gallery. Perhaps in some corner of a room there is some insignificant detail, such as a gilded cornice, that is the same as in the last gallery. This will be seen and recognized, but the feeling of recognition, instead of being confined to the one detail, may be spread over the whole room. In that case, I may not consciously understand just what brings the feeling of recognition, but feel that I am recognizing the whole. (Humphrey, 1923, p. 140)

Several researchers evaluating their personal déjà vu experiences conclude that most, if not all, can be attributed to minimal clues in the setting that connect to old information or memories not consciously accessible at the moment (Gregory, 1923; James, 1890; Leeds, 1944). Scott (1890) alludes to this hypothesis in describing a personal déjà vu experience with a group of friends, sitting around the table at dinner time. He suggests spending many prior experiences with the same group of old friends this setting created numerous opportunities for various implicit memories to have been implanted that now connect with the present reality. Humphrey (1923) proposes that odors are particularly likely to be the unidentified but familiar element eliciting a déjà vu because one may not be aware of the smell, and odors have such strong associative connections.

MacCurdy (1925) presents a reasonable problem with this particular interpretation of déjà vu. If a match with implicit (unconscious) memory is all that is needed for a déjà vu to occur, then we should be having déjà vu experiences all of the time because most elements of our present experience resemble aspects of our prior experiences. MacCurdy presents a complex (and difficult to understand) rationalization of why only certain implicit memories reach a higher level of activation (co-consciousness) necessary to elicit a déjà vu experience. It may be parsimonious to assume that the select subset of implicit memories that connect with the present experience with sufficient strength to elicit a déjà vu is determined by experiential variables such as frequency of prior exposure, length of time since the last exposure, and personal significance (or importance) of the environmental elements.

As a variation of the single-element familiarity position, Sno and Linszen (1990) propose a holographic model of déjà vu (cf. Meurs & Hes, 1993). Each unique memory (first kiss; favorite song) is represented as a unique, global waveform pattern of neural activation involving the entire cortex (cf. Pribram, 1969). If any perceptual element(s) in a new scene happens to overlap one (or more) elements of a previously stored memory, then this fractional component of the holistic wave pattern may reactivate the entire waveform of the prior experience (Kafka, 1989, 1991). If only the familiarity component of that prior experience is reactivated, a déjà vu results. If the entire prior experience is reactivated, the present setting simply reminds one of a past event.

Imagined Elements

Although a perceptual element from a prior real experience may be imbedded in the present setting, it is also possible that this element may match an imagined (rather than real) experience from a dream, day-dream, or story. For instance, if a *dream* contained a setting, object, person, or spoken words that corresponds to one experienced in the moment, a déjà vu may result (Allin, 1896a; Baldwin, 1889; Ellis, 1911; Findler, 1998; Freud, 1914; Fukuda, 2002; Holmes, 1891; Johnson, Kahan, & Raye, 1984; Lapie, 1894; MacCurdy, 1925; Myers, 1895; Osborn, 1884; Sully, 1887; Wickelgren, 1977; Zuger, 1966). Following this same line of reasoning, Fukuda (2002) proposes that a precognitive dream results from faulty backward reasoning, and only occurs to the individual after they encounter an element in their present experience that matches an earlier dream fragment. In support of his speculation, he discovered that déjà vu is significantly more likely among those who claim to have pre-cognitive dreams, compared to those who do not make this claim.

MacCurdy (1925) describes a personal déjà vu experience that he later determined was due to a dream fragment experienced the night before. Radenstock (1879) kept a detailed dream diary and discovered that his déjà vu experiences frequently matched the content of prior dreams. Interestingly, the very act of recording his dreams may have strengthened the memory sufficiently to make their connection to subsequent waking stimuli more probable. That a vivid dream would be missing its source tag is certainly reasonable, especially if it is reflected on during the hyp-nopompic state—a diminished period of conscious awareness as one is rousing from sleep (Ellis, 1911; Osborn, 1884).

In an extension of this dream interpretation, Ferenczi (1912, cited in Sno & Linszen, 1990) suggests that dreams and déjà vu represent similar and reciprocal mechanisms in the sleep and awake states, respectively. A dream manifests the residual cognitive processing of events that hap-pened during the prior waking state, whereas a waking déjà vu manifests the processing of the content of the prior night's dreams.

The above speculation is based on the assumption that a portion of a dream is consciously remembered, but it is also possible that the present experience connects with a portion of a dream beyond one's conscious awareness. Similar to Freud's (1914) suggestion that all déjà vu experiences result from our present situation linking to unconscious fantasies, one could speculate that dream elements not consciously remembered are still encoded in some form. Research on implicit memory (Richardson-Klavehn & Bjork, 1988; Roediger & McDermott, 1993; Schacter, 1987) has focused primarily on material experienced during conscious awareness, but couldn't information from dreams be similarly registered?

> One can be sure that many dreams are not only forgotten but are never even fleetingly recalled. Even so, they could have a trace sufficient to produce the feeling of familiarity when the moment is actually lived. (Rhine, 1961, p. 108)

Research indicates that information experienced under anesthesia is retained in memory and has the capacity to influence performance on subsequent implicit memory tests (Bonebakker, Bonke, Klein, Wolters, Stijnen, Passchier, & Merikle, 1996). It also would seem possible that the mental experiences while asleep have a similar potential to connect with subsequent waking events, thus eliciting a déjà vu.

Another source of imagined elements which could potentially elicit déjà vu experiences are *daydreams*, or waking fantasy (Allin, 1896a; Chapman & Mensh, 1951; Lapie, 1894; Osborn, 1884). As Chapman and Mensh (1951) suggest, "the present experience may have occurred only in fantasy previously, and now is being experienced in reality" (p. 174). Titchener (1928) makes an even stronger case for this speculation: He claims that one's imaginings leave a *more* vivid memory impression than actual experiences, making them especially likely to trigger a subsequent déjà vu. However, Chapman and Mensh's (1951) survey yielded little evidence that déjà vu and daydreaming were related. Whereas it may be difficult to imagine a correspondence between objective reality and imagined elements sufficiently strong to elicit the sense of familiarity usually accompanying déjà vu, the strange and ephemeral quality associated with a daydream (or dream) may engender the sense of unreality characteristic of déjà vu. In line with such speculation, perhaps we construct an idealized mental representation of certain events, situations, or settings, and when a real experience closely resembles such an idealized prototype, we experience déjà vu.

It was noted earlier that well-crafted *literary descriptions* may etch entire scenes in our memory so vividly that we later may mistake them for being real. It is also conceivable that this works on a smaller scale. Phrase fragments, an individual's facial features, or a distinctive object described in literature may later connect with actual experience, eliciting a déjà vu.

> Habitual novel-readers often catch themselves mistaking the echo of some passage in a good story for the trace left by an actual event. A person's name, a striking saying, and even an event itself, when we first come across it or experience it, may for a moment seem familiar to us, and to recall some past like impression ... (Sully, 1887, p. 279)

The many descriptions of déjà vu found throughout literature (see Chapter 5) most likely stem from an author's personal experiences, and Sully (1887) proposes that writers may experience déjà vu frequently because of the richness of their imaginations (cf. Burnham, 1889). Details of experiences imagined or dreamt become more distinctly registered in a writer's memory, and achieve a texture similar to real events, thus subsequently triggering déjà vu experiences (cf. Lapie, 1894). However, Zangwill (1945) finds this explanation implausible, and argues that if this were true, a gifted writer would be "...incapable of distinguishing fantasy from reality and of making valid judgments of recognition" (p. 250).

Implanted Memories

The idea that one's imagination can take on a texture close to reality ties in with the research on implanted memories. Loftus and her colleagues (Loftus, 1993; Loftus & Ketcham, 1994; Loftus & Pickrell, 1995) have done extensive research on how telling someone about a false episode concerning their personal past can be experienced as a real "memory" by that individual at a later time. Similarly, reading a fictitious account could create a memory difficult to differentiate from a real experience with the passage of time. Hyman and his colleagues (Hyman, Husband, & Billings, 1995; Hyman & Billings, 1998; Hyman & Pentland, 1996) have demonstrated that mental imagery ability is strongly, and positively, related to the likelihood of the implantation of false memories in children (cf. Schacter, 1996). Could the ability to form mental images also be positively related to the likelihood of experiencing déjà vu?

False Memory Effect

A number of investigations have also clearly shown that a single (target) word can be implanted in one's memory if a sufficient number of words are studied which are each closely related to that particular target word. More specifically, if one studies a list of words related to "sleep" (awake, tired, snooze, dream, rest, bed, snore, slumber, nap, doze, wake, blanket), there is a high probability that one will later recall the word sleep even though it never appeared in the list. This intriguing "false memory" phenomenon, originally discovered by Deese (1959) and later modified and extended by Roediger and McDermott (1995), has stimulated a considerable amount of research, aimed at explaining or eliminating the effect (Seamon, Goodkind, Dumey, Dick, Aufseeser, Strickland, Woulfin, & Fung, 2003). Extending this finding to the déjà vu illusion, it is conceivable that one may construct a prototypical conversational exchange, restaurant setting, or hotel lobby, from the converging elements of many different but related experiences. When this abstract representation, which has emerged strictly from the melding of strongly associated elements, happens to correspond to the present experience, a déjà vu may be the outcome.

Poetzl Phenomenon

The single-element interpretation of a déjà vu is also related to the Poetzl phenomenon (1917, 1960) where elements of a briefly presented stimulus are later produced in response to an unstructured generation task (cf. Dixon, 1971). Poetzl's (1917, 1960) early experimental work consisted of two techniques to restrict stimulus comprehension: a subthreshold presentation of a simple stimulus, and a brief suprathreshold presentation of a complex (multi-element) visual scene. The Poetzl phenomenon occurs when stimulus elements not immediately accessible (remembered) are produced in subsequent free associations to word or pictorial stimuli (Allers & Teler, 1924; Erdelyi, 1970; Haber & Erdelyi, 1967; Shevrin & Fritzler, 1968; Silverman & Silverman, 1964). Although usually evaluated with recall procedures, the Poetzl phenomenon could occur during the act of recognition and underlie the déjà vu experience. Interestingly, the effect is more likely to occur during a relaxed or fatigued state (Fiss, 1966; Fisher & Paul, 1959; Pine, 1964), similar to the increase in déjà vu under conditions of diminished physical energy (see Chapter 5).

Multiple Element Familiarity

The single element familiarity explanation of déjà vu is based on *one* element triggering a déjà vu, but several familiar elements also could be involved (Findler, 1998; Fleminger, 1991; Lampinen, 2002; Wohlgemuth, 1924). Findler (1998) presents a computer model of déjà vu based on the overlap in a number of elements between two different visual scenes. Also, Fleminger (1991) suggests that because common structural codes are shared by different faces, the overlap of a few features of a new acquaintance's face with those found in one or more old friends may occasionally result in a déjà vu experience. Fleminger's speculation also could reasonably be extended to the structural elements of inanimate objects.

Wohlgemuth (1924) carefully analyzed one of his personal déjà vu experiences and discovered elements from three different previous episodic memories to be present in the current setting. He speculated that the summation of the multiple familiar elements could produce the exaggerated feeling of familiarity in déjà vu, whereas one single but unrecognized element might not have a sufficient familiarity to exceed the threshold for a déjà vu. Multiple elements may summate their common feeling of familiarity, while the competition among the different contextual associations linked with each single element blocks access to any specific one of these episodic memories. Or perhaps none of the individual elements' contextual association is sufficiently strong to reach threshold, while the more homogeneous and shared sensations of familiarity can summate to yield an inappropriately strong sense of past. This mechanism is similar to that proposed by Hintzman (1988) in his MINERVA model of memory, and Lampinen (2002) provides a description of how this could work, with reference to a global matching model of memory:

> Imagine you are shown pictures of various people in my family. Afterward, you happen to bump into me and think, "Hey, that guy looks familiar." Although nobody in my family looks just like me, they all look somewhat like me, and according to global matching models the similarity tends to summate. (p. 103)

One problem with the single- and multiple-element familiarity positions is that the déjà vu experience should be especially prevalent with chronic amnesics. Cutting and Silzer (1990) note that it is strange that individuals with pervasive anterograde amnesia (Korsakoff's syndrome) have difficulty with familiarity evaluations for past events (Huppert & Piercy, 1976), yet do not appear to be particularly prone to déjà vu. Given that amnesics are still able to acquire implicit familiarity, it is puzzling why these individuals do not experience frequent déjà vu. However, one could argue that amnesics suffer from chronic hypofamiliarity, such that no present experience can elicit a level of familiarity sufficient to exceed that threshold necessary for a déjà vu experience.

Redintegration and Restricted Paramnesia

Two explanations of déjà vu are closely related to the single-element familiarity hypothesis (Neppe, 1983a, 1983e) and represent opposite perspectives, with the "memory glass" being either half full (redintegration) or half empty (restricted paramnesia). The concept of redintegration was introduced in the mid-19th century but was first applied to déjà vu by Neppe (1983a):

> ... if A and B occur in situation Y, and A and C in situation Z, Z may appear like Y because the common factor A (actually only a "part") has mistakenly caused the "whole" (Y and Z) to appear the same even though actually B and C are different. As a concrete example, a subject may have seen an enormous steel gate with gothic architectural design some years before while touring a castle overseas. He may then visit a war museum near his home for the first time, and it may have the same kind of gate. He may feel the whole museum, not just the gate, is familiar and he may be perplexed because he knows he has never been there before. (p. 26)

The problem with this explanation is that the concept of redintegration actually refers to the complete reconstruction of the prior memory—content plus context—and the above example represents a *failure* of redintegration (cf. Horowitz & Prytulak, 1969). As in earlier examples provided with single-element familiarity, only part of the prior memory is dredged up and this fallacious connection with the present context resurrects the familiarity but not the episodic experience.

The second interpretation, restricted paramnesia, is the opposite of redintegration in that some element in the present situation is only partially recognized, but the individual has forgotten most details of the prior encounter (Neppe, 1983a). This particular explanation of déjà vu also seems insufficiently connected with the déjà vu experience. First, if an individual is aware that a particular object has been encountered before but fails to recognize the episodic context, this partial awareness should prevent déjà vu. Recognizing someone familiar (bank teller) in a different context (restaurant) and knowing that you know them from somewhere else never results in a déjà vu experience. A second difficulty with the restricted paramnesia interpretation is that Neppe (1983a) claims that such a déjà vu emerges in two stages. Initially, only a part of the scene/setting is imbued with familiarity, and then this segues into a feeling that the whole scene is familiar. This two-step emergence of déjà vu does not fit with any empirical or anecdotal accounts of the experience.

☐ Processing Fluency

Clearly, the most puzzling dimension of the déjà vu experience is the subjective sensation of oldness or familiarity in the absence of objective evidence to support that impression. Research on perceptual fluency can provide a mechanism whereby an impression of familiarity is derived from the speed with which the information is processed rather than the objective properties of the stimulus. Jacoby and Dallas (1981) proposed that processing fluency may be a key dimension whereby we infer familiarity. When a previously experienced stimulus is encountered again it is processed more rapidly and efficiently than the first time, and we infer from this facilitated processing that the item has been experienced previously.

This enhanced reprocessing can result in other behavioral effects such as reduced naming times (Mitchell & Brown, 1988) or lower perceptual identification threshold (Jacoby & Dallas, 1981), and this increased fluency may bias an individual to interpret a stimulus as louder (Jacoby et al., 1988), more credible (Brown & Nix, 1996), or more famous (Jacoby, Woloshyn, & Kelley, 1989) than one less fluently processed. This facilitated processing enabled by a single prior encounter may persist for a month or longer (Mitchell & Brown, 1988; Mitchell, Brown, & Murphy, 1990), while conscious recognition drops off precipitously across a few days. Thus, the contrast between an undiminished processing fluency and a progressively decreasing conscious recognition becomes more pronounced with time, and may lay the foundation for surprising familiarity of unrecognized stimuli at long intervals after the initial encounter.

Whittlesea and Williams (1998) propose that a processing fluency basis of familiarity occurs in the real world *only* if the previously experienced object or person is encountered in an unexpected context. If simple prior exposure is sufficient to facilitate subsequent processing, then meeting your spouse in your own kitchen should engender considerable processing fluency leading to an overwhelmingly strong familiarity response. However, this does not occur. In fact, such encounters curiously elicit no sense of familiarity. By contrast, spotting your spouse sitting in the middle of your classroom as you lecture would arouse an intense and immediate sense of familiarity. Similarly, seeing your postal delivery person at your front door arouses no sense of familiarity, but seeing her at the movie theater evokes a strong sense of familiarity because of the novel context (Reed, 1979).

Applying this interpretation to déjà vu, if we experience an old but recognized element in an unfamiliar setting, and this information is processed fluently below our level of awareness or while distracted, this may elicit a déjà vu from the unique mix of fluent processing and unfamiliar context:

> ... a bus-ride through an unfamiliar part of town engenders the expectation that no stimulus will be processed with especially high

fluency.... The unexpectedly fluent processing requires an explanation; attributed to past experience, it produces a powerful feeling of
familiarity. (Whittlesea & Williams, 1998, p. 159)

☐ Affective Association

Much of the above speculation within the memory perspective has cen-
tered on a specific physical aspect of the present setting eliciting an
implicit sense of familiarity. It is also possible that the sense of familiarity
results from a reinterpretation of an affective response evoked by the current situation. If something in the present environment triggers a strong
affective response and the source cannot be identified, a déjà vu may
result. Within this framework, the strange feeling that accompanies déjà
vu is not a byproduct of the illusion, but the cause of it (Angell, 1908;
Reed, 1974).

There are two different interpretations of how an emotional response
could elicit a déjà vu. First, the emotional reaction could be positive and
misinterpreted as familiarity. Second, the emotional reaction could be
negative and a sense of familiarity is used to buffer this uncomfortable
reaction.

Positive Affect as Familiarity

Under most circumstances, individuals can identify the particular environmental stimulus that elicits an emotional reaction: seeing a person,
hearing a name, or smelling a perfume. On occasion, one may have an
implicit emotional reaction to a perceptual experience but be unable to
explicitly connect it to a particular stimulus (Zeidenberg, 1973). The person misinterprets the emotional arousal as familiarity, and when unexpected or inappropriate, a déjà vu may result (Allin, 1896a; Baldwin, 1889;
Hodgson, 1865; Pagliaro, 1991; Siomopoulos, 1972; Zeidenberg, 1973).

For example, you enter a hotel you have never been in before and a
couch in the corner of the lobby is identical to one that is in your grand-
parents' house. This item of furniture elicits a strong emotionally positive
reaction but you fail to explicitly recognize the item embedded in a complex perceptual milieu (Hodgson, 1865). Allin (1896a) describes such a
déjà vu experience on first encountering a stranger.

Upon closer examination, I found a pleasurable feeling that arose
through the partial resemblance of that person's countenance with

the countenance of one of my friends. I believe that the characteristic upon which the classification of know-again-ness was based was in this case the pleasurable feeling. (Allin, 1896a, p. 261)

Pagliaro (1991) suggests that a flashback and déjà vu may have similar etiologies, with the déjà vu representing a situation where an emotional trigger in the present environment provides an incomplete restitution of the prior experience (but see Sno and Linszen, 1991, for a different opinion). Zeidenberg (1973) takes a similar stance, but views déjà vu as resulting from a mixture of two different states of awareness: a flashback, which consists of reexperiencing a prior emotional event, coupled with an ongoing cognitive awareness of the present situation.

Siomopoulos (1972) speculates that affective reactions are especially likely to trigger déjà vu experiences because an implicit emotional response may persist long after conscious recollection has disappeared. Thus, a disparity between the affective and recollective responses to a given object/situation/person grows wider with passing time, and this discrepancy may be an important ingredient to the déjà vu experience. Giving empirical credibility to this particular interpretive framework, Johnson, Kim, and Risse (1985) have demonstrated that the affective and cognitive dimensions of a particular prior experience can become completely disconnected. More specifically, Korsakoff's amnesics may experience affective reactions to stimuli in the absence of any explicit recollection of the object, person, or setting.

Another perspective on the affective response is that it is a byproduct of processing fluency (see Chapter 15). Rather than the positive affect arising from some association with the stimulus, it stems from the manner in which the stimulus is processed. Reber, Winkielman, and Schwarz (1998) have found that manipulations of fluency lead to enhanced positive affect, or liking, for a particular stimulus. If one assumes that this liking then translates into familiarity, as speculated above, then one outcome of reprocessing an unrecognized, but old, stimulus could be a déjà vu experience through a four-step chain: reprocessing leads to (a) fluency, then (b) positive affect, then (c) familiarity, and, finally, (d) déjà vu.

Negative Affect Masked by Familiarity

The second version of an affective etiology of déjà vu is that the emotional reaction is not positive, but is ambiguous, confusing, or negative. Under these circumstances, the discomfort created by an unsettling emotional reaction that cannot be immediately connected with the present experience is dispelled or dismissed by the feeling of familiarity.

MacCurdy (1928) speculates that there are always two components of a nominal recognition response: an initial affective reaction, derived from the feeling of familiarity attached to the object, followed by the memory activation. These two stages usually follow in quick and seamless succession, and are essentially indistinguishable as separate processes. However, a déjà vu experience results when the initial affective (familiarity) stage is not followed by a clear, second-stage memory match:

> ... the subject is harrowed by a feeling of familiarity attaching to some bit of cognitive experience without being able to recall the antecedent experience of which the present one seems to be an identical reproduction. (MacCurdy, 1928, p. 113)

MacCurdy argues that the memory may be repressed, but his position is also viable if the memory attached to this emotional reaction is simply momentarily inaccessible. Fleminger (1991) similarly suggests that the affective and cognitive channels of information processing usually work in concert, but the occasional déjà vu may be the result of "... aberrant activity in the pathway responsible for affective interpretation of percepts" (p. 1418). Such a two-stage model in which affect precedes cognition corresponds to similar speculation by Zajonc (1980). It should also be noted that this interpretation resembles some of the dual process explanations presented in Chapter 12. However, the current interpretation is distinct from these in that some particular aspect of the current experience is triggering the dangling affective response. The dual process interpretations all assume a processing glitch that occurs independently of any particular characteristic of the present situation.

Taking this affective position to a physiological level, Linn (1953) speculates that the anxiety evoked by some aspect of the present situation disrupts the normal functioning of the reticular activating system (RAS) to dampen the intensity of the experience. This is a mild form of fainting, in which the emotional arousal is overwhelming and feels impossible to cope with. With the RAS activity reduced, one's cognitive ability to evaluate the present information is diminished, thus precipitating a déjà vu. Linn's interpretation focuses on a *change* in arousal level as the central mechanism which elicits a déjà vu.

These interpretations of déjà vu based on negative affect resemble some clinical interpretations (see Chapter 11). Myers and Grant (1972) suggest an association between déjà vu and agoraphobia, such that the déjà vu dampens a fear response that may lead to a full-blown panic attack. When something potentially anxiety evoking is perceived, the agoraphobic responds with an exaggerated familiarity response to defuse the anxiety. Extending this perspective, Mayer and Merckelbach (1999) suggest that most stimuli that we encounter elicit an extremely rapid initial emotional reaction, followed by a slower, conscious, cognitive evaluation. This model is used to frame how anxiety disorders may maintain themselves (Öhman & Soares, 1994; Soares & Öhman, 1993), but it also applies to the present discussion of déjà vu. The rapid, initial, and unaware emotional reaction to a specific environmental stimulus may be interpreted by subsequent cognitive processing as global familiarity with the present setting. The rapid, and rough-cut, affective reaction usually segues easily into the slow-and-sophisticated cognitive evaluation, but when this emotional process is particularly intense it may become a central focus of perception and be misinterpreted as familiarity. Mayer and Merckelbach (1999) use negative affect (or anxiety) as the core of their speculation, but it seems reasonable that positive affective reactions could also be part of this preliminary affective response leading to déjà vu.

Subliminal Mere Exposure

These affect-based interpretations of the déjà vu are related to research on subliminal mere exposure, where unfamiliar stimuli exposed at levels below perceptual threshold are later preferred over nonexposed stimuli, even though individuals are unable later to recognize these stimuli as previously seen (Bornstein, 1992; Kunst-Wilson & Zajonc, 1980). Seamon et al. (1983b) specifically relate their findings on subliminal mere exposure to déjà vu. In their study, participants were shown 10 geometric shapes repeated five times each, at a 5 ms exposure duration. The usual threshold level at which an individual can merely detect the presence of some stimulus, much less identify what it is, is usually between 35 to 50 ms. Thus, this particular exposure duration is well below the visual perceptual threshold.

Following these subliminal presentations, participants are shown pairs of stimuli (one old, one new) and pick the one they prefer. They also are asked to identify which member of each old/new pair was previously shown. The recognition and preference tests are both given immediately, 1 day or 1 week following input. Recognition accuracy does not differ from chance (50%) in any of the three retention groups (ranging from 51% to 56%), but liking preference for previously exposed shapes is consistently and significantly above chance (ranging from 60% to 65%). Thus, subthreshold exposure enhances affective evaluation in the absence of conscious recognition.

> The experience of déjà vu … is an expression of the familiarity of a similar stimulus without the retrieval of that earlier event or its context into conscious awareness.… Essentially, the same outcome was

observed in this study: people liked familiar stimuli without recognizing the basis for their familiarity. In this respect, the finding of target selection by affect in the absence of recognition is similar to the well-known, but poorly understood, phenomenon. (Seamon et al. 1983b, p. 188)

Seamon et al. (1983a, 1983b) actually propose that familiarity provides the basis on which the affective (preference) judgments are made, which is opposite to most others supporting the affective basis of déjà vu, who see affect as eliciting familiarity.

This parallel with subliminal mere exposure may be strained because what is typically measured in mere-exposure research is preference or liking—a modest affective response, at best. What is needed to connect this paradigm more closely to the phenomenon of déjà vu is the intense affective reaction characteristic of déjà vu. Both number of exposures and test delay are directly related to level of preference in the subliminal mere exposure research (Bornstein, 1989), so perhaps a large number of subliminal exposures and long input-to-test delay could intensify the affective response to a level closer to that experienced with déjà vu.

☐ Gestalt Familiarity

It is possible that the general visual *organization* of the elements in a scene, rather than any specific item(s), has the capacity to evoke a sense of familiarity. When the present array of stimuli is configured similarly to one experienced previously, this gestalt arrangement could trigger an inappropriate positive recognition response to the entire setting (Grasset, 1904; Reed, 1974; Sander, 1874). To illustrate this using a previous example, it is not the grandfather clock in the living room of your friend's new home that is familiar but, rather, that the room has a layout similar to the one in your aunt's house: a sofa to the right of the love seat, with a stairway going up the left wall, a grandfather clock against the back wall, and an oriental rug on the floor. Although none of the individual elements in the newly entered living room duplicates familiar ones, the particular configuration fits the same template from the prior setting.

> A friend ... experiences the sensation of déjà vu when wandering through a ruined castle where she has never been before. Now, in the features that strike the ordinary observer, one ruined castle, with its broken staircases, its silent courtyard, its empty echoes, its dungeons, is most certainly just like another, so that in this instance the

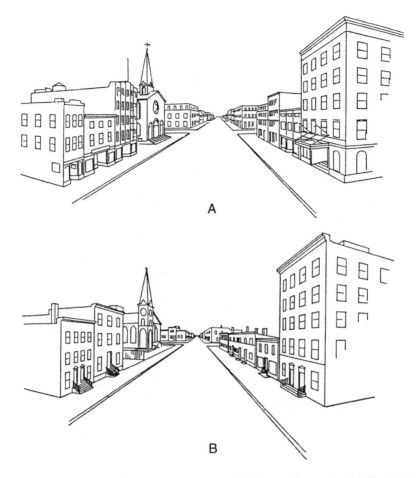

A

B

FIGURE 14.1. Gestalt interpretation of déjà vu (from Dashiell, 1937, p. 433).

reminiscence has its basis in ill-recollected actual previous states. (Kinnier Wilson, 1929, p. 61).

Dashiell (1928; 1937) presents a vivid visual illustration of this gestalt interpretation in his two textbooks on general psychology (cf. Findler, 1998). Referring to Figure 112 in the 1937 edition of his book (p. 433), which is reproduced in Figure 14.1, Dashiell (1937) says:

… assume that Mr. Smith upon facing a street vista in city [A] … is strangely moved to act as if in an old environment. He partially recognizes the scene spread before him, although … he has never been within a hundred miles of this city [A] before. A careful canvassing of his past life may, however, brings out the fact that at one time he was often in the foreground of the scene in city [B].... To be sure, the majority of the items present differ in the two scenes, but there are a few ... similarities in the position of a church and steeple over on the left, in the position of a large loft building on the near right, and in the more general character of a business block ... (p. 433–444)

Sno and Linszen (1990) suggest that different scenes and individuals often overlap in many structural details, and when perception is degraded through fatigue or inattention, the general framework of a prior experience may correspond considerably with the present one. Gloor (1990) also uses this gestalt analogy in speculating about déjà vu experiences in the pre-seizure aura of TLEs. Drawing on the parallel distributed processing model of Rumelhart and McClelland (1986), Gloor (1990) suggests that the erratic firing of neurons in the temporal lobe prior to the seizure gives rise to spurious matches between the present visual scene and prior visual experiences. Under the interpretations provided by both Sno and Linszen (1990) and Gloor (1990), a degree of perceptual degradation is likely to facilitate such mental matches, and such sensory degradation is more likely under conditions of diminished energy or stress (see Chapter 5).

Levitan (1969) puts a slightly different slant on the gestalt perspective. When recognizing a setting, we automatically break it down into simpler perceptual forms—cubes, triangles, and circles—a process similar to that of the cubist painters. Thus, the untoward sense of familiarity in an unfamiliar setting may arise because these reduced forms match those from prior familiar experiences. Levitan's (1969) speculation relates to Biederman's (1987) notion that all perceptual experience can be reduced to a relatively small set of "geons" that represent the range of all primitive perceptual forms.

☐ Summary

A variety of different memory explanations have been proposed for the déjà vu experience. The simplest perspective is that an individual actually has experienced this situation or place before when very young (infantile amnesia), in a media presentation (picture, TV show), or a literary description. It is also possible that the processing of the present experience, rather than the content, duplicates the mental processing of a similar prior experience. Déjà vu could also result when one aspect (object) in the present setting is identical to one that is familiar, but explicit identification is occluded by the changed context and the familiarity overgeneralizes to the entire experience. The familiar element(s) could come from either actual or imagined (dream, daydream, literature) experiences. An enhancement in processing fluency because of a previous encounter may drive the déjà vu experience. A déjà vu also may occur as a result of an emotional association to a particular, unidentified item. With a positive emotional association, the affect is misidentified as familiarity. With a negative association, the familiarity may mask the affect. Finally, it may be the overall framework, or gestalt, of the present experience (e.g., room layout) that closely resembles one encountered before, thus eliciting a déjà vu.

Double Perception Explanations of Déjà Vu

This category of déjà vu explanations centers on a brief break in one's ongoing perceptual processing that gives rise to an impression of two separate and duplicated experiences. With the glue of normal continuity missing, the two experiences appear disconnected from each other by an indeterminate period of time, suggesting that the presently perceived stimulus is repeated. More important, we are unaware that this sense of "oldness" derives from the correspondence between the present perception and a previous, semi-aware duplicate impression received only moments before.

There are four ways in which this double perception can supposedly occur. The first is a perceptual gap, where some physical or environmental distraction slices through an ongoing perceptual experience dissecting it into two, apparently separate experiences. The second form is where an initial perceptual experience is degraded, perhaps by diminished energy, and immediately followed by a full perception of the same scene. The third variety of double perception is when a perceptual impression is registered peripherally as we focus first on a different aspect of the current experience. Our full attention is then shifted toward the previously peripheral dimension, and this full registration matches one made incidentally only moments ago. A final version of double perception explanations involves one's internal perception of an emotional reaction.

When a rapid recycling of an emotional response to the present situation occurs, the second (or subsequent) waves of emotion are duplications resulting in a heightened sense of familiarity.

☐ Perceptual Gap

One of the oldest scientific interpretations of déjà vu posits that an ongoing stream of perceptual experience is split into two separate perceptions through a momentary lapse of attention or distraction by some environmental stimulus. An initial perception of a scene under full attention is followed immediately by a second perception also under full attention, and when the second impression matches that experienced moments earlier, the current experience feels like a repetition. The individual fails to identify the source of the prior event as moments ago, but rather attributes it to a more distant past.

Many researchers have espoused different versions of this interpretation (Allin, 1896a; Anjel, 1878; Conklin, 1935; Dugas, 1894; Heymans, 1904; Krijgers Janzen, 1958; Lalande, 1893; Leeds, 1944; Osborn, 1884; Ribot, 1882; Tiffin et al., 1946; Wigan, 1844), and Titchener (1928) provides the following, oft-cited description:

> ... you are about to cross a crowded street, and you take a hasty glance in both directions to make sure of a safe passage. Now your eye is caught, for a moment, by the contents of a shop window; and you pause, though only for a moment, to survey the window before you actually cross the street ... the preliminary glance up and down, that ordinarily connects with the crossing in a single attentive experience, is disjointed from the crossing; the look at the window, casual as it was, has been able to disrupt the associative tendencies. As you cross, then, you think "Why, I crossed this street just now"; your nervous system has severed two phases of a single experience, both of which are familiar, and the latter of which appears accordingly as a repetition of the earlier. (pp. 187–188)

Conklin (1935) provides a similar illustration of a mountain climber whose fleeting glimpse of the scene ahead results in partial recognition of the whole scene encountered moments later. Leeds (1944) calls this split-perception, and suggests that an eyeblink could possibly divide one's ongoing visual experience into two successive and separate perceptions. Tiffin et al. (1946) further suggest that a momentary distraction could be of an auditory (strange noise) or visual (picture on the wall) nature.

Krijgers Janzen (1958) speculates that an initial and unattended eidetic image matches a regular perception moments later. He believes that all people experience eidetic imagery occasionally, and the fact that regular eidetic imagers consistently experience déjà vu supports this position. Krijgers Janzen (1958) also notes that both eidetic imagery and déjà vu are more common in younger than older adults. Ribot (1882, cited in Kinnier Wilson, 1929) proposed a similar explanation. Without using the term eidetic, he suggests that an image of an experience formed immediately *after* the sensory impression can be so powerful that it becomes a reality that matches the immediately preceding sensation.

> The real impression is relegated to a secondary place as a recollection; the image becomes the reality and the reality the recollection. … The illusory state does not efface the real impression, but as it is detached from it and produced by it, it appears as a second experience. (Kinnier Wilson, 1929, p. 65)

According to Allin (1896a), what makes the attentional break between the perception and reperception (moments later) so powerful is that the reprocessing is much quicker than the original processing. Thus, the déjà vu experience does not simply stem from an immediate reperception identical to the first. Instead, the second perception is more rapid because enhanced processing fluency makes it more distinctive and attention grabbing. He suggests that there is a

> … great rapidity and often surprising ease and quickness of the act of perceiving, due to preceding practice … [and] often a second idea-presentation of the object arises immediately after the perception. (Allin, 1896a, p. 263)

Mentally Induced Gap

Lalande (1893, translated by Myers, 1895, and Allin, 1986a) proposes that the distraction that causes the "break" in the continuous perception could be mental, rather than in the external world. We take in much more information than we are ever aware of in our moment-to-moment perceptions, and when briefly distracted by our own thoughts and inward reflections, our time sense becomes considerably distorted and extended while "lost in thought." On returning our awareness to the immediate scene, we are likely to notice details that escaped us the first time and that now strike us as familiar because we processed them moments ago.

> You are presented with a new landscape, and you receive thence a
> mass of images that your intelligence does not at once comprehend,
> but that enter therein none the less, like an instantaneous photo-
> graph. Suppose then a distraction of the tenth of a second, during
> which your thoughts fly elsewhere.... What will happen when you
> return from the distraction? You will behold and recognise the scene
> that your thought quitted for a moment, but you will not refer the
> first act of perception to its right place in time. (Lalande, 1893,
> quoted in Myers, 1895, p. 345)

Ellis (1911) agrees that our inward reflections disconnect us from our
usual ongoing time sense, and on our conscious return to external reality,
it appears that a much longer period of time has passed. He likens this to
what happens when we are just aroused out of sleep during hypnopompic period: "When we become conscious that we are awake it always
seems to us that we are already awake, awake for an indefinite time, and
not that we have just awakened" (p. 251).

Finally, De Pury (1902) uses a more complex metaphor to illustrate this
interpretation of déjà vu, based on the assumption that an individual is
confronted by two versions of the same perception. As translated by Ellis
(1911), De Pury argues that an "anteriorisation of actual perception"
causes déjà vu like

> ... the nature of a double refraction such as that simultaneously pro-
> duced on two faces of a prism by the same image ... an image
> appears for the moment on the plane both of the past and of the
> present, and psychically we see double just as physically we see
> double when the parallelism of our visual rays is disturbed. (Ellis,
> 1911, pp. 251–252)

These mental distraction versions of the perceptual gap explanation
are very similar to ones based on environmental distraction, but there are
two important distinctions. First, the mental distraction that occurs
between the two successive perceptions alters the perceptual landscape
when we refocus on it. We are in a slightly changed mental framework
because of the brief inward reflection. Second, the mental break distorts
and extends our sense of time, making the illusory gap between the
present and prior experience appear subjectively to be much longer.

Revelation Effect

A cognitive phenomenon potentially related to the perceptual gap interpretation of déjà vu is the revelation effect (Peynircioglu & Watkins, 1993;

Watkins & Peynircioglu, 1990). When a word is partially revealed prior to full exposure (e.g., letter by letter), it is more likely to be called "old" than when revealed all at once (Watkins & Peynircioglu, 1990). Applying this to the déjà vu experience, assume that an individual perceives some (but not all) elements of a scene in the first glance, and then takes in more aspects of the same scene in the reperception, immediately after. The partial revelation prior to a more complete impression then exaggerates the sense of familiarity or "oldness," characteristic of the déjà vu experience. Interestingly, older adults (63 to 82 years old) fail to show a revelation effect (Prull, Light, Collett, & Kennison, 1998) and also have a lower incidence of déjà vu (see Figures 6.1, 6.2, and 6.3).

☐ Degraded Initial Perception

For the perceptual gap interpretations of déjà vu in the prior section, the critical stimulus element is clearly visible and under full attention, but the continuous perceptual flow is made discontinuous, cut into two separate experiences. A déjà vu also may result from a diminished initial perceptual experience followed by a second perception of full clarity. This degradation can be the result of either a reduction in the clarity or quality of the initial perception (occlusion) or through distraction or attention directed elsewhere (diminished attention).

Perceptual Occlusion

The possibility of déjà vu produced by an initial perceptual experience that is indistinct or unclear was evaluated experimentally by Jacoby and Whitehouse (1989):

> Our experiments were aimed at producing a memory illusion of the sort described by Titchener. We arranged a situation in such a way that a 'hasty glance' at a word immediately before its presentation for a recognition memory test might produce the illusion that the test word was one of the words presented in an earlier list. (p. 126)

This study is unique in cognitive literature in that déjà vu was a primary construct around which the experiment was designed. Jacoby and Whitehouse (1989) conducted two experiments to address Titchener's interpretation. In Experiment 1, participants were first presented with 90 words for 1 s. each on a computer screen, and told to study them for a subsequent memory test. The later test consisted of a mix of both old (90) and new (90) words, presented one at a time, with the participant judging whether each word was old or new. Each test trial consisted of the following sequence: (1) a premask ("&&&") for 500 ms, (2) a context stimulus (word or nonword), (3) a postmask ("&&&&") for 500 ms, (4) a blank screen for 300 ms, and (5) the test word. The context stimulus was either a word identical to the test word that immediately followed it (match), a word different from the test word (nonmatch), or a nonword. Context stimuli (words or nonwords) were either presented at a supraliminal (200 ms) or a subliminal (50 ms) exposure. In the subliminal condition, new words preceded by that same word (match) were mistakenly called "old" significantly more often than new words preceded by a nonmatch word or nonword. Jacoby and Whitehouse (1989) suggest that the more fluid processing evoked by the immediately prior subliminal presentation (the "glance") caused individuals to be more likely to incorrectly assess the new word as being old, with old defined as having appeared in the prior list. To further assure that the subliminal context word really was below the level of awareness, Jacoby and Whitehouse (1989) reduced the subliminal exposure duration from 50 to 35 ms. in Experiment 2, and replicated the outcome from Experiment 1.

Jacoby and Whitehouse (1989) note that this fluency bias precipitates the common experience of having a word appear to "jump out from the page" when reading (Jacoby & Dallas, 1981, p. 333). Perhaps this perceptual surprise may initiate a déjà vu under conditions when a primed perceptual element suddenly and forcefully stands out, in the absence of an immediately identifiable source for this fluency. Jacoby and Whitehouse (1989) also speculate that just as facilitation of fluency could lead to enhanced familiarity (déjà vu), a disruption of processing, or disfluency, could conversely lead to a feeling of strangeness and lack of familiarity, or jamais vu (see Chapter 9). If this were true, then the recognition judgment for new test word preceded by a nonmatch word might make processing the test word *less* fluid than one preceded by no word (nonword), causing a *reduction* in spurious false positives (false alarms) to these test words. In line with this prediction, the mismatch condition did decrease false alarms for new test words (relative to the nonword condition) in Experiment 1, but this difference did not replicate in Experiment 2. Thus, Jacoby and Whitehouse (1989) found consistent support for processing fluency increasing false alarms, but only partial support for processing disfluency decreasing false alarms.

While Jacoby and Whitehouse (1989) relate this finding directly to the déjà vu phenomenon, the paradigm is lacking the element of surprise so characteristic of déjà vu. The participant must reasonably (but mistakenly) assume that any word assessed as familiar occurred in the prior word list (also see Whittlesea, 1993; Whittlesea, Jacoby, & Girard, 1990), which would not support the sense of incongruity ("this could not have happened here before") necessary for a true déjà vu experience.

Although this paradigm provides a reasonable framework to model the inappropriate familiarity of the déjà vu experience, there is debate over whether participants are consciously aware of the masked prime word. Bernstein and Welch (1991) suggest that this supposedly subliminal stimulus presentation is actually supraliminal, and tested this idea by adding a condition in which participants made a match/nonmatch decision concerning the correspondence between the context and target words. They replicated Jacoby and Whitehouse's (1989) finding of an increase in false alarms to new words following match context words but they also found that a second group of participants could make match and nonmatch decisions at above chance levels, suggesting that some information about the context word is being consciously processed.

It is important to emphasize that Bernstein and Welch (1991) did not disagree with Jacoby and Whitehouse (1989) concerning the importance or reliability of their findings. Instead, Bernstein and Welch (1991) contend that the context word does *not* have to be subliminal to produce the effect. Joordens and Merikle (1992) also assessed whether subliminal exposure was necessarily occurring in this paradigm by evaluating participants' recognition performance for context words. As with Jacoby and Whitehouse (1989) and Bernstein and Welch (1991), they found higher false alarm rates for new words in the match, compared to the nonmatch and nonword condition. However, they discovered that the effect occurred both when participants were at chance (Experiment 1) and above chance (Experiments 2 and 3) on recognition for context words. Joordens and Merikle (1992) echoed Bernstein and Welch's (1991) assertion that while Jacoby and Whitehouse's (1989) empirical finding is reliable and important, their conclusion is flawed: Subliminal perception of the context word is not necessary to produce the effect.

This particular debate does not lessen the potential relevance of this paradigm as a model of empirical explorations of the déjà vu phenomenon. In fact, Bernstein and Welch (1991) point out that an above-threshold perceptual experience corresponds more closely to Titchener's (1928) illustration (provided earlier) and that the "glance" is a supraliminal perceptual act processed at a very shallow level. What may be more important is the brief separation between the two successive perceptual experiences (the "gap"), rather than the temporal duration of the initial perception.

Diminished Attention

Another way that an initial perceptual experience can be degraded is by a momentary reduction in attentional resources. If one's attention to the present perceptual experience is momentarily diminished, and if this is followed by a second perception under full and focused attention, a déjà vu could result. The attentional lapse may have a variety of different causes, such as daydreaming, distraction, or reduced energy. It is important to point out the distinction between this position and the earlier interpretation based on a perceptual gap caused by mental distraction. More specifically, under the prior (perceptual gap) position, both of the perceptions were under full awareness, whereas the present interpretation posits that the initial perception is not as clear or thoroughly processed as the second, subsequent perception.

Allin (1896a) suggests that déjà vu *only* occurs when mental fatigue causes our attentional capacity to falter, and we become only slightly attentive to our current sensory experiences. When pulled back into the present moment by a strong or sudden stimulus, we feel that the current experience is a repetition of the past. Kraepelin (1887, cited in Parish, 1897) postulates that when individuals become fatigued, this has two consequences: it reduces their ability to stop "... the stream of vague, indistinct images hastening through the mind" (p. 280), and it lessens their ability to focus their attention on the external world. With daydreaming enhanced and attention reduced, there is a tendency to confuse the external stimuli with prior less-distinct images.

West (1948) speculates that his personal déjà vu experiences are because of an extended form of such inattention where we tend to distract ourselves. In normal conversation, individuals often repeat themselves, saying the same thing several times in succession with perhaps a different twist each time. Our attention may wander during the first statement, perhaps formulating what to say next. When we fully re-engage our attention to what we are saying during the second statement, a déjà vu can occur (West, 1948). Dugas (1902, translated by Ellis, 1911) also suggests that when we are somehow distracted during our initial perception, that particular diminished perception immediately works its way back into conscious awareness as we return our perceptual focus to the stimulus at hand. When confronted with two perceptions—one processed moments ago while unaware, and one presently processed while fully aware—the version that reaches conscious awareness indirectly through the subconscious route assumes a "dreamlike" and distant aura.

One of the common aspects of all the diminished attention interpretations of déjà vu is that the initial and subsequent perception of the present experience are qualitatively different. The first is degraded because of shallow processing, and the second is clearer with more detail and focus. The fact that the initial impression is indistinct enhances the misimpression that it is a distant memory rather than a recent perception.

☐ Indirect Initial Perception

Another way in which an ongoing perceptual experience can be separated into two different components is by an initial perception that is peripheral, followed by a subsequent perception in which the stimulus which was first peripheral now becomes focal. The two previous double-perception explanations (perceptual gap; degraded initial perception) assume that both the first and second perceptions involve the same focal material. In contrast, the interpretations in this section assume that the critical stimulus is first perceived peripherally, and then focally immediately after, and the indirect peripheral processing of the stimulus primes the subsequent focal perception, resulting in a déjà vu.

Inattentional Blindness

Individuals can potentially miss perceiving objects that are in clear view in front of them, if they are focused on some other object in the environment. This inattentional blindness has been extensively documented in a book by Mack and Rock (1998), and could explain how an initial brief perception of a scene or object can go undetected. In their basic paradigm, the participant focuses on a fixation point on a computer monitor for 1500 ms. Then, a brief (200 ms) suprathreshold presentation of a cross (+) occurs at some random location in the display. After the critical stimulus disappears, the participant evaluates whether the horizontal or vertical bar of the cross is longer. On some trials, this target cross is accompanied by an extraneous stimulus—a shape, object, or word—in a different part of the screen. On those particular trials, after the participant makes their decision about which line of the cross is longer, they are asked if anything else was presented along with the cross. Most individuals (about 60%) fail to detect the presence of the extraneous stimulus accompanying the target, and this "blindness" is assumed to be because of lack of attention, or misdirected attention, hence the term inattentional blindness.

A paradigm such as this, where the stimulus is above threshold but unattended, rather than subthreshold or degraded, better models our natural perceptual experience (Merikle, Smilek, & Eastwood, 2001) and provides a good framework for studying the déjà vu experience in the real world.

> ... it is very common for people to be in situations where there are many unattended stimuli outside their immediate focus of attention that are not consciously experienced.... For this reason, the experimental conditions in studies in which unattended stimuli are presented at spatial locations removed from the current focus of attention more closely resemble the conditions under which visual stimuli are perceived in everyday situations ... (p. 122)

An even stranger aspect of inattentional blindness is that the magnitude of the effect is larger when the ignored stimulus is *directly in front of the individual*. More specifically, when the target stimulus is presented off to one side of the visual field (periphery) and the extraneous stimulus is presented directly in the center of the visual field (fovea), the magnitude of the inattentional blindness is larger than when the attended stimulus is in the fovea and the extraneous stimulus is in the periphery. Restated, when a visual element X is directly in front of you and you are focused on visual element Y off to one side of your visual field, you are *less* likely to notice X than when X is in the periphery and you focus on Y directly in front of you.

It is important to add that while participants claim that they don't notice the extraneous stimulus, it still gets processed. For participants who fail to notice a word presented along with the target, their subsequent performance on a five-alternative forced-choice recognition test is significantly above chance (20%) at 47% (Mack & Rock, 1998). In addition, the "blind" participants will show priming, with word stem completion performance significantly greater (36%) than for control participants not previously exposed to that particular word (4%). Applying this laboratory phenomenon to the real world setting, assume that you walk into a hotel lobby looking for the front desk (the target stimulus). Many other stimuli in the environment (plant in the corner; crystal chandelier; coat rack) are processed by you without your direct attention. When you rapidly redirect your attention toward your surroundings and one (or more) of these other environmental element(s) (the chandelier) becomes focal, you may be gripped by a strong sense of familiarity because of the match with the immediately prior implicit peripheral processing.

This inattention blindness also could conceivably occur where the focus of attention is mental (one's thoughts) rather than external. For example, one may enter a room talking on a cell phone or thinking about an upcoming meeting while looking directly at a picture on the wall. When you hang up the cell phone moments later, this picture is consciously perceived leading to the second or duplicated perception eliciting a déjà vu. Perhaps one of the most blatant examples of inattention to suprathreshold stimuli is the "time gap" experience where one's entire perceptual experience over several minutes of driving down an interstate highway is unrecallable (Reed, 1979). A milder version of this diminished attention under distraction has been demonstrated with cell phone use while driving an automobile (Strayer, Drews, & Johnston, 2003; Strayer & Johnston, 2001).

Also related to inattentional blindness is change blindness, where individuals fail to notice that a *change* has occurred to a stimulus that they are paying direct attention to (Simons, 2000; Simons & Levin, 1998). More specifically, if one individual is replaced by another in a succession of photos or scenes in a movie, fewer than half of the people will recognize the change even though the switch involved individuals who are clearly discriminable from each other. This same level of obliviscence even occurs when talking face to face and one's conversational partner is replaced as workmen move between two persons holding an occluding door! Thus, if we are so unaware of details of objects and persons that we are focused on, it seems reasonable that when a particular detail does pop onto our focal radar it could result in déjà vu from being processed below full awareness moments before.

Perceptual Inhibition

An explanation similar to inattentional blindness was suggested by Dixon (1971), using an extension of the Poetzl phenomenon (see Chapter 14). Poetzl originally suggested that during the initial brief stimulus exposure, there is "… a rapid fragmentation of the sensory information, wherein 'inhibition by interference' causes parts of the stimulus field to interfere with the development of other parts" (Dixon, 1971, p. 106). Certain elements in the stimulus array may suppress or block the perception of others, similar to lateral inhibition in the visual system (cf. Martindale, 1981). A second glance at the scene immediately after the first may elicit a déjà vu as the initially inhibited portion of the visual scene is now disinhibited. This explanation of the déjà vu gains some credibility from the fact that there is an age-related decline in inhibitory processes (Craik & Byrd, 1982) which parallels the decrease in déjà vu experience with age.

Another type of inhibitory effect germane to the present discussion is *negative priming* interference. In the negative priming paradigm, an inappropriate response that is inhibited on one trial is more difficult to generate as a correct response on the immediately succeeding trial. In the usual demonstration of this effect with the Stroop paradigm, one must read the color of ink in which color words are printed (say "red" to a BLUE word printed in red ink). If the next trial has the word GREEN printed in blue ink, the correct response of "blue" is slowed down because this response was suppressed on the immediately preceding trial. Whereas this negative priming effect is substantial with younger adults, it is much smaller with older adults (Hasher, Stoltzfus, Zacks, & Rypma, 1991). If the magnitude of visual inhibition of parafoveal elements similarly decreases with age, this would reduce the likelihood that such unprocessed features would subsequently elicit a déjà vu in older adults.

☐ Emotional Reverberation

The last double perception explanation of déjà vu relates to our inner, affective world and how we monitor our emotional reactions. A current experience can appear to be a duplication of a prior experience based on an emotional rather than a cognitive repetition of a prior response. Lewes (1879, cited in Kinnier Wilson, 1929) suggests that an emotional reaction to a situation will occasionally come in cycles, and repeat itself beyond the cessation of the eliciting stimulus.

> Now when a wave of feeling has swept through us, and another similar though fainter wave succeeds, the secondary feeling will naturally be taken for a vague remembrance, the resemblance between the two being accompanied by a difference in intensity that throws the second … into the distance. (Lewes, 1879, p. 129)

Thus, the secondary wave of emotion is experienced as slightly different as the ongoing stream of events gradually evolves, and it is this apparent duplication of an emotional reaction that gives rise to the déjà vu sensation. One simply misinterprets the external context as duplicated, whereas this fallacious sense of repetition actually stems from the re-experiencing of an affective state that occurred moments before.

☐ Subjective Interpretations

A number of explanations for the déjà vu experience have been provided in the last four chapters. Before leaving this topic, several survey studies have solicited opinions from laypersons concerning what causes déjà vu. Whereas most frame the query within a paranormal perspective, a survey by Leeds (1944) is an exception. He sampled a broad range of persons using an open-ended question. Paranormal explanations predominate, and include dreams and prophesy (28%), reincarnation (15%), and wandering of the spirit (4%). However, a number of respondents suggest cognitive and physiological interpretations similar to those covered in Chapters 12 through 15. These include "similarity of elements of situation with past experience" (34%) (Chapter 14), daydreaming or imagination (12%) (Chapter 14), a "pause in brain operation" (2%) (Chapter 13) or "just bad memory" (4%). Osborn (1884) also asked participants if "... any satisfactory explanation of this experience ever suggested itself to you" (p. 478), but found that few respondents had any ideas on the subject.

☐ Summary

Double perception explanations of déjà vu are all based on the premise that an individual perceives a particular situation twice in quick succession. In the perceptual gap interpretation, a continuous perceptual experience under full awareness becomes divided into two apparently separate perceptions after a glance away, or a quick retreat into one's thoughts, and these perceptions are misinterpreted as occurring separated in time. It is also possible that the initial perception is degraded by occlusion or diminished attention, or that the first perception is peripheral with attention first directed away from, and then directly at, the critical stimulus. The phenomena of inattentional blindness and lateral inhibition may underlie how an indirect initial perception followed by a subsequent direct perception may evoke a déjà vu. Finally, a double perception could consist of a quick recycling of one's emotional response, which is misperceived as a duplication of the external experience.

CHAPTER 16

It's Like Déjà Vu All Over Again

In this chapter is a recap the findings on the déjà vu experience. In addition, a general road map is sketched out for future explorations of the phenomenon, focusing on the more important issues in déjà vu research and the paradigms that hold the most potential for clarifying these questions.

☐ Summary: Déjà Vu Findings

Most subjective evaluations of déjà vu in the literature suggest that it is a common experience, and the survey data back this up. Across more than 50 surveys conducted across 120 years, about two thirds of respondents have experienced a lifetime déjà vu. Although there is considerable variation, the incidence tends to be higher in more recent surveys, and in those with younger respondents. If one has experienced déjà vu, it is highly likely that there have been multiple experiences. These experiences are rated as seldom to occasional, and tend to occur every one to six months. The general physical setting is the most likely trigger for a déjà vu experience, although spoken words (one's own and others') is also a frequent cause. Stress and fatigue may make the experience more likely to occur, and déjà vu occurs primarily indoors, while recreating/relaxing, and in the company of friends. The experience typically lasts under 30 s, and is more likely in the afternoon or evening, and toward the end of the week.

Surprise, curiosity, and confusion are typical reactions to déjà vu, although a wide variety of positive and negative reactions are experienced. Time also seems to slow down during the illusion.

Déjà vu is experienced by a higher proportion of younger than older persons, and the frequency of déjà vu among those who do experience it decreases with age. The illusion is more likely in individuals who (a) have more education, (b) have higher incomes, (c) travel (vs. don't), and (d) remember their dreams (vs. don't). Déjà vu is less common in individuals of conservative (vs. liberal) political persuasion and among those with fundamentalist (vs. moderate) religious beliefs.

☐ Important Issues Concerning Déjà Vu

There are a number of different aspects of the déjà vu illusion that should be given priority among those investigating the phenomenon from either survey or laboratory approaches.

Déjà Vu in Unique Versus Ordinary Settings: Different Mechanisms?

One can divide déjà vu reports into two general varieties: those that occur in new settings where one has never been before, and those that occur in familiar or routine locations. The three déjà vu experiences at the start of Chapter 1 provide examples of both the unique (dancing in Downtown Disney with two girls from Brazil) and routine (home with parents, doing school work) varieties. A primary hallmark of the déjà vu experience is subjectively unjustified hyperfamiliarity, but it seems likely that the familiarity in these two situations may be evoked in different ways. More specifically, an inordinately high familiarity response is more likely to be noticed in a foreign, compared to a routine, setting. In other words, one should have a much lower threshold for noticing a feeling of familiarity when in the middle of a strange situation. The literature on déjà vu is silent on this issue, but it may prove useful to explore such differences in future surveys.

Why Does Déjà Vu Happen during Mundane Activities?

Regardless of whether the setting is unique or routine, most déjà vu experiences occur while we are engaged in ordinary activities. Ultimately, this may be one of the most puzzling aspects of the illusion (Crichton-Browne, 1895):

... the condition that seems to be the duplicate of a former one is often very trivial—one that might have presented itself a hundred times. (Holmes, 1891, p. 74)

Put another way, why does such an unusual experience so often occur when nothing out of the routine seems to be happening to us?

Are Auditory and Visual Déjà Vu Experiences Comparable?

Scientific interpretations of déjà vu rely heavily on visual aspects of the experience. Although the physical setting is the most common eliciting factor with déjà vu (see Table 5.1), spoken words are oft-noted triggers to déjà vu illusions. While the physiological (Chapter 13) and dual process (Chapter 12) explanations can handle both visually- and auditorily-based déjà vu experiences, memory (Chapter 14) and double perception (Chapter 15) explanations are primarily focused on visual processing. Thus, extensions of the memory and double perception interpretations to the realm of auditory processing should be encouraged.

What Elicits the Subjective Sense of Precognition?

Although parapsychological interpretations of déjà vu are problematic, a sense of precognition is associated with a sufficiently large number of déjà vu reports that this needs to be clearly addressed, rather than dismissed. Several scientific perspectives can potentially demystify this subjective impression. For instance, a slight increase in the temporal gap between two successive sensory messages along different tracks could theoretically result in both déjà vu—when attending to the lagging message—and precognition—when focusing on the leading message (see Chapter 13). If one rapidly switches between the two impressions, then illusions of déjà vu and precognition could intermingle with each other. Similarly, a faulty temporal tagging mechanism could elicit both inappropriate past-ness (déjà vu) and futureness (precognition) during the same experience (see Chapter 12). In short, any complete scientific explanation should attempt to address this subjective aspect of the illusion.

Why Does Déjà Vu Decrease with Age?

One of the most reliable findings in the déjà vu literature is an inverse relationship between déjà vu and age in both (a) the percentage claiming a lifetime experience, and (b) the frequency of déjà vu among experients. The first finding is apparently because of an increase in the cultural acceptability of the illusion over recent decades, but this needs to be scientifically addressed in a direct rather than post hoc manner. No satisfactory explanation has been proposed for second finding, and its pervasiveness may be an important litmus test for the credibility of any explanation.

How Does Déjà Vu Relate to Memory Deficits?

There are numerous neurological dysfunctions that involve some sort of memory disability, such as Alzheimer's, Parkinson's, multiple sclerosis, Huntington's, and closed head injuries. These patient groups have been extensively studied by cognitive scientists, but little has been noted concerning déjà vu among these individuals. The incidence of déjà vu logically should be elevated in these disabilities, and there is some evidence of this with closed head injury (see Chapter 7). More careful interviews with these patient groups may be of value in clarifying the nature of the illusion.

How Are Individual Differences to Be Explained?

There are several individual differences that appear to be reliably related to the déjà vu experience, including political orientation, socioeconomic status, religious leanings, income level, alcohol consumption, and education. Is there some aspect of these different groups of individuals that elicit differing numbers of déjà vu experiences, or are these groups experientially the same and simply differ in their willingness to admit to having the illusion? Incidentally, the large NORC data base plus statistical tools are publically available on the Web (see Chapter 6), allowing one to investigate personally the relationship between déjà vu and various demographic and attitudinal variables.

Can Drugs Reliably Elicit Déjà Vu?

A number of studies point to a possible connection between déjà vu and various prescription, nonprescription, and recreational drugs (e.g., Crosby & Gottlieb, 1988). Especially intriguing is Taiminen and Jääskeläinen's (2001) finding that prescription flu medication caused a dramatic increase in déjà vu experiences, which they attributed to excessive dopamine in the mesial temporal lobe (see Chapter 7). Could other medications that increase dopamine (agonists) in the brain (e.g., L-DOPA) also elicit déjà vu as a side-effect? Also, benzodiazepine medications appear to differentially affect explicit remember responses but not familiarity (know) (Bishop & Curran, 1995; Curran, Gardiner, Java, & Allen, 1993). Given that such a memorial disparity appears to underlie the déjà vu experience, it may be worth pursuing research with this particular pharmacological agent.

☐ Questionnaire Development

Although a wide variety of surveys and questionnaires on the déjà vu experience have been used, serious problems exist with the development and application of such queries. Many focus on possible psychodynamic (depersonalization) and parapsychological (belief in mystical experience) corollaries of déjà vu, or embed the déjà vu question among items that relate to such phenomena. Prior surveys and questionnaires are generally not well refined or validated, and results are rarely summarized in a thorough or readily accessible form. The extensive questionnaire instruments are often overly long, complex, and repetitive, and many survey samples are more convenient than representative.

Thus, a thorough redesign of the retrospective survey is needed, tied in with the cognitive literature. Survey results should be published with a large and representative sample of individuals across a wide range of age, racial, ethnic, and cultural backgrounds. It is important to evaluate the déjà vu experiences in people of non-Western religions, cultures, and ethnic backgrounds. Do individuals in cultures more tolerant of mystical experiences tend to report more déjà vu experiences (cf. Stevenson, 1987)? Any survey should include questions concerning acute personal physical stressors (recent illness, accident), chronic disease processes, psychological traumas, recent family events (illness, birth, death, divorce), prescription medication useage, recreational drug habits, recent changes in residence or work, and belief in paranormal phenomena. In fact, the domain of life circumstances preceding the déjà vu—changes in recent days or weeks—may be a critical dimension in understanding what causes déjà vu.

An open-ended question should request a personal definition of déjà vu, what the respondent believes *causes* it, and their view on the societal acceptance of the illusion (cf. Leeds, 1944). The déjà vu experience should be thoroughly examined in individuals with TLE, seizure disorders, various neurological conditions (cf. Richardson & Winocur, 1968), amnesics (Cutting and Silzer, 1990; Weinstein et al., 1962), split-brain patients (cf. Kirshner, 1973) and individuals receiving electroconvulsive therapy. The incidence of depersonalization, dissociation, jamais vu, and hypnogogic/hypnopompic imagery also should be evaluated in survey respondents, as well as whether they remember their dreams, read fiction on a regular basis, and have vivid mental imagery ability.

It would be ideal to combine retrospective and prospective question-naires in one study, because even the most recent déjà vu experience is likely to be many months old with details of the physical and personal experience having faded (Brown et al., 1994; Chapman & Mensh, 1951; Harper, 1969; Neppe, 1983e). One potentially fruitful avenue for harvest-ing déjà vu experiences is to interview individuals who have recently undergone a major move. After more than a decade living in Dallas, a departmental colleague took a job at another university hundreds of miles (and several states) away. A month after the move, she informed me that she was having frequent déjà vu experiences in her new circumstances. Confronting a new physical surrounding may provide an ideal context for triggering déjà vu experiences, especially when there is considerable over-lap in the features of both settings (university to university). The stress of job change also may increase the likelihood of such experiences. Other groups of individuals undergoing similar transitions could be evaluated: college freshmen, professionals starting their first job out of school (doc-tors, lawyers, professors), military personnel reassigned bases, and busi-nesspersons transferred within the company to a different city.

☐ Future Laboratory Research

The previous four chapters of this book clearly demonstrate that the déjà vu experience has spawned a healthy variety of plausible scientific expla-nation, tracing back into the middle of the 18th century. The amorphous nature of déjà vu is especially conducive to speculation by creative and observant scientifically oriented individuals, and a brief summary of these positions is provided in Appendix B. With the exception of Jacoby and Whitehouse (1989), however, there has been no empirically focused effort to identify the possible mechanisms underlying déjà vu, or to develop cognitive models to subsume the illusion. Some have expressed pessimism about the possibility of scientifically analyzing déjà vu because of the phenomenon's transient and unpredictable nature (Sno & Linzen, 1991) and association with mundane experiences lacking clearly identifiable eliciting stimuli (Funkhouser, 1983a, 1983b; Green, 1966; Osborn, 1884). Furthermore, research scientists may naturally gravitate toward those phenomena that they personally experience. For example, the tip-of-the-tongue state probably receives research attention (Brown, 1991) in part because the incidence is reasonably high among middle age (or older) cognitive researchers (Brown, 2000). In contrast, the decline in déjà vu with age may reduce the likelihood that this phenomenon holds much personal relevance or interest for most mature research specialists.

Whereas producing a "full-blown" déjà vu in the laboratory may be problematic, a reasonable goal is to create conditions that approximate the subjectively inappropriate familiarity characteristic of a déjà vu. In short, what is needed is to simultaneously create two opposing evaluations: a strong feeling of familiarity *and* a belief that this familiarity cannot logically be connected with the present stimulus. In past research touching on the déjà vu experience, the experiential context has *not* been novel (Banister & Zangwill, 1941a, 1941b; Jacoby & Whitehouse, 1989; Seamon et al., 1983b) in that both study and test procedures occur in the *same* laboratory setting with relatively homogeneous stimuli.

Among the four categories of scientifically based explanations, the dual processing interpretations (Chapter 12) are the least amenable to a scientific test. They frame the déjà vu experience in a more abstract manner, several steps removed from the actual behaviors that could be tied in with the illusion, and would take considerable effort to appropriately operationalize in a way that could provide an adequately test. The physiological positions (Chapter 13) would seem to require sophisticated equipment to measure brain activity, or simulate the neurological dysfunctions that could underlie the déjà vu illusion. A possible way to procedurally approximate the two pathway asynchrony would be to present a single stimulus in both the right and left visual fields (or the right and left ears) but in a manner that is slightly delayed to one field (ear). This might simulate the slight discordance that could precipitate an impression that the stimulus is old.

The memory and double perception categories of explanation are more closely tied in with cognitive paradigms that are currently being explored, and provide possible paradigms that are more technically feasible for modeling the déjà vu illusion.

Memory Approaches

A number of different memory paradigms may lend themselves especially well to evaluating the déjà vu experience. For instance, the subliminal mere exposure research (Seamon et al., 1983b), suggests a large number of below-threshold exposures plus a long input-to-test delay could substantially increase the magnitude of an affective response (Bornstein, 1992) making it more closely resemble the intensity of reaction typically found in déjà vu. Also, posthypnotic suggestion holds some potential (Banister & Zangwill, 1941a, 1941b) for establishing implicit familiarity while eliminating contextual memory for a previously encountered stimulus. Individuals exposed to unique stimuli (symbols, faces, short stories, songs) under hypnosis, along with a posthypnotic suggestion to forget, could later be given a recognition test in a different lab setting. The evaluations of each item could include context-free familiarity (know) plus a context-specific recognition (remember). And given Marcuse et al.'s (1945) observation that responses to posthypnotic suggestion may be accompanied by a sense of déjà vu, a more systematic assessment of individuals' subjective interpretations of these experiences may be useful.

The single-element familiarity position also holds some promise. Using complex visual scenes (living room, hotel lobby, courtyard) with a continuous recognition task, single elements from prior scenes (chair, wall picture, fountain) could be digitally inserted into "new" scenes in an attempt to elicit an overgeneralized sense of familiarity. The gestalt position could be similarly tested via new pictures that duplicate earlier-presented ones in the arrangement of (but not specific) objects. Virtual reality technology applied to such a paradigm could enhance the verisimilitude, better duplicating the naturalistic environment in which déjà vu usually occurs. Finally, one could attempt to establish "memories" through descriptive passages, guided imagery, or false memory lists. A recognition test on a subsequent (and apparently unrelated) occasion could involve real pictures of scenes described earlier in prose.

Double Perception Approaches

The domain of perception without full awareness seems to hold a tremendous potential to elucidate the mechanism underlying the déjà vu experience. As Merikle et al. (2001) so cogently point out,

> … how does information that is perceived without awareness influence conscious experience? This question has received relatively little attention in experimental studies to date because the goal of the vast majority of studies has been simply to demonstrate perception without awareness. (p. 128–129)

It has repeatedly been found that dividing attention during study can have a deleterious effect on later explicit memory, leaving implicit familiarity relatively unaffected (Jacoby, 1991). A flanker task where a focal (attended) stimulus is presented in the center of a computer screen with flanker (unattended) stimuli presented either above, below, left, or right of the focal stimulus (Hawley & Johnston, 1991; Mulligan & Hornstein, 2000) may prove especially useful in modeling déjà vu. A flanker stimulus on trial N that becomes the target on trial N + 1 may elicit the type of false familiar response characteristic of a déjà vu. A more complex array involving many flanker stimuli surrounding the focal stimulus, may better represent the type of complex visual setting in which a déjà vu is often experienced.

Research on inattentional blindness would suggest a stronger effect if the flanker(s) appear in the middle of the screen with the target presented at a location off center. Also, complex natural scenes could be used where the participant's attention is directed to one particular feature of an anticipated scene ("is there a bird's nest in the tree?"), and a nonfocal feature (a pond) on trial N is presented focally on trial N + 1. Recognition decisions could include confidence ratings, as well as source evaluations on whether the scene is an intraexperimental (recent or remote trial) or extraexperimental (cf. Schacter et al., 1984) duplication.

Descriptions of Déjà Vu Experiences

There are many descriptions of déjà vu provided in the research literature and these generally are of three different types.

Routine Examples

The first set includes descriptions of déjà vu episodes culled from non-clinical individuals, and meant to illustrate various features of the normal déjà vu experience.

> Neppe (1983e; pp. 3, 54–55, 65–66, 111, 112, 114, 115, 118, 119, 120, 124, 126, 127–128, 129, 131, 131–132),
> Osborn (1884, p. 479)
> Pickford (1940, p. 154, 153–155)
> Reed (1974, p. 105)
> Smith (1913, p. 56)
> Stern (1938, p. 208–209)
> White (1973, p. 44)

Clinical Case Study Examples

A second group of déjà vu descriptions are derived from individuals with serious psychopathology (e.g., schizophrenics) and are meant to provide a contrast with more routine examples.

Kirshner (1973, pp. 247–248; three cases)
Neppe (1983e, p. 34, 50, 137–138, 139–140, 141, 142, 144, 146, 147, 149, 159–160, 162, 163, 166)

Psychoanalytic Examples

The psychodynamic literature is especially rich in detailed personal stories illustrating déjà vu. Not only is the specific déjà vu experience described, often across several pages, there is typically extensive background about the individual to set the stage for interpreting the psychodynamic basis of the particular déjà vu. As Arlow (1959) points out following an 11-page analysis of two déjà vu experiences, "Like a dream, the experience of déjà vu can perhaps be analyzed inexhaustibly" (p. 624).

Arlow (1959, p. 614–624)
Arlow (1992, p. 72)
Arnoud (1896, p. 460; cited in Marková & Berrios, 2000)
Bergler (1942, pp. 166–170)
Freud (1901/1914, psychopathology of everyday life)
Kirshner (1973, pp. 247–248)
Oberndorf (1941, pp. 322–325)
Pacella (1975, pp. 308–312)
Schneck (1961, pp. 91–92; 1962, pp. 49–51)
Shapiro (1978, pp. 309–314)
Sno (1994, pp. 145–146)

Summary of Scientific Explanations of Déjà Vu

Dual Processing

Retrieval and familiarity: familiar occurs spontaneously, independent of retrieval

Retrieval and temporal tags: time tag of "old" gets spuriously generated

Encoding and retrieval: retrieval is inadvertently activated during encoding

Perception and encoding: memory formation overlaps with perception

Sensation and recollection: sensation is degraded, and appears as a memory

Sensation and perception: gap between sensation and perception is briefly widened

Dual consciousness: two alternating conscious states become simultaneously active

Subliminal awareness: a secondary state of consciousness comes to the fore

Neurological

General seizure: a momentary, global seizure causes a memory dysfunction

Parahippocampal firing: spurious activation of this structure elicits familiarity

Single pathway delay: briefly slowed neuronal message is interpreted as old

Single pathway acceleration: briefly speeded neuronal message is interpreted as old

Dual pathway, secondary delay: slowed secondary track creates "separate" messages

Dual pathway, primary delay: slowed primary message arrives after the secondary one

Memory

Episodic forgetting: person forgot the prior experience

Literary description: experience or setting was read about in a literary passage

Childhood amnesia: experience occurred very early in childhood, and is inaccessible

Media source confusion: present setting was experienced through some form of media

Duplication of processing: present mental process replicates previous processing

Single element familiarity: unrecognized familiarly to one element overgeneralizes

Dream element duplication: unrecognized element occurred in a prior dream

Daydream element duplication: unrecognized element occurred in daydream/imagination

Literary element duplication: unrecognized element was read about in literary passage

Multiple element familiarity: several aspects of setting are unrecognized but familiar

Processing fluency: speeded processing of implicit old elements elicits familiarity

Positive affective association: implicit positive emotional reaction interpreted as familiarity

Negative affective association: implicit negative affect is buffered by familiarity interpretation

Gestalt familiarity: configuration of elements, not the elements themselves, is familiar

Double Perception

Perceptual gap: an ongoing perceptual experience is split into two parts

Revelation effect: partial, followed by full, perception elicits familiarity

Degraded initial perception: diminished first glance precedes full perception

Indirect initial perception: peripheral first impression precedes focal full perception

Diminished energy: reduced physical energy erodes initial perception

Emotional reverberation: emotional reaction rapidly recycles a second time

References

Abercrombie, J. (1836). *Inquiries concerning the intellectual powers and the investigation of truth*. New York: Harper & Brothers.

Adachi, N., Adachi, T., Kimura, M., Akanuma, N., & Kato, M. (2001). Development of the Japanese version of the Inventory of *Déjà vu* Experiences Assessment (IDEA). *Seishin Igaku (Clinical Psychiatry), 43,* 1223–1231.

Adachi, N., Adachi, T., Kimura, M., Akanuma, N., Takekawa, Y., & Kato, M. (2003). Demographic and psychological features of déjà vu experiences in a nonclinical Japanese population. *Journal of Nervous and Mental Disease, 191,* 242–247.

Adachi, N., Koutroumanidis, M., Elwes, R. D. C., Polkey, C. E., Binnie, C. D., Reynolds, E. H., Barrington, S. F., Maisey, M. N., & Panayiotopoulos, C. P. (1999). Interictal [18]FDG PET findings in temporal lobe epilepsy with *déjà vu*. *Journal of Neuropsychiatry & Clinical Neurosciences, 11,* 380–386.

Allers, R., & Teler, J. (1924). On the utilization of unnoticed impressions in associations. In Monograph 7, *Psychological Issues, 2,* 121–154.

Allin, A. (1896a). Recognition. *American Journal of Psychology, 7,* 249–273.

Allin, A. (1896b). The "recognition-theory" of perception. *American Journal of Psychology, 7,* 237–248.

Amster, H. (1964). Semantic satiation and generation: Learning? Adaptation? *Psychological Bulletin, 62,* 273–286.

Anderson, B. F. (1975). *Cognitive psychology*. New York: Academic Press.

Anderson, J. R. (1980). *Cognitive psychology and its implications*. New York: W. H. Freeman.

Angell, J. R. (1908). *Psychology*. New York: Henry Holt.

Anjel (no initial) (1878). Beitrag zum Capitel über Erinnerugstäuschungen. *Archiv für Psychiatrie und Nervenkrankheiten, 8,* 57–64.

Antoni, N. (1946). Dreamy states, epileptic aura, depersonalization and psychaesthenic fits: A few comments and reflections. *Acta Psychiatrica et Neurologia Scandinavia, 21,* 1–20.

Ardila, A., Montañes, P., Bernal, B., Serpa, A., & Ruiz, E. (1986). Partial psychic seizures and brain organization. *The International Journal of Neuroscience, 30,* 23–32.

Ardila, A., Niño, C. R., Pulido, E., Rivera, D. B., & Vanegas, C. J. (1993). Episodic psychic symptoms in the general population. *Epilepsia, 34,* 133–140.

Arlow, J. A. (1959). The structure of the *déjà vu* experience. *Journal of the American Psychoanalytic Association, 7,* 611–631.

Arlow, J. A. (1986). Psychoanalysis and time. *Journal of the American Psychoanalytic Association, 34,* 507–528.

Arlow, J. A. (1992). Altered ego states. *Israel Journal of Psychiatry & Related Sciences, 29,* 65–76.

Arnaud, F. L. (1896). Un cas d'illusion du 'déjà vu' ou de 'fausse mémoire'. *Annales Médico-Psychologiques, 3,* 455–471.

Ascherson, W. L. (1907). Mental state in alcoholism. *Mott's Archives of Neurology, 3,* 23–41.

Ashcraft, M. H. (2002). *Cognition*. Upper Saddle River, NJ: Prentice-Hall.

Baddeley, A. (1976). *The psychology of memory*. New York: Basic Books.

Baddeley, A. (1990). *Human memory: Theory and practice*. Boston: Allyn and Bacon.

Baldwin, J. M. (1889). *Handbook of psychology*. New York: Henry Holt.

Bancaud, J., Brunet-Bourgin, F., Chauvel, P., & Halgren, E. (1994). Anatomical origin of *déjà vu* and vivid "memories" in human temporal lobe epilepsy. *Brain, 117,* 71–90.

Banister, H., & Zangwill, O. L. (1941a). Experimentally induced olfactory paramnesias. *British Journal of Psychology, 32,* 155–175.

Banister, H., & Zangwill, O. L. (1941b). Experimentally induced visual paramnesias. *British Journal of Psychology, 32,* 30–51.

Bartlett, F. C. (1932). *Remembering*. Cambridge: Cambridge University Press.

Barton, J. L. (1979). Depersonalization. *Southern Medical Journal, 72,* 770.

Bayen, U. J., Murnane, K., & Erdfelder, E. (1996). Source discrimination, item detection, and multinomial models of source monitoring. *Journal of Experimental Psychology: Learning, Memory, & Cognition, 22,* 197–215.

Belbin, E. (1950). The influence of interpolated recall upon recognition. *Quarterly Journal of Experimental Psychology, 2,* 163–169.

Bendit, L. J. (1944). *Paranormal cognition*. London: Faber & Faber.

Benson, D. F., & Stuss, D. T. (1990). Frontal lobe influences on delusions: A clinical perspective. *Schizophrenia Bulletin, 16,* 403–411.

Bergler, E. (1942). A contribution to the psychoanalysis of *déjà vu*. *Psychoanalytic Quarterly, 11,* 165–170.

Bergson, H. (1908). Le souvenir du présent et la fausse reconnaissance. *Revue Philosophique, 66,* 561–593.

Bergson, H. (1911). *Matter and memory*. London: George Allen and Unwin.

Bernhard-Leroy, E. (1898). *L'illusion de fausse reconnaissance*. Paris: F. Alcan.

Bernstein, E. M., & Putnam, F. W. (1986). Development, reliability, and validity of a dissociation scale. *Journal of Nervous and Mental Disease, 174,* 727–735.

Bernstein, I. H., & Welch, K. R. (1991). Awareness, false recognition, and the Jacoby-Whitehouse effect. *Journal of Experimental Psychology: General, 120,* 324–328.

Berndt-Larsson, H. (1931). Ueber das déjà vu und andere Täuschungen des Bekanntheistgefühls. *Zeitschrift fur Gesamte Neurologie, 133,* 521–543

Berrios, G. E. (1995). Déjà vu in France during the 19th century: A conceptual history. *Comprehensive Psychiatry, 36,* 123–129.

Berson, R. J. (1983). Capgras' syndrome. *American Journal of Psychiatry, 140,* 969–978.

Best, J. B. (1986). *Cognitive psychology*. St. Paul, MN: West Publishing.

Biederman, I. (1987). Recognition by components: A theory of human image understanding. *Psychological Review, 94,* 115–117.

Bird, B. (1957). Feelings of unreality. *International Journal of Psychoanalysis, 38,* 256–265.

Bishop, K., & Curran, H. V. (1998). An investigation of the effects of benzodiazepine receptor ligands and of scopolamine on conceptual priming. *Psychopharmacology, 140,* 345–353.

Blake, M. (1973). Prediction of recognition when recall fails: Exploring the feeling-of-knowing phenomenon. *Journal of Verbal Learning and Verbal Behavior, 12,* 311–319.

Boesky, D. (1969). The reversal of *déjà reconte*. *Journal of the American Psychoanalytic Association, 17,* 1114–1141.

Boirac, E. (1876). Correspondance. *Review Philosophique, 1,* 430–431.

Boltz, M. G. (1998). Task predictability and remembered duration. *Perception & Psychophysics, 60,* 768–784.

Bonebakker, A. E., Bonke, B., Klein, J., Wolters, G., Stijnen, T., Passchier, J., & Merikle, P. M. (1996). Information processing during general anesthesia: Evidence for unconscious memory. *Memory and Cognition, 24,* 766–776.

Boring, E. G., Langfeld, H. S., & Weld, H. P. (1935). *Psychology: A factual textbook*. New York: John Wiley & Sons.

Bornstein, R. F. (1989). Exposure and affect: Overview and meta-analysis of research, 1968–1987. *Psychological Bulletin, 106*, 265–289.

Bornstein, R. F. (1992). Subliminal mere exposure effects. In R. F. Bornstein & T. S. Pittman (Eds.), *Perception without awareness*. New York: Guilford Press. pp. 191–210.

Bourdon, B. (1893). La reconnaissance de phénomènes nouveaux. *Revue Philosophique, 36*, 629–631.

Bourne, L. E., Dominowski, R. L., & Loftus, E. F. (1979). *Cognitive processes*. Englewood Cliffs, NJ: Prentice-Hall.

Bowers, K. S., & Hilgard, E. R. (1988). Some complexities in understanding memory. In H. M. Pettinati (Ed.), *Hypnosis and memory*. New York: Guilford.

Brauchi, J. T., & West, L. J. (1959). Sleep deprivation. *Journal of the American Medical Association, 171*, 11–14.

Brauer, R., Harrow, M., & Tucker, G. J. (1970). Depersonalization phenomena in psychiatric patients. *British Journal of Psychiatry, 117*, 509–515.

Breese, B. B. (1921). *Psychology*. New York: Charles Scribner's Sons.

Brickner, R. M., & Stein, A. (1942). Intellectual symptoms in temporal lobe lesions, including "déjà pensée." *Journal of the Mount Sinai Hospital, 9*, 344–348.

Brown, A. S. (1991). A review of the tip of the tongue phenomenon. *Psychological Bulletin, 109*, 204–223.

Brown, A. S. (2000). Aging and the tip-of-the-tongue experience. American Psychological Society Convention, Miami Beach.

Brown, A. S. (2002). Consolidation theory and retrograde amnesia in humans. *Psychonomic Bulletin and Review, 9*, 403–425.

Brown, A. S. (2003). A review of the déjà vu experience. *Psychological Bulletin, 129*, 394–413.

Brown, A. S., & Halliday, H. E. (1991). Cryptomnesia and source memory difficulties. *American Journal of Psychology, 104*, 475–490.

Brown, A. S., Jones, E. M., & Davis, T. L. (1995). Age differences in conversational source monitoring. *Psychology and Aging, 10*, 111–122.

Brown, A. S., & Murphy, D. R. (1989). Cryptomnesia: Delineating inadvertent plagiarism. *Journal of Experimental Psychology: Learning, Memory, and Cognition, 15*, 432–442.

Brown, A. S., & Nix, L. A. (1996). Turning lies into truths: Referential validation of falsehoods. *Journal of Experimental Psychology: Learning, Memory, and Cognition, 22*, 1088–1100.

Brown, A. S., Porter, C. L., & Nix, L. A. (1994). A questionnaire evaluation of the déjà vu experience. Midwestern Psychological Association Convention, Chicago.

Brown, J. W. (1988). *The life of the mind*. Hillsdale, NJ: Erlbaum.

Brown, R., & Kulik, J. (1977). Flashbulb memories. *Cognition, 5*, 73–99.

Buck, L. A. (1970). Varieties of consciousness: Comparison of some cognitive characteristics. *Perceptual & Motor Skills, 30*, 183–186.

Buck, L. A., & Geers, M. B. (1967). Varieties of consciousness: I. Intercorrelations. *Journal of Clinical Psychology, 23*, 151–152.

Burke, D. M., & Light, L. L. (1981). Memory and aging: The role of retrieval processes. *Psychological Bulletin, 90*, 513–546.

Burke, D. M., MacKay, D. G., Worthley, J. S., & Wade, E. (1991). On the tip of the tongue: What causes word finding failures in young and older adults? *Journal of Memory and Language, 30*, 237–246.

Burnham, W. H. (1889). Memory, historically and experimentally considered. III. Paramnesia. *American Journal of Psychology, 2*, 431–464.

Burnham, W. H. (1903). Retroactive amnesia: Illustrative cases and a tentative explanation. *American Journal of Psychology, 14*, 382–396.

Cahill, C., & Frith, C. (1995). Memory following electroconvulsive therapy. In A. D. Baddeley & B. A. Wilson (Eds), *Handbook of memory disorders*. New York: Wiley (pp. 319–335).

Calkins, M. W. (1916). *An introduction to psychology*. New York: Macmillan.

Carlson, E. B., & Putnam, F. W. (1993). An update on the Dissociative Experiences Scale. *Dissociation, 6*, 16–27.

Carlson, E. B., Putnam, F. W., Ross, C. A., Anderson, G., Clark, P., Torem, M., Coons, P., Bowman, E., Chu, J. A., Dill, D., Lowenstein, R. J., & Braun, B. G. (1991). Factor analysis of the Dissociative Experiences Scale: A multicenter study. In B. G. Braun & E. B. Carlson (Eds.), *Proceedings of the eighth international conference on multiple personality and dissociative states*. Chicago: Rush.

Carrington, H. (1931). "Déjà-vu": The sense of the "already seen." *Journal of the American Society of Psychical Research, 25,* 301–306.

Carmichael, L. (1957). *Basic psychology: A study of the modern healthy mind*. New York: Random House.

Carpenter, W. B. (1874). *Principles of mental physiology*. New York: D. Appleton Co.

Chapman, A. H., & Mensh, I. N. (1951). Déjà vu experience and conscious fantasy in adults. *Psychiatric Quarterly Supplement, 25,* 163–175.

Chari, C. T. K. (1962). Paramnesia and reincarnation. *Proceedings of the Society for Psychical Research, 53,* 264–286.

Chari, C. T. K. (1964). On some types of *déjà vu* experiences. *Journal of the American Society of Psychical Research, 58,* 186–203.

Claparède, E. (1951). Recognition and "me-ness." In D. Rapaport (Ed.), *Organization and pathology of thought*. New York: Columbia University Press.

Cole, M., & Zangwill, O. L. (1963). *Déjà vu* in temporal lobe epilepsy. *Journal of Neurology, Neurosurgery & Psychiatry, 26,* 37–38.

Coleman, S. M. (1944). Psychopathology. *Journal of Mental Science, 90,* 152–192.

Comfort, A. (1977). Homuncular identity-sense as a *déjà vu* phenomenon. *British Journal of Medical Psychology, 50,* 313–315.

Conklin, E. S. (1935). *Principles of abnormal psychology*, 2nd Ed. New York: Henry Holt.

Cotard, J. (1880). Du délire hypochondriaque dan une forme grave de la melancolie. *Annals Méd Psychol, 38,* 168–174.

Cotard, J. (1882). Du délire des négations. *Archives of Neurology, 4,* 152–170.

Council, J. R., & Edwards, P. W. (1987). Survey of traumatic childhood events. Unpublished measure. Fargo: North Dakota State University.

Courbon, P., & Fail, G. (1927). Syndrome "d'illusion de Frégoli" et schizophrenie. *Annals of Medical Psychology, 85,* 289–290.

Courbon, P., & Tusques, J. (1932). Illusions d'intermetamorphose et de la charme. *Annals of Medicopsychology, 90,* 401–406.

Craik, F. I. M., & Byrd, M. (1982). Aging and cognitive deficits: The role of attentional resources. In F. I. M. Craik & S. E. Trehub (Eds.), *Aging and cognitive processes*. New York: Plenum.

Crichton-Browne, J. (1895). The Cavendish Lecture on dreamy mental states. *Lancet, 2,* 1–5.

Critchley, E. M. R. (1989). The neurology of familiarity. *Behavioural Neurology, 2,* 195–200.

Crosby, D., & Gottlieb, C. G. (1988). *Long time gone: The autobiography of David Crosby*. London: Mandarin Paperbacks.

Crowder, R. G. (1976). *Principles of learning and memory*. Hillsdale, NJ: Erlbaum.

Curran, H. V., Gardiner, J. M., Java, R., & Allen, D. J. (1993). Effects of lorazepam on recollective experience in recognition memory. *Psychopharmacology, 110,* 374–378.

Cutting, J., & Silzer, H. (1990). Psychopathology of time in brain disease and schizophrenia. *Behavioural Neurology, 3,* 197–215.

Dashiell, J. F. (1928). *Fundamentals of objective psychology*. Boston: Houghton Mifflin Company.

Dashiell, J. F. (1937). *Fundamentals of general psychology*. Boston: Houghton Mifflin Company.

Davidson, G. M. (1941). A syndrome of time-agnosia. *Journal of Nervous and Mental Diseases, 94,* 336–343.

Davis, G. A., Peterson, J. M., & Farley, F. H. (1974). Attitudes, motivation, sensation seeking, and belief in ESP as predictors of creative behavior. *Journal of Creative Behavior, 8,* 31–39.

Dawson, M. R. W. (1998). *Understanding cognitive science*. Malden, MA: Blackwell Publishers.

Deese, J. (1959). On the prediction of occurrence of particular verbal intrusions in immediate recall. *Journal of Experimental Psychology, 58*, 17–22.

de Lamartine, M. A. (1835). Souvenirs, impressions pensées et paysages pendant un voyage en orient 1832–1834. *Oeuvre Complètes, Vol. 5*. Paris: Charles Gosselin.

de Nayer, A (1979). Le "déjà vu": élaboration d'un modèle d'approche hypothétic. *Psychiatria Clinica, 12*, 92–96.

De Pury, J. (1902). *Archives de Psychologie*. (cited in H. Ellis, 1911)

Devereux, G. (1967). *Fausse non-reconnaissance*: Clinical sidelights on the role of possibility in science. *Bulletin of the Menninger Clinic, 31*, 69–78.

Dixon, J. C. (1963). Depersonalization phenomena in a sample population of college students. *British Journal of Psychiatry, 109*, 371–375.

Dixon, N. F. (1971). *Subliminal perception: The nature of a controversy*. London: McGraw-Hill.

Dodd, D. H., & White, R. M. (1980). *Cognition: Mental structures and processes*. Boston: Allyn and Bacon.

Donaldson, W. (1996). The role of decision processes in remembering and knowing. *Memory & Cognition, 24*, 523–533.

Drever, J. (1952). *A dictionary of psychology*. Baltimore, MD: Penguin Books.

Dugas, L. (1894). Observations sur la fausse mémoire. *Revue Philosophique, 38*, 34–45.

Dugas, L. (1902). Sur l'interpretation des faits de paramnésie. *Revue Philosophique, 46*, 51–58.

Dugas, L. (1908). Observations sur les erreurs formelles de la mémoire. *Revue Philosophique, 66*, 79–84.

Dunlap, K. (1922). *The elements of scientific psychology*. St. Louis: C. V. Mosby.

Dywan, J. (1984). Hypermnesia and accuracy in recall. Paper presented at the 45th annual convention of the Canadian Psychological Association, Ottawa, Canada.

Ebbinghaus, H. (1885). Über das Gedächtnis. H. R. Dunker & C. E. Bussenius (Trans.), *Memory*. New York: Teachers College Press, 1913.

Efron, R. (1956). The effect of olfactory stimuli in arresting uncinate fits. *Brain, 79*, 267–281.

Efron, R. (1963). Temporal perception, aphasia, and déjà vu. *Brain, 86*, 403–424.

Ellinwood, E. H., Jr. (1968). Amphetamine psychosis: II. Theoretical implications. *International Journal of Neuropsychiatry, 4*, 45–54.

Ellis, H. (1897). A note on hypnagogic paramnesia. *Mind, 6*, 283–287.

Ellis, H. (1911). *The world of dreams*. London: Constable and Company.

Ellis, H. C., & Hunt, R. R. (1972). *Fundamentals of human memory and cognition*. Dubuque, IA: W. C. Brown.

Ellis, H. D., Luauté, J. P., & Retterstøl, N. (1994). Delusional misidentification syndromes. *Psychopathology, 27*, 117–120.

Emmons, C. F., & Sobal, J. (1981). Paranormal beliefs: Testing the marginality hypothesis. *Sociological Focus, 14*, 49–56.

Epstein, A. W., & Collie, W. R. (1976). Is there a genetic factor in certain dream types? *Biological Psychiatry, 11*, 359–362.

Epstein, A. W., & Freeman, N. R. (1981). The uncinate focus and dreaming. *Epilepsia, 22*, 603–605.

Erdelyi, M. H. (1970). Recovery of unavailable perceptual input. *Cognitive Psychology, 1*, 99–113.

Ey, H., Bernard, P., & Brisset, C. (1978). *Manuel de psychiatrie*, 5th edition. Paris: Masson.

Farina, B., & Verrienti, D. (1996). Il fenomeno "déjà vu" tra psicopatologia ed opera letteraria. *Minerva Psichiatrica, 37*, 99–106.

Federn, P. (1952). *Ego psychology and the psychoses*. New York: Basic Books.

Fenichel, O. (1945). *The psychoanalytic theory of neurosis*. New York: Norton.

Ferenczi, S. (1912). Ein Fall von "déjà vu." *Zeitschrift fur Psychologie, 2*, 648–649.

Ferenczi, S. (1955). *Final contributions to the problems and methods of psychoanalysis*. New York: Basic Books.

Ferenczi, S. (1969). *Further contributions to the theory and technique of psycho-analysis*. London: Hogarth Press.

Feuchtersleben, E. (1845). *Lehrbuch der ärztlichen Seelenkunde.* Vienna: C. Gerold Verlag.

Feuchtersleben, E. (1847). *The principles of medical psychology.* London: Sydenham Society.

Findler, N. V. (1998). A model-based theory for déjà vu and related psychological phenomena. *Computers in Human Behavior, 14,* 287–301.

Fish, D. R., Gloor, P., Quesney, F. L., & Oliver, A. (1993). Clinical responses to electrical brain stimulation of the temporal and frontal lobes in patients with epilepsy: Pathophysiological implications. *Brain, 116,* 397–414.

Fisher, C., & Paul, I. H. (1959). The effect of subliminal visual stimulation on imagery and dreams. A validation study. *Journal of the American Psychoanalytical Association, 7,* 35–83.

Fiss, H. (1966). The effects of experimentally induced changes in alertness on response to subliminal stimulation. *Journal of Personality, 34,* 577–595.

Fleminger, S. (1991). "The déjà vu experience: Remembrance of things past?": Comment. *American Journal of Psychiatry, 148,* 1418–1419.

Förstl, H., Almeida, O. P., Owen, A. M., Burns, A., & Howard, R. (1991). Psychiatric, neurological and medical aspects of misidentification syndromes: A review of 260 cases. *Psychological Medicine, 21,* 905–910.

Fox, J. W. (1992). The structure, stability, and social antecedents of reported paranormal experiences. *Sociological Analysis, 53,* 417–431.

Fraisse, P. (1964). *The psychology of time.* London: Eyre & Spottiswoode.

Freud, S. (1901/1960). Psychopathology of everyday life. *Standard Edition, 6.* London: Hogarth Press.

Freud, S. (1914/1955). Fausse reconnaissance (déjà raconté) in psycho-analytic treatment. *Standard Edition, 13.* London: Hogarth Press.

Freud, S. (1936/1964). A disturbance of memory on the Acropolis. *Standard Edition, 22.* London: Hogarth Press.

Freud, S. (1933). Fausse reconnaissance (déjà raconté) in psychoanalytic treatment. *Collected papers.* London: Hogarth Press (2: 334–342).

Freud, S. (1959). Fausse reconnaissance in psychoanalytic treatment. *Collected Papers,* Vol. 2. New York: Basic Books.

Fukuda, K. (2002). Most experiences of precognitive dream could be regarded as a subtype of déjà-vu experiences. *Sleep and Hypnosis, 4,* 111–114.

Funkhouser, A. T. (1983a). A historical review of déjà vu. *Parapsychological Journal of South Africa, 4,* 11–24.

Funkhouser, A. T. (1983b). The "dream" theory of déjà vu. *Parapsychological Journal of South Africa, 4,* 107–123.

Gallagher, C., Kumar, V. K., & Pekala, R. J. (1994). The Anomalous Experiences Inventory: Reliability and validity. *Journal of Parapsychology, 58,* 402–428.

Gallup, G. H., & Newport, F. (1991). Belief in paranormal phenomena among adult Americans. *The Skeptical Inquirer, 15,* 137–146.

Garbutt, J. C., & Gillette, G. M. (1988). Apparent complex partial seizures in a bipolar patient after withdrawal of carbamazepine. *Journal of Clinical Psychiatry, 49,* 410–411.

Gardiner, J. M. (1988). Functional aspects of recollective experience. *Memory & Cognition, 16,* 309–313.

Gardiner, J. M., & Parkin, A. J. (1990). Attention and recollective experience in recognition memory. *Memory & Cognition, 18,* 579–583.

Gaynard, T. J. (1992). Young people and the paranormal. *Journal of the Society for Psychical Research, 58,* 165–180.

Gazzaniga, M. S. (1985). *The social brain: Discovering the networks of the mind.* New York: Basic Books.

Geldard, F. A. (1963). *Fundamentals of psychology.* New York: Wiley.

Gibbs, F. A., Gibbs, E. L., & Lennox, W. G. (1937). Epilepsy: A paroxysmal cerebral dysrhythmia. *Brain, 60,* 377–388.

Gil-Nagel, A., & Risinger, M. W. (1997). Ictal semiology in hippocampal versus extrahippocampal temporal lobe epilepsy. *Brain, 120,* 183–192.

Glass, A. L., Holyoak, K. J., & Santa, J. L. (1979). *Cognition*. Reading, MA: Addison Wesley.

Gloor, P. (1990). Experiential phenomena of temporal lobe epilepsy: Facts and hypotheses. *Brian, 113*, 1673–1694.

Gloor, P. (1991). Neurobiological substrates of ictal behavioral changes. In D. B. Smith, D. M. Treiman, & M. R. Trimble (Eds.), *Neurobehavioral problems in epilepsy* (pp. 1–34). New York: Raven Press.

Gloor, P. (1997). *The temporal lobe and limbic system*. New York: Oxford University Press.

Gloor, P., Olivier, A., Quesney, L. F., Andermann, F., & Horowitz, S. (1982). The role of limbic system in experiential phenomena of temporal lobe epilepsy. *Annals of Neurology, 12*, 129–144.

Good, M. I. (1998). Screen reconstructions: Traumatic memory, conviction, and the problem of verification. *Journal of the American Psychoanalytic Association, 46*, 149–183.

Goodale, M. A., & Milner, A. D. (1992). Separate visual pathways for perception and action. *Trends in Neuroscience, 15*, 20–25.

Gordon, A. (1921). Illusion of "the already seen" (paramnesia) and of "the never seen" (agnosia). *Journal of Abnormal Psychology, 15*, 187–192.

Graf, P., Squire, L. R., & Mandler, G. (1984). The information that amnesic patients do not forget. *Journal of Experimental Psychology: Learning, Memory, and Cognition, 10*, 164–178.

Grasset, J. (1904). La sensation du "déjà vu." *Journal de psychologie, normale et pathologique, 1*, 17.

Greeley, A. M. (1975). *The sociology of the paranormal: A reconnaissance*. Beverly Hills, CA: Sage.

Greeley, A. M. (1987). Mysticism goes mainstream. *American Health*, Jan/Feb, 47–49.

Green, C. E. (1966). Spontaneous "paranormal" experiences in relation to sex and academic background. *Journal of the Society for Psychical Research, 43*, 357–363.

Greene, R. L. (1992). *Human memory: Paradigms and paradoxes*. Hillsdale, NJ: Erlbaum.

Gregg, V. H. (1986). *Introduction to human memory*. London: Routledge & Kegan Paul.

Gregory, J. C. (1923) Memory, forgetfulness, and mistakes of recognition in waking and dreaming. *Monist, 33*, 15–32.

Greyson, B. (1977). Telepathy in mental illness: Deluge or delusion? *Journal of Nervous and Mental Disease, 165*, 184–200.

Grimmer, M. R., & White, K. D. (1990). The structure of paranormal beliefs among Australian psychology students. *Journal of Psychology, 124*, 357–370.

Groh, L. A. (1968). Interhemispheric integration of identity relationships. *Psychiatria, Neurologia, Neurochirurgia, 71*, 185–191.

Gupta, A. K, Jeavons, P. M., Hughes, R. C., & Covanis, A. (1983). Aura in temporal lobe epilepsy: Clinical and electroencephalographic correlation. *Journal of Neurology, Neurosurgery, and Psychiatry, 46*, 1079–1083.

Haber, R. N., & Erdelyi, M. H. (1967). Emergence and recovery of initially unavailable perceptual material. *Journal of Verbal Learning and Verbal Behavior, 6*, 618–628.

Haberlandt, K. (1994). *Cognitive psychology*. Boston: Allyn and Bacon.

Hakim, H., Verma, N. P., & Greiffenstein, M. F. (1988). Pathogenesis of reduplicative paramnesia. *Journal of Neurology, Neurosurgery & Psychiatry, 51*, 839–841.

Halgren, E., Walter, R. D., Cherlow, D. G., & Crandall, P. H. (1978). Mental phenomena evoked by electrical stimulation of the human hippocampal formation and amygdala. *Brain, 101*, 83–117.

Harper, M. A. (1969). Déjà vu and depersonalization in normal subjects. *Australian and New Zealand Journal of Psychiatry, 3*, 67–74.

Harper, M., & Roth, M (1962). Temporal lobe epilepsy and the phobic anxiety-depersonalization syndrome: Part I: A comparative study. *Comprehensive Psychiatry, 3*, 129–161.

Harriman, P. L. (1947). *Dictionary of psychology*. New York: Philosophical Library.

Hartocollis, P. (1975). Time and affect in psychopathology. *Journal of the American Psychoanalytic Association, 23*, 383–395.

Hasher, L., Stoltzfus, E. R., Zacks, R. T., & Rypma, B. (1991). Age and inhibition. *Journal of Experimental Psychology: Learning, Memory, and Cognition, 17*, 163–169.

Hawley, K. J., & Johnston, W. A. (1991). Long-term perceptual memory for briefly exposed words as a function of awareness and attention. *Journal of Experimental Psychology: Human Perception and Performance, 17*, 807–815.

Hawthorne, N. (1863). *Our old home*. London: Smith, Elder & Co.

Head, H. (1920). *Studies in neurology*. London: Frowde.

Hearn, L. (1927). *Gleanings in buddha-fields*. London: Johathan Cape.

Hennessy, M. J., & Binnie, C. D. (2000). Photogenic partial seizures. *Epilepsia, 41*, 59–64.

Hermann, K., & Strömgren, E. (1944). Paroxysmal disturbances of consciousness in verified localised brain affections. *Acta Psychiatrica et Neurologia Scandinavia, 19*, 175–194.

Heymans, G. (1904). Eine enquete und depersonalisation und 'fausse reconnaissance.' *Zeitschrift fur Psychologie, 36*, 321–343.

Heymans, G. (1906). Weitere daten uber depersonalisation und'fausse reconnaissance.' *Zeitschrift fur psychologie, 43*, 1–17.

Hill, D. (1956). Clinical applications of EEG in psychiatry. *Journal of Mental Science, 102*, 264.

Hintzman, D. L. (1988). Judgments of frequency and recognition memory in a multiple-trace memory model. *Psychological Review, 95*, 528–551.

Hirshman, E., & Henzler, A. (1998). The role of decision processes in conscious recollection. *Psychological Science, 9*, 61–65.

Hoch, P. H. (1947). Some psychopathological aspects of organic brain damage. *Proceedings: American Psychopathological Association, 36*, 149–162.

Hodgson, S. H. (1865). *Time and space*. London: Longman, Green.

Hoffman, H. G. (1997). Role of memory strength in reality monitoring decisions: Evidence from source attribution biases. *Journal of Experimental Psychology: Learning, Memory, and Cognition, 23*, 371–383.

Holmes, O. W. (1891). *The autocrat of the breakfast table*. Boston: Houghton Mifflin.

Horowitz, L. M., & Prytulak, L. S. (1969). Redintegrative memory. *Psychological Review, 76*, 519–531.

Horton, D. L., & Turnage, T. W. (1976). *Human learning*. Englewood Cliffs, NJ: Prentice-Hall.

Houston, J. P. (1981). *Fundamentals of learning and memory*. New York: Academic Press.

Hulse, S. H., Deese, J., & Egeth, H. (1975). *The psychology of learning*. New York: McGraw-Hill.

Humphrey, G. (1923). *The story of man's mind*. Boston: Small, Maynard, & Co.

Hunter, I. M. L. (1957). *Memory*. Baltimore: Penguin Books.

Huppert, F. A., & Piercy, M. (1976). Recognition memory in amnesic patients: Effect of temporal context and familiarity of material. *Cortex, 12*, 3–30.

Hyman, I. E., Husband, T. H., & Billings, F. J. (1995). False memories of childhood experiences. *Applied Cognitive Psychology, 9*, 181–197.

Hyman, I. E., & Pentland, J. (1996). The role of mental imagery in the creation of false childhood memories. *Journal of Memory and Language, 35*, 101–107.

Hyman, I. E., & Billings, F. J. (1998). Individual differences in the creation of false childhood memories. *Memory, 6*, 1–20.

Ide, M., Mizukami, K., & Suzuki, T., & Shiraishi, H. (2000). A case of temporal lobe epilepsy with improvement of clinical symptoms and single photon emission computed tomography findings after treatment with clonazepam. *Psychiatry and Clinical Neurosciences, 54*, 595–597.

Inoue, Y., Mihara, T., Matsuda, K., Tottori, T., Otsubo, T., & Yagi, K. (2000). Absence of simple partial seizure in temporal lobe epilepsy: Its diagnostic and prognostic significance. *Epilepsy Research, 38*, 133–138.

Irwin, H. J. (1993). Belief in the paranormal: A review of the empirical literature. *Journal of the American Society for Psychical Research, 87*, 1–39.

Irwin, H. J. (1996). Childhood antecedents of out-of-body and déjà vu experiences. *Journal of the American Society for Psychical Research, 90*, 157–173.

Jackson, J. H. (1876). Lectures on epilepsy. *Medical Times and Gazette*, Dec. 23, 702.

Jackson, J. (1888). On a particular variety of epilepsy ("intellectual aura"), one case with symptoms of organic brain disease. *Brain, 11*, 179–207.

Jackson, J., & Colman, W. S. (1898). Case of epilepsy with tasting movements and "dreamy state"—very small patch of softening in the left uncinate gyrus. *Brain, 21*, 580–590.

Jacoby, L. L. (1988). Memory observed and memory unobserved. In U. Neisser & E. Winograd (Eds.), *Remembering reconsidered: Ecological and traditional approaches to the study of memory* (pp. 145–177). Cambridge: Cambridge University Press.

Jacoby, L. L. (1991). A process dissociation framework: Separating automatic from intentional uses of memory. *Journal of Memory and Language, 30*, 513–541.

Jacoby, L. L., Allan, L. G., Collins, J. C., & Larwill, L. K. (1988). Memory influences subjective experience: Noise judgments. *Journal of Experimental Psychology: Learning, Memory, and Cognition, 14*, 240–247.

Jacoby, L. L., & Dallas, M. (1981). On the relationship between autobiographical memory and perceptual learning. *Journal of Experimental Psychology: General, 110*, 306–340.

Jacoby, L. L., Kelley, C. M., & Dywan, J. (1989). Memory attributions. In H. L. Roediger & F. I. M. Craik (Eds.), *Varieties of memory and consciousness: Essays in honour of Endel Tulving.* Hillsdale, NJ: Erlbaum, pp. 391–422.

Jacoby, L. L., & Whitehouse, K (1989). An illusion of memory: False recognition influenced by unconscious perception. *Journal of Experimental Psychology: General, 118*, 126–135.

Jacoby, L. L., Woloshyn, V., & Kelley, C. M. (1989). Becoming famous without being recognized: Unconscious influences of memory produced by dividing attention. *Journal of Experimental Psychology, 118*, 115–125.

James, W. (1890). *The principles of psychology.* New York: Henry Holt.

Jasper, H. H. (1936). Localised analyses of the function of the human brain by the electroencephalogram. *Archives of Neurology and Psychiatry, 36*, 1131–1134.

Jensen (no initial) (1868). Ueber Doppelwahrnehmungen in der gesunden, wie in der kranke Psyche. *Allgemeine Zeitschrift für Psychiatrie, 25*, 48–63.

Jessen, P. (1855). *Versuch einer wissenschaftlichen Psychologie.* Berlin: Verlag von Veit & Co.

Johnson, M. K. (1983). A multiple-entry, modular memory system. In G. H. Bower (Ed.), *The psychology of learning and motivation: Advances in research and theory* (Vol. 17). New York: Academic Press, pp. 81–123.

Johnson, M., K., Hashtroudi, S., & Lindsay, D. S. (1993). Source monitoring. *Psychological Bulletin, 114*, 3–28.

Johnson, M. K., Kahan, T. L., & Raye, C. L. (1984). Dreams and reality monitoring. *Journal of Experimental Psychology: General, 113*, 329–343.

Johnson, M. K., Kim, J. K., & Risse, G. (1985). Do alcoholic Korsakoff's syndrome patients acquire affective reactions? *Journal of Experimental Psychology: Learning, Memory, and Cognition, 11*, 22–36.

Joordens, S., & Merikle, P. M. (1992). False recognition and perception without awareness. *Memory & Cognition, 20*, 151–159.

Jordan, T. R. (1986). Testing the BOSS hypothesis: Evidence for position-insensitive orthographic priming in the lexical decision task. *Memory & Cognition, 14*, 523–532.

Jung, C. G. (1963). *Memories, dreams, reflections.* New York: Pantheon Books.

Kafka, J. S. (1989). *Multiple realities in clinical practice.* New Haven, CT: Yale University Press.

Kafka, J. S. (1991). Déjà vu and synesthesia. *American Journal of Psychiatry, 148*, 951–952.

Kausler, D. H. (1974). *Psychology of verbal learning and memory.* New York: Academic Press.

Keschner, M., Bender, M. B., & Strauss, I. (1936). Mental symptoms in cases of tumor of the temporal lobe. *Archives of Neurology and Psychiatry, 35*, 572–596.

Kinnier Wilson, S. A. (1929). *Modern problems in neurology.* New York: William Wood.

Kirshner, L. A. (1973). The mechanism of déjà vu. *Diseases of the Nervous System, 34*, 246–249.

Kintsch, W. (1970). *Learning, memory, and conceptual processes.* New York: Wiley.

Klatzky, R. L. (1975). *Human memory: Structures and processes.* San Francisco: W. H. Freeman.

Knight, E. F. (1895) *Where three empires meet: A narrative of recent travel in Kashmir, western Tibet, Gilgit, and adjoining countries.* London: Longmans, Green, and Co.

Knowlton, B. J., & Squire, L. R. (1995). Remembering and knowing: Two different expressions of declarative memory. *Journal of Experimental Psychology: Learning, Memory, and Cognition, 21*, 699–710.

Kohn, S. R. (1983). A "déjà vu" review: "Where or when": Still mystery and magic in the guise of "déjà vu." *Parapsychological Journal of South Africa, 4,* 70–82.

Kohn, S. R. (1991). Déjà vu phenomenon. *American Journal of Psychiatry, 148,* 1417–1418.

Kohr, R. L. (1980). A survey of psi experiences among members of a special population. *Journal of the American Society for Psychical Research, 74,* 395–412.

Kolers, P. A. (1973). Remembering operation. *Memory & Cognition, 1,* 347–355.

Kolers, P. A., & Roediger, H. L. (1984). Procedures of mind. *Journal of Verbal Learning and Verbal Behavior, 23,* 425–449.

Kraepelin, E. (1887). Ueber Erinnerungsfälschungen. *Archiv für Psychiatrie, 18,* 395–436.

Krijgers Janzen, E. (1958). Déjà vu and eidetics. *Folia Psychiatrica Neurologica et Neurochirurgica Neerlandica, 61,* 170–177.

Kuiper, P. C. (1973). *Hoofdsom der psychiatrie.* Utrecht: Bijleveld.

Kunst-Wilson, W. R., & Zajonc, R. B. (1980). Affective discrimination of stimuli that cannot be recognized. *Science, 207,* 557–558.

Lalande, A. (1893). Des paramnesies. *Revue Philosophique, 36,* 485–497.

La Lorrain, J. (1894). A propos de la paramnésie. *Revue Philosophique, 37,* 208–210.

Lampinen, J. M. (2002). What exactly is déjà vu? *Scientific American, 287* (No. 3), 103.

Langdon, R., & Coltheart, M. (2000). The cognitive neuropsychology of delusions. *Mind & Language, 15,* 184–218.

Lapie, P. (1894). Note sur la fausse mémoire. *Revue Philosophique, 37,* 551–552.

Leeds, M. (1944). One form of paramnesia: The illusion of déjà vu. *Journal of the American Society for Psychical Research, 38,* 24–42.

Lennox, W. G., & Cobb, S. (1933). Aura in epilepsy: A statistical review of 1359 cases. *Archives of Neurology and Psychiatry, 30,* 374–387.

Léon-Kindberg, M. (1903). Le sentiment du déjà vu. *Revue de Psychiatrie, 4,* 221–236. (in Ellis, 1911)

Levin, J. S. (1993). Age differences in mystical experience. *The Gerontologist, 33,* 507–513.

Levitan, H. (1967). Depersonalization and the dream. *Psychoanalytic Quarterly, 36,* 157–171.

Levitan, H. (1969). The depersonalizing process. *Psychoanalytic Quarterly, 38,* 97–109.

Lewis, D. O., Feldman, M., Greene, M., & Martinez-Mustardo, Y. (1984). Psychomotor epileptic symptoms in six patients with bipolar mood disorders. *American Journal of Psychiatry, 141,* 1583–1586.

Linn, L. (1953). Psychological implications of the "activating system." *American Journal of Psychiatry, 110,* 61–65.

Linn, L. (1954). The discriminating function of the ego. *Psychoanalytic Quarterly, 23,* 38–47.

Loftus, E. F. (1993). The reality of repressed memories. *American Psychologist, 48,* 518–537.

Loftus, E. F., & Ketcham, K. (1994). *The myth of repressed memory: False memories and allegations of sexual abuse.* New York: St. Martin's Press.

Loftus, E. F., & Pickrell, J. E. (1995). The formation of false memories. *Psychiatric Annals, 25,* 720–725.

Loftus, G. R., & Loftus, E. F. (1976). *Human memory.* Hillsdale, NJ: Erlbaum.

MacCurdy, J. T. (1924). The psychology of déjà vu. *Report of the Meeting of the British Association for the Advancement of Science,* 442.

MacCurdy, J. T. (1925). *The psychology of emotion.* New York: Harcourt Brace.

MacCurdy, J. T. (1928). *Common principles in psychology and physiology.* New York: Macmillan.

Mack, A., & Rock, I. (1998). *Inattentional blindness.* Cambridge, MA: MIT Press.

Maeterlinck, M. (1919). *Mountain paths.* New York: Dodd, Mead, and Co.

Marcovitz, E. (1952). The meaning of *déjà vu. Psychoanalytic Quarterly, 21,* 481–489.

Marcuse, F. L., Hill, A., & Keegan, M. (1945). Identification of posthypnotic signals and responses. *Journal of Experimental Psychology, 35,* 163–166.

Marková, I. S., & Berrios, G. E. (2000). Paramnesias and delusions of memory. In G. E Berrios & J. R. Hodges (Eds.), *Memory disorders in psychiatric practice* (pp. 313–337). New York: Cambridge University Press.

Marsh, R. L., & Bower, G. H. (1993). Eliciting cryptomnesia: Unconscious plagiarism in a puzzle task. *Journal of Experimental Psychology: Learning, Memory, & Cognition, 19,* 673–688.

Martindale, C. (1981). *Cognition and consciousness.* Homewood, IL: The Dorsey Press.

Martindale, C. (1991). *Cognitive psychology: A neural-network approach.* Pacific Grove, CA: Brooks/Cole Publishing.

Matlin, M. (1983*). Cognition.* New York: Holt, Rinehart, and Winston.

Maudsley, H. (1889). The double brain. *Mind, 14,* 161–187.

Mayer, B., & Merckelbach, H. (1999). Unconscious processes, subliminal stimulation, and anxiety. *Clinical Psychology Review, 19,* 571–590.

McClenon, J. (1988). A survey of Chinese anomalous experiences and comparison with western representative national samples. *Journal for the Scientific Study of Religion, 27,* 421–426.

McClenon, J. (1994). Surveys of anomalous experience: A cross-cultural analysis. *Journal of the American Society for Psychical Research, 88,* 117–135.

McCready, W. C., & Greeley, A. M. (1976). *The ultimate values of the American population.* Beverly Hills, CA: Sage.

McKellar, A. (1978). Depersonalization in a 16-year-old boy. *Southern Medical Journal, 71,* 1580–1581.

McKellar, P. (1957). *Imagination and thinking.* New York: Basic Books.

McKellar, P., & Simpson, L. (1954). Between wakefulness and sleep: Hypnagogic imagery. *British Journal of Psychology, 45,* 266–276.

Medin, D. L., & Ross, B. H. (1992). *Cognitive psychology.* Forth Worth, TX: Harcourt Brace Jovanovich.

Merikle, P. M., Smilek, D., & Eastwood, J. D. (2001). Perception without awareness: Perspectives from cognitive psychology. *Cognition, 79,* 115–134.

Metcalfe, J. (2000). Metamemory: Theory and data. In E. Tulving & F. I. M. Craik (Eds.), *The Oxford handbook of memory* (pp. 197–211). New York: Oxford University Press.

Meurs, E. J. A., & Hes, R. (1993). Déjà vu and holographic images. *American Journal of Psychiatry, 150,* 679–680.

Milner, A. D., & Goodale, M. A. (1995). *The visual brain in action.* Oxford: Oxford University Press.

Mitchell, D. B., & Brown, A. S. (1988). Persistent repetition priming in picture naming and its dissociation from recognition memory. *Journal of Experimental Psychology: Learning, Memory and Cognition, 14,* 213–222.

Mitchell, D. B., Brown, A. S., & Murphy, D. R. (1990). Dissociations between procedural and episodic memory: Effects of time and aging. *Psychology and Aging, 5,* 264–276.

Morgan, J. J. B. (1936). *The psychology of abnormal people with educational applications.* Longmans, Green & Co.

Morris, C. D., Bransford, J. D., & Franks, J. J. (1977). Levels of processing versus transfer appropriate processing. *Journal of Verbal Learning and Verbal Behavior, 16,* 519–533.

Mullan, S., & Penfield, W. (1959). Illusions of comparative interpretation and emotion. *Archives of Neurology and Psychiatry, 81,* 269–284.

Mulligan, N. W., & Hornstein, S. L. (2000). Attention and perceptual implicit memory. *Journal of Experimental Psychology: Learning, Memory and Cognition, 26,* 626–637.

Multhaup, K. S. (1995). Aging, source, and decision criteria: When false fame errors do and do not occur. *Psychology and Aging, 10,* 492–497.

Murdock, B. B. (1974). *Human memory:* Theory and data. Hillsdale, NJ: Erlbaum.

Murphy, G. (1933). *General psychology.* New York: Harper & Brothers.

Murphy, G. (1951). *An introduction to psychology.* Westport, CT: Greenwood Press.

Myers, D. H., & Grant, G. (1972). A study of depersonalization in students. *British Journal of Psychiatry, 121,* 59–65.

Myers, F. W. H. (1895). The subliminal self. *Proceedings of the Incorporated Society for Psychical Research, 11,* 334–407.

Myers, S. A., & Austrin, H. R. (1985). Distal eidetic technology: Further characteristics of the fantasy-prone personality. *Journal of Mental Imagery, 9,* 57–66.

Myers, W. A. (1977). Micropsia and testicular retractions. *Psychoanalytic Quarterly, 46,* 580–604.

Neath, I., & Surprenant, A. M. (2003). *Human memory.* Belmont, CA: Wadsworth/Thompson.

Neisser, U. (1982). Memory: What are the important questions? In U. Neisser (Ed.), *Memory observed* (pp. 3–19). San Francisco: W. H. Freeman.

Nelson, K. (1990). Remembering, forgetting, and childhood amnesia. In R. Fivush & J. A. Hudson (Eds.), *Knowing and remembering in young children* (pp. 301–316). Cambridge: Cambridge University Press.

Nelson, T. O., & Dunlosky, J. (1991). When people's judgments of learning (JOLs) are extremely accurate at predicting subsequent recall: The "Delayed-JOL Effect." *Psychological Science, 2,* 267–270.

Nelson, T. O., & Dunlosky, J. (1992). How shall we explain the delayed-judgement-of-learning effect? *Psychological Science, 3,* 317–318.

Nemiah, J. (1989). Dissociative disorders. In H. I. Kaplan & B. J. Sadock (Eds.), *Comprehensive textbook of psychiatry, Vol. 5.* Baltimore, MD: Williams & Wilkins.

Neppe, V. M. (1979). An investigation of the relationship between subjective paranormal experience and temporal lobe symptomatology. M. Med. (Psych.), University of the Witwatersrand, Johannesburg.

Neppe, V. M. (1981). Is *déjà vu* a symptom of temporal lobe epilepsy? *South African Medical Journal, 60,* 907–908.

Neppe, V. M. (1983a). The causes of déjà vu. *Parapsychological Journal of South Africa, 4,* 25–35.

Neppe, V. M. (1983b). The concept of déjà vu. *Parapsychological Journal of South Africa, 4,* 1–10.

Neppe, V. M. (1983c). The different presentations of the déjà vu phenomenon: New research. *Parapsychological Journal of South Africa, 4,* 124–139.

Neppe, V. M. (1983d). The incidence of déjà vu. *Parapsychological Journal of South Africa, 4,* 94–106.

Neppe, V. M. (1983e). *The psychology of déjà vu: Have I been here before?* Johannesburg: Witwatersrand University Press.

Nisbett, R. E., & Wilson, T. D. (1977). Telling more than we know: Verbal reports on mental processes. *Psychological Review, 84,* 231–259.

Norman, D. A. (1969). *Memory and attention.* New York: John Wiley and Sons.

Oberndorf, C. P. (1941). Erroneous recognition. *Psychiatric Quarterly, 15,* 316–326.

O'Connor, W. A. (1948). *Psychiatry.* Bristol: John Wright.

Öhman, A., & Soares, J. J. F. (1994). "Unconscious anxiety": Phobic responses to masked stimuli. *Journal of Abnormal Psychology, 103,* 231–240.

Osborn, H. F. (1884). Illusions of memory. *North American Review, 138,* 476–486.

Ouspensky, P. D. (1931). *A new model of the universe.* London: Paul Trench, Trubner & Co.

Pacella, B. L. (1975). Early ego development and the *déjà vu. Journal of the American Psychoanalytic Association, 23,* 300–318.

Pacia, S. V., Devinsky, O., Perrine, K., Ravdin, L., Luciano, D., Vazquez, B., & Doyle, W. K. (1996). Clinical features of neocortical temporal lobe epilepsy. *Annals of Neurology, 40,* 724–730.

Pagliaro, L. (1991). The déjà vu experience: Remembrance of things past? Reply. *American Journal of Psychiatry, 148,* 1418.

Palmer, J. (1979). A community mail survey of psychic experiences. *Journal of the American Society for Psychical Research, 73,* 221–251.

Palmer, J., & Dennis, M. (1975). A community mail survey of psychic experience. In J. D. Morris, W. G. Roll, & R. L. Morris (Eds.), *Research in parapsychology 1974.* Metuchen, NJ: Scarecrow, pp. 130–133.

Palmini, A., & Gloor, P. (1992). The localizing value of auras in partial seizures: A prospective and retrospective study. *Neurology, 42,* 801–808.

Parish, E. (1897). *Hallucinations and illusions.* London: Walter Scott.

Parkin, A. J. (1993). *Memory: Phenomena, experiment, and theory.* Oxford: Blackwell Publishers.

Pashler, H. (1994). Dual-task interference in simple tasks: Data and theory. *Psychological Bulletin, 116,* 220–244.

Penfield, W. (1955). The twenty-ninth Maudsley lecture: The role of the temporal cortex in certain psychical phenomena. *Journal of Mental Science, 101,* 451–465.

Penfield, W., & Mathieson, G. (1974). Memory. Autopsy findings and comments on the role of hippocampus in experiential recall. *Archives of Neurology, 31,* 145–154.

Penfield, W., & Perot, P. (1963). The brain's record of auditory and visual experience. *Brain, 86,* 596–695.

Pethö, B. (1985). Chronophrenia—a new syndrome in functional psychoses. *Psychopathology, 18,* 174–180.

Peynircioglu, Z. F., & Watkins, M. J. (1993). Revelation effect: Effort or priming does not create the sense of familiarity. *Journal of Experimental Psychology: Learning, Memory, and Cognition, 19,* 382–388.

Phillips, D. E. (1913). *An elementary psychology.* Boston: Ginn and Company.

Pick, A. (1903) Clinical studies. *Brain, 26,* 242–304.

Pickford, R. W. (1940). Three related experiences of déjà vu. *Character & Personality, 9,* 153–159.

Pickford, R. W. (1942a). A restricted paramnesia of complex origin. *British Journal of Medical Psychology, 19,* 186–191.

Pickford, R, W. (1942b). Rossetti's "Sudden Light" as an experience of *déjà vu. British Journal of Medical Psychology, 19,* 192–200.

Pickford, R. W. (1944). *Déjà vu* in Proust and Tolstoy. *International Journal of Psycho-analysis, 25,* 155–165.

Pillsbury, W. B. (1915). *The essentials of psychology.* New York: Macmillan.

Pine, F. (1964). The bearing of psychoanalytic theory on selected issues in research on marginal stimuli. *Journal of Nervous and Mental Disease, 138,* 205–222.

Poetzl, O. (1926). Zur Metaphychologie des "déjà vu." *Imago, 12,* 393–402.

Poetzl, O. (1917/1960). The relationship between experimentally induced dream images and indirect vision. *Psychological Issues Monograph, 2* (3, VII), 46–106. (Original work published 1917).

Posner, M. I. (1973). *Cognition: An introduction.* Glenview, IL: Scott, Foresman.

Pribram, K. (1969). The neurophysiology of remembering. *Scientific American, 220,* 73–86.

Probst P., & Jansen, J. (1994). Depersonalization and déjà vu: Prevalence in non-clinical samples. *The German Journal of Psychology, 18,* 363–364.

Prull, M. W., Light, L. L., Collett, M. E. & Kennison, R. F. (1998). Age-related differences in memory illusions: Revelation effect. *Aging, Neuropsychology, and Cognition, 5,* 147–165.

Quaerens (1870). A prognostic and therapeutic indication in epilepsy. *The Practitioner, 4,* 284–285.

Rapaport, D. (1959). *Emotions and memory.* New York: International Universities Press.

Read, J. D., Vokey, J. R., & Davidson, M. (1991, November). Knowing who's new: The phenomenon of jamais vu. Paper presented at the 32nd annual meeting of the Psychonomic Society, San Francisco.

Reason, J. T., & Lucas, D. (1984). Using cognitive diaries to investigate naturally occurring memory blocks. In J. E. Harris & P. E. Morris (Eds.), *Everyday memory, actions and absentmindedness* (pp. 53–69). San Diego, CA: Academic Press.

Reber, R., Winkielman, P, & Schwarz, N. (1998). Effects of perceptual fluency on affective judgments. *Psychological Science, 9,* 45–48.

Reed, G. (1974). *The psychology of anomalous experience.* Boston: Houghton Mifflin (p. 104–111).

Reed, G. (1979). Everyday anomalies of recall and recognition. In J. F. Kihlstrom & F. J. Evans (Eds.), *Functional disorders of memory*. Hillsdale, NJ: Wiley, pp. 1–32.

Reed, S. K. (1982). *Cognition: Theory and applications*. Monterey, CA: Brook/Cole Publishing.

Reisberg, D. (1997). *Cognition: Exploring the science of the mind*. New York: W. W. Norton & Co.

Reynolds, A. G., & Flagg, P. W. (1983). *Cognitive psychology*. Boston: Little, Brown.

Rhine, L. E. (1961). *Hidden channels of the mind*. New York: William Sloane Associates.

Ribot, T. (1882). *The diseases of memory*. London: Kegan Paul, Trench & Co.

Richardson, T. F. & Winokur, G. (1968). Déjà vu—As related to diagnostic categories in psychiatric and neurosurgical patients. *Journal of Nervous and Mental Disease, 146*, 161–164.

Richardson, T. F. & Winokur, G. (1967). Déjà vu in psychiatric and neurosurgical patients. *Archives of General Psychiatry, 17*, 622–625.

Richardson-Klavehn, A., & Bjork, R. A. (1988). Measures of memory. *Annual Review of Psychology, 39*, 475–543.

Riley, K. C. (1988). Measurement of dissociation. *Journal of Nervous and Mental Disease, 176*, 449–450.

Roberts, R. J., Varney, N. R., Hulbert, J. R., Paulsen, J. S., Richardson, E. D., Springer, J. A., Shepherd, J. S., Swan, C. M., Legrand, J. A., Harvey, J. H., & Struchen, M. A. (1990). The neuropathology of everyday life: The frequency of partial seizure symptoms among normals. *Neuropsychology, 4*, 65–85.

Roediger, H. L. (1996). Memory illusions. *Journal of Memory and Language, 35*, 76–100.

Roediger, H. L., & McDermott, K. B. (1993). Implicit memory in normal human subjects. In F. Boller & J. Grafman (Eds.), *Handbook of neuropsychology, Vol. 8*. Amsterdam: Elsevier. pp. 63–131.

Roediger, H. L., & McDermott, K. B. (1995). Creating false memories: Remembering words not presented in lists. *Journal of Experimental Psychology: Learning, Memory, & Cognition, 21*, 803–814.

Roediger, H. L., & McDermott, K. B. (2000). Tricks of memory. *Current Directions in Psychological Science, 9*, 123–127.

Roediger, H. L., Weldon, M. S., & Challis, B. H. (1989). Explaining dissociations between implicit and explicit measures of retention: A processing account. In H. L. Roediger & F. I. M. Craik (Eds.), *Varieties of memory and consciousness: Essays in houour of Endel Tulving*. Hillsdale, NJ: Erlbaum, pp. 3–41.

Rosen, D. S. (1991). The déjà vu experience: Remembrance of things past? Comment. *American Journal of Psychiatry, 148*, 1418.

Rosen, D. S., Smith, S. M., Huston, H. I., & Gonzales, G. (1991). Empirical study of associations between symbols and their meanings: Evidence of collective unconscious (archetypal) memory. *Journal of Analytical Psychology, 36*, 211–228.

Ross, C. A., Heber, S., Norton, G. R., Anderson, D., Anderson, G., & Barchet, P. (1989). The Dissociative Disorders Interview Schedule: A structured interview. *Dissociation, 2*, 169–189.

Ross, C. A., & Joshi, S. (1992). Paranormal experiences in the general population. *The Journal of Nervous and Mental Disease, 180*, 357–361.

Roth, M. (1959). The phobic anxiety-depersonalization syndrome. *Proceedings of the Royal Society of Medicine, 52*, 587–595.

Rumelhart, D. E., & McClelland, J. L. (1986). *Parallel distributed processing: Explorations in the microstructure of cognition. Vol. 1, Foundations*. Cambridge, MA: MIT Press.

Salthouse, T. A. (1998). Cognitive and information-processing perspectives on aging. In I. H. Nordhus, G. R. VandenBos, S. Berg & P. Fromholt (Eds.), *Clinical geropsychology*. Washington, DC: APA. pp. 49–54.

Sander, W. (1874). Ueber erinnerungstäuschungen. *Archiv für Psychiatrie und Nervenkrankheiten, 4*, 244–253.

Schacter, D. L. (1987). Implicit memory: History and current status. *Journal of Experimental Psychology: Learning, Memory, and Cognition, 13*, 501–518.

Schacter, D. L. (1996). *Searching for memory: The brain, the mind, and the past*. New York: Basic Books.

Schacter, D. L. (2001). *The seven sins of memory: How the mind forgets and remembers*. Boston: Houghton Mifflin.

Schacter, D. L., Harbluk, J. L., & McLaughlin, D. R. (1984). Retrieval without recollection: An experimental analysis of source amnesia. *Journal of Verbal Learning and Verbal Behavior, 23*, 593–611.

Scheyer, R. D., Spencer, D. D., & Spencer, S. S. (1995). Letter. *Epilepsia, 36*, 522.

Schilder, P. (1936). Psychopathology of time. *Journal of Nervous and Mental Disease, 83*, 530–546.

Schneck, J. M. (1961). A contribution to the analysis of déjà vu. *Journal of Nervous and Mental Disease, 132*, 91–93.

Schneck, J. M. (1962). The psychodynamics of "déjà vu." *Psychoanalysis and the Psychoanalytic Review, 49*, 48–54.

Schneck, J. M. (1964). Dreams and déjà vu. *Psychosomatics, 5*, 116–118.

Schneider, G. E. (1969). Two visual systems: Brain mechanisms for localization and discrimination are dissociated by tectal and cortical lesions. *Science, 163*, 895–902.

Scott, W. (1890). *The journal of Sir Walter Scott, Vol. II*. Edinburgh: D. Douglas.

Seamon, J. G. (1980). *Memory and cognition*. New York: Oxford University Press.

Seamon, J. G., Brody, N., & Kauff, D. M. (1983a). Affective discrimination of stimuli that are not recognized: Effects of shadowing, masking, and cerebral laterality. *Journal of Experimental Psychology: Learning, Memory, and Cognition, 9*, 544–555.

Seamon, J. G., Brody, N., & Kauff, D. M. (1983b). Affective discrimination of stimuli that are not recognized: II. Effect of delay between study and test. *Bulletin of the Psychonomic Society, 21*, 187–189.

Seamon, J. G., Goodkind, M. S., Dumey, A. D., Dick, E., Aufseeser, M. S., Strickland, S. E., Woulfin, J. R., & Fung, N. S. (2003). "If I didn't write it, why would I remember it?" Effects of encoding, attention, and practice on accurate and false memory. *Memory & Cognition, 31*, 445–457.

Searleman, A., & Herrmann, D. (1994). *Memory from a broader perspective*. New York: McGraw-Hill.

Sengoku, A., Toichi, M., & Murai, T. (1997). Dreamy states and psychoses in temporal lobe epilepsy: Mediating role of affect. *Psychiatry and Clinical Neurosciences, 51*, 23–26.

Shelley, P. B. (1880). Speculations on metaphysics. In H. B. Forman (Ed.), *The works of Percy Bysshe Shelley in verse and prose*. London: Reeves & Turner.

Shevrin, H., & Fritzler, D. E. (1968). Visual evoked response correlates of unconscious mental processes. *Science, 161*, 295.

Silberman, E. K., Post, R. M., Nurnberger, J., Theodore, W., & Boulenger, J. (1985). Transient sensory, cognitive, and affective phenomenon in affective illness: A comparison with complex partial epilepsy. *British Journal of Psychiatry, 146*, 81–89.

Silbermann, I. (1963). The *jamais* phenomenon with reference to fragmentation. *Psychoanalytic Quarterly, 32*, 181–191.

Silverman, L. H., & Silverman, D. K. (1964) A clinical-experimental approach to the study of subliminal stimulation. *Journal of Abnormal and Social Psychology, 69*, 158–172.

Simmons, M. B. (1895). Prevalence of paramnesia. *Psychological Review, 2*, 329–330.

Simon, D. A., & Bjork, R. A. (2001). Metacognition in motor learning. *Journal of Experimental Psychology: Learning, Memory, and Cognition, 27*, 907–912.

Simons, D. J. (2000). Current approaches to change blindness. *Visual Cognition, 7*, 1–15.

Simons, D. J., & Levin, D. T. (1998). Failure to detect changes to people during a real-world interaction. *Psychonomic Bulletin & Review, 4*, 501–506.

Siomopoulos, V. (1972). Derealization and déjà vu: Formal mechanisms. *American Journal of Psychotherapy, 26*, 84–89.

Slamecka, N. J. (1985). Ebbinghaus: Some associations. *Journal of Experimental Psychology: Learning, Memory, and Cognition, 11*, 414–435.

Slochower, H. (1970). Freud's *déjà vu* on the Acropolis. *Psychoanalytic Quarterly, 39*, 90–102.

Smith, T. L. (1913). Paramnesia in daily life. *American Journal of Psychology, 24*, 52–65.

Sno, H. N. (1994). A continuum of misidentification symptoms. *Psychopathology, 27*, 144–147.

Sno, H. N. (2000). Déjà vu and jamais vu. In G. E. Berrios & J. R. Hodges (Eds.), *Memory disorders in psychiatric practice* (pp. 338–347). Cambridge: Cambridge University Press.

Sno, H. N., & Draaisma, D. (1993). An early Dutch study of déjà vu experiences. *Psychological Medicine, 23*, 17–26.

Sno, H. N., & Linszen, D. H. (1990). The déjà vu experience: Remembrance of things past? *The American Journal of Psychiatry, 147*, 1587–1595.

Sno, H. N., & Linszen, D. H. (1991). "The déjà vu experience: Remembrance of things past?": Reply. *The American Journal of Psychiatry, 148*, 1419.

Sno, H. N., Linszen, D. H., & de Jonghe, F. (1992a). Art imitates life: *Déjà vu* experiences in prose and poetry. *British Journal of Psychiatry, 160*, 511–518.

Sno, H. N., Linszen, D. H., & de Jonghe, F. (1992b). *Déjà vu* experiences and reduplicative paramnesia. *British Journal of Psychiatry, 161*, 565–568.

Sno, H. N., Schalken, H. F. A., & de Jonghe, F. (1992c). Empirical research on déjà vu experiences: A review. *Behavioural Neurology, 5*, 155–160.

Sno, H. N., Schalken, H. F. A., de Jonghe, F., & Koeter, M. W. J. (1994). The inventory for déjà vu experiences assessment. *The Journal of Nervous and Mental Disease, 182*, 27–33.

Soares, J. J. F., & Öhman, A (1993). Backward masking and skin conductance responses after conditioning to nonfeared but fear-relevant stimuli in fearful subjects. *Psychophysiology, 30*, 460–466.

Sobal, J., & Emmons, C. F. (1982). Patterns of belief in religious, psychic, and other paranormal phenomena. *Zetetic Scholar, 9*, 7–17.

Solso, R. L. (1979). *Cognitive psychology.* New York: Harcourt Brace Jovanovich.

Spatt, J. (2002). Déjà vu: Possible parahippocampal mechanisms. *Journal of Neuropsychiatry & Clinical Neurosciences, 14*, 6–10.

Squire, L. R., Chace, P. M., & Slater, P. C. (1976). Retrograde amnesia following electroconvulsive therapy. *Nature, 260*, 775–777.

Stanford, R. G. (1982). Is scientific parapsychology possible? *Journal of Parapsychology, 46*, 231–271.

Stanford, R. G. (1983). Correspondence. *Journal of Parapsychology, 47*, 184–185.

Stern, L. (1985). *The structures and strategies of human memory.* Homewood, IL: Dorsey Press.

Stern, W. (1938). *General psychology: From a personalistic standpoint.* New York: Macmillan.

Sternberg, R. J. (2003). *Cognitive psychology.* Belmont, CA: Wadsworth/Thompson.

Stevens, J. R. (1990). Psychiatric consequences of temporal lobectomy for intractable seizures: A 20–30-year follow-up of 14 cases. *Psychological Medicine, 20*, 529–545.

Stevenson, I. (1960). The evidence for survival from claimed memories of former incarnations. Part I. *Journal of the American Society for Psychical Research, 54*, 51–71.

Stevenson, I. (1987). *Children who remember previous lives: A question of reincarnation.* Charlottesville: University Press of Virginia.

Strayer, D. L., Drews, F. A., & Johnston, W. A. (2003). Cell phone-induced failures of visual attention during simulated driving. *Journal of Experimental Psychology: Applied, 9*, 23–32.

Strayer, D. L., & Johnston, W. A. (2001). Driven to distraction: Dual-task studies of simulated driving and conversing on a cellular telephone. *Psychological Science, 12*, 462–466.

Sully, J. (1887). *Illusions: A psychological study.* London: Kegan Paul, Trench.

Sutherland, S. (1989). *The international dictionary of psychology.* New York: Continuum.

Taiminen, T., & Jääskeläinen, S. K. (2001). Intense and recurrent déjà vu experiences related to amantadine and phenylpropanolamine in a healthy male. *Journal of Clinical Neuroscience, 8*, 460–462.

Takaoka, K., Ikawa, N., & Niwa, N. (2001). "Alice in Wonderland" syndrome as a precursor of delusional misidentification syndromes. *International Journal of Psychiatry in Clinical Practice, 5*, 149–151.

Tarpy, R. M., & Mayer, R. E. (1978). *Foundations of learning and memory*. Dallas, TX: Scott, Foresman.

Taylor, G. R. (1979). *The natural history of the mind*. London: E. P. Dutton.

Taylor, J. (1931). *Selected writings of J. H. Jackson. Vol. 1*. London: Hodder & Stoughton.

Thompson, D. M., & Tulving, E. (1970). Associative encoding and retrieval: Weak and strong cues. *Journal of Experimental Psychology, 86*, 255–262.

Tiffin, J., Knight, B. F., & Asher, E. J. (1946). *The psychology of normal people*. Boston, MA: D. C. Heath & Co.

Titchener, E. B. (1924). *A beginner's psychology*. New York: Macmillan.

Titchener, E. B. (1928). *A text-book of psychology*. New York: Macmillan.

Tobacyk, J. J., & Milford, G. (1983). Belief in paranormal phenomena: Assessment instrument development and implications for personality. *Journal of Personality and Social Psychology, 44*, 1029–1037.

Tulving, E. (1968). Theoretical issues in free recall. In T. R. Dixon and D. L. Horton (Eds.), *Verbal behavior and general behavior theory*. Englewood Cliffs, NJ: Prentice-Hall.

Tulving, E. (1985). Memory and consciousness. *Canadian Psychologist, 26*, 1–12.

Tulving, E., & Thompson, D. M. (1973). Encoding specificity and retrieval processing in episodic memory. *Psychological Review, 80*, 352–373.

Turner, J. (1910). Alcoholic insanity. *Journal of Mental Science*, pp. 25–63.

Underwood, B. J. (1969). Attributes of memory. *Psychological Review, 76*, 559–573.

Underwood, B. J. (1983). *Attributes of memory*. Glenview, IL: Scott, Foresman.

van Paesschen, W., King, M. D., Duncan, J. S., & Connelly, A. (2001). The amygdala and temporal lobe simple partial seizures: A prospective and quantitative MRI study. *Epilepsia, 42*, 857–862.

Walter, W. G. (1960). *The neurophysiological aspects of hallucinations and illusory experience*. London: Society for Psychical Research.

Ward, J. (1918). *Psychological principles*. Cambridge: Cambridge University Press.

Warren, H. C. (1934). *Dictionary of psychology*. Boston: Houghton Mifflin.

Warren, H. C., & Carmichael, L. (1930). *Elements of human psychology*. Boston: Houghton Mifflin.

Warrington, E. K., & Weiskrantz, L. (1968). New method of testing long-term retention with special reference to amnesic patients. *Nature, 217*, 972–974.

Warrington, E. K., & Weiskrantz, L. (1970). Amnesic syndrome: Consolidation or retrieval? *Nature, 228*, 629–630.

Watkins, M. J., & Peynircioglu, Z. F. (1990). The revelation effect: When disguising test items induces recognition. *Journal of Experimental Psychology: Learning, Memory, and Cognition, 16*, 1012–1020.

Weinand, M. E., Hermann, B., Wyler, A. R., Carter, L. P., Oommen, K. J., Labiner, D., Ahern, G., & Herring, A. (1994). Long-term subdural strip electrocorticographic monitoring of ictal déjà vu. *Epilepsia, 35*, 1054–1059.

Weinstein, E. A. (1969). Patterns of reduplication in organic brain disease. In P. J. Vinken & G. W. Bruyn (Eds.), *Handbook of Clinical Neurology, Vol. 3*. Amsterdam: North-Holland. pp. 251–257.

Weinstein, E. A., Kahn, R. L., & Sugarman, L. A. (1952). Phenomenon of reduplication. *Archives of Neurology and Psychiatry, 67*, 808–814.

Weinstein, E. A., Marvin, S. L., & Keller, N. J. A. (1962). Amnesia as a language pattern. *Archives of General Psychiatry, 6*, 259–270.

Weizkrantz, L. (1986). *Blindsight: A case study and implications*. Oxford: Oxford University Press.

West, D. J. (1948). The investigation of spontaneous cases. *Proceedings of the Society for Psychical Research, 48*, 264–300.

White, R. (1973). The mystery of déjà vu: Who knows where or when? *Psychic, 4*, 44–49.

Whittlesea, B. W. A. (1993). Illusions of familiarity. *Journal of Experimental Psychology: Learning, Memory, and Cognition, 19*, 1235–1253.

Whittlesea, B. W. A., Jacoby, L. L., & Girard, K. (1990). Illusions of immediate memory: Evidence of an attributional basis for feelings of familiarity and perceptual quality. *Journal of Memory and Language, 29*, 716–732.

Whittlesea, B. W. A., & Williams, L. D. (1998). Why do strangers feel familiar, but friends don't? A discrepancy-attribution account of feelings of familiarity. *Acta Psychologica, 98*, 141–165.

Wickelgren, W. A. (1977). *Learning and memory.* Englewood Cliffs, NJ: Prentice-Hall.

Wickelgren, W. A. (1979). *Cognitive psychology.* Englewood Cliffs, NJ: Prentice-Hall.

Wigan, A. L. (1844). *The duality of the mind.* London: Longman, Brown, & Green.

Wilmer Brakel, L. A. (1989). Understanding negative hallucination: Toward a developmental classification of disturbances in reality awareness. *Journal of the American Psychoanalytic Association, 37*, 437–463.

Wingfield, A. (1979). *Human learning and memory: An introduction.* New York: Harper & Row.

Wohlgemuth, A. (1924). On paramnesia. *Mind, 33*, 304–310.

Wolf, H. (1940). Die Entstehung der Wiedererkennungstaeuschung. *Zeitschrift fuer Psychologie, 149*, 306–320. (Cited in PsycINFO.)

Wolfradt, U. (2000). Déjà vu-Erfahrungen: Theoretische Annahmen und empirische Befunde. *Zeitschrift fuer Klinische Psychologie, Psychiatrie und Psychotherapie, 48*, 359–376.

Woodworth, R. S. (1940). *Psychology.* New York: Henry Holt.

Woodworth, R. S. (1948). *Psychology.* London: Methuen.

Yager, J. (1989). Clinical manifestations of psychiatric disorders. In H. I. Kaplan, & B. J. Sadock (Eds.), *Comprehensive textbook of psychiatry, 5th edition.* Baltimore, MD: Williams & Wilkins, pp. 569–570.

Yager, J., & Gitlin, M. J. (1995). Clinical manifestations of psychiatric disorders. In H. I. Kaplan, & B. J. Sadock (Eds.), *Comprehensive textbook of psychiatry, 6th edition.* Baltimore, MD: Williams & Wilkins, pp. 652–654.

Yamashita, H., Yoshida, T., Yoneda, Y., Mori, E., & Yamadori, A. (1994). Encephalic amnesia presenting déjà vu experiences limited to people. *Seishin Igaku (Clinical Psychiatry), 36*, 89–95.

Zajonc, R. B. (1980). Feeling and thinking: Preferences need no inferences. *American Psychologist, 35*, 151–175.

Zangwill, O. L. (1945). A case of paramnesia in Nathaniel Hawthorne. *Character and Personality, 13*, 246–260.

Zechmeister, E. B., & Nyberg, S. E. (1982). *Human memory.* Monterey, CA: Brooks/Cole.

Zeidenberg, P. (1973). Flashbacks. *Psychiatric Annals, 3*, 14–19.

Zuger, B. (1966). The time of dreaming and the déjà vu. *Comprehensive Psychiatry, 7*, 191–196.

Author Index

A

Abercrombie, J. 148–149
Adachi, N. 28, 61, 63, 67–70, 73, 76–77, 87–88, 94, 100–101, 103, 107
Adachi, T. 28, 61
Ahern, G. 82
Akanuma, N. 28, 61
Allan, L. G. 140
Allen, D. J. 190
Allers, R. 160
Allin, A. 2, 47, 48, 82, 140, 157–158, 164–165, 174–175, 180
Almeida, O. P. 110
Amster, H. 109
Andermann, F. 83
Anderson, B. F. 6
Anderson, G. 107
Anderson, J. R. 6
Angell, J. R. 113, 164
Anjel 47. 131–132, 174
Antoni, N. 82, 84
Ardila, A. 19, 27, 40, 89, 103–104, 139
Arlow, J. A. 47, 55, 100, 121–124
Arnaud, F. L. 11, 95–96
Ascherson, W. L. 94
Ashcraft, M. H. 6
Aufseeser, M. S. 160
Austrin, H. R. 77

B

Baddeley, A. 6
Baldwin, J. M. 75, 157, 164
Bancaud, J. 82, 85–86, 89, 91, 94, 103, 138–139

Banister, H. 122, 148, 151–153, 155, 193
Bartlett, F. C. 2
Barton, J. L. 100
Bayen, U. J. 151
Belbin, E. 108–109
Bender, M. B. 83
Bendit, L. J. 117
Benson, D. F. 111
Bergler, E. 123
Bergson, H. 47, 130–131
Bernal, B. 89
Bernard, P. 103
Bernhard-Leroy, E. 33, 61, 70, 82, 94, 98, 100
Bernstein, E. M. 102, 107
Bernstein, I. H. 6, 179
Berndt-Larsson, H. 96
Berrios, G. E. 2, 10, 11, 47, 98, 116, 142
Berson, R. J. 110
Best, J. B. 6
Biederman, I. 170
Billings, F. J. 159
Binnie, C. D. 83–84
Bird, B. 100, 122
Bishop, K. 190
Bjork, R. A. 4, 147, 158
Blake, M. 4
Boesky, D. 122–123
Boirac, E. 11, 155
Boltz, M. G. 52
Bonebakker, A. E. 158
Bonke, B. 158
Boring, E. G. 155
Bornstein, R. F. 167–168, 193
Boulenger, J. 20
Bourdon, B. 155
Bourne, L. E. 6
Bower, G. H. 110

221

Bowers, K. S. 149
Bowman, E. 107
Bransford, J. D. 154
Brauchi, J. T. 48
Brauer, R. 19, 21, 25, 39, 61, 100–101
Braun, B. G. 107
Breese, B. B. 11, 103, 109, 155
Brickner, R. M. 91
Brisset, C. 103
Brody, N. 6
Brown, A. S. 4, 40–41, 45–47, 51–52, 54,
 56–57, 67, 70–71, 75, 100, 139,
 148–149, 163, 192
Brown, J. W. 97
Brown, R. 28
Brunet-Bourgin, F. 82
Buck, L. A. 16, 20–21, 25, 41, 75–77, 100–101
Burke, D. M. 28, 148
Burnham, W. H. 10–12, 47, 51, 55, 61, 75,
 77, 96, 103, 106, 116, 132,
 140–141, 150
Burns, A. 110
Byrd, M. 183

C

Cahill, C. 107
Calkins, M. W. 11–12, 95
Carlson, E. B. 107,
Carrington, H. 12, 95, 116–117, 130–131
Carmichael, L. 114
Carpenter, W. B. 148
Carter, L. P. 82
Chace, P. M. 107
Challis, B. H. 154
Chapman, A. H. 12, 20–22, 26, 33, 40, 61–63,
 67–71, 73, 76, 148, 158, 192
Chari, C. T. K. 11, 16, 42, 96, 103, 116–118,
 155
Chauvel, P. 82
Cherlow, D. G. 83
Chu, J. A. 107
Claparède, E. 118, 129
Clark, P. 107
Cobb, S. 83
Cole, M. 82–84, 87–88, 91
Coleman, S. M. 55, 122
Collie, W. R. 75, 138
Collett, M. E. 177
Collins, J. C. 140
Colman, W. S. 82

Coltheart, M. 98
Comfort, A. 143–144
Conklin, E. S. 47, 103, 106, 155
Connelly, A. 19
Coons, P. 107
Cotard, J. 103,106
Council, J. R. 101
Courbon, P. 111
Covanis, A. 83
Craik, F. I. M. 183
Crandall, P. H. 83
Crichton-Browne, J. 12, 26, 58, 65, 67, 69,
 82–84, 87, 96, 98, 118, 155, 188
Critchley, E. M. R. 103, 106
Crosby, D. 94, 190
Crowder, R. G. 6
Curran, H. V. 190
Cutting, J. 11, 87, 95–97, 103–105, 138, 161,
 191

D

Dallas, M. 163, 177
Dashiell, J. F. 11, 169–170
Davidson, G. M. 97
Davidson, M. 108
Davis, G. A. 27
Davis, T. L. 67
Dawson, M. R. W. 6
Deese, J. 6, 159
de Jonghe, F. 3, 95
de Lamartine 117
de Nayer, A. 47, 130
Dennis, M. 20
De Pury, J. 176
Devereux, G. 103
Devinsky, O. 83
Dick, E. 160
Dill, D. 107
Dixon, J. C. 21, 61, 100–101
Dixon, N. F. 160, 183
Dodd, D. H. 6
Dominowski, R. L. 6
Donaldson, W. 129
Doyle, W. K. 83
Draaisma, D. 28, 48, 103, 109
Drever, J. 12
Drews, F. A. 183
Duncan, J. S. 19
Dugas, L. 2, 11, 47, 61, 67, 116, 131, 174, 180
Dumey, A. D. 160

Dunlap, K. 110
Dunlosky, J. 4
Dywan, J. 109

E

Eastwood, J. D. 181
Ebbinghaus, H. 2
Edwards, P. W. 101
Efron, R. 117, 142, 144
Egeth, H. 6
Ellinwood, E. H., Jr. 93, 106, 143
Ellis, H. 11–12, 47, 55, 67, 75, 82, 113,
          131–132, 141, 149, 151, 155, 157,
          176
Ellis, H. C. 6
Ellis, H. D. 98, 106
Emmons, C. F. 25, 77–78, 115
Epstein, A. W. 75, 83, 138
Erdelyi, M. H. 160
Erdfelder, E. 151
Ey, H. 103

F

Farina, B. 58
Farley, F. H. 27
Federn, P. 100, 125
Feldman, M. 98
Fenichel, O. 122
Ferenczi, S. 12, 123, 157
Feuchtersleben, E. 118
Findler, N. V. 11, 104, 108, 155, 157, 160
Fish, D. R. 83, 85–87, 89–90
Fisher, C. 160
Fiss, H. 160
Flagg, P. W. 6
Fleminger, S. 160, 166
Förstl, H. 110
Fox, J. W. 67, 74, 115
Fraisse, P. 97
Franks, J. J. 154
Freeman, N. R. 83, 138
Freud, S. 12, 47, 100, 118, 122–125, 157
Frith, C. 107
Fritzler, D. E. 160
Fukuda, K. 66, 157
Fung, N. S. 160
Funkhouser, A. T. 5, 10–11, 114, 116–118, 192

G

Gallagher, C. 27, 115
Gallup, G. H. 19–20, 23–25, 63, 66–67,
          69–70, 77–78, 114
Garbutt, J. C. 93
Gardiner, J. M. 128, 190
Gaynard, T. J. 16, 20–22, 24, 41, 70, 77–78,
          114
Gazzaniga, M. S. 134
Geers, M. B. 16, 20–21, 25, 41, 75–77,
          100–101
Gibbs, E. L. 89
Gibbs, F. A. 89
Gillette, G. M. 93
Gil-Nagel, A. 83–84, 89
Girard, K. 179
Gitlin, M. J. 103
Glass, A. L. 6
Gloor, P. 83–90, 103, 128, 138, 170
Gonzales, G. 119
Good, M. I. 123
Goodale, M. A. 143
Goodkind, M. S. 160
Gordon, A. 11, 47, 98, 103, 106
Gottlieb, C. G. 94, 190
Graf, P. 151
Grant, G. 21, 25, 33, 70, 100, 103, 106–107,
          122, 124, 166
Grasset, J. 55, 132, 140, 155, 168
Greeley, A. M. 20, 22, 31, 39, 61, 63, 114
Green, C. E. 19–21, 39, 70, 114, 192
Greene, M. 98
Greene, R. L. 6
Gregg, V. H. 6
Gregory, J. C. 148, 155–156
Greiffenstein, M. F. 98
Greyson, B. 19–21, 33, 97, 114
Grimmer, M. R. 27
Groh, L. A. 47
Gupta, A. K. 83–84, 87–88

H

Haber, R. N. 160
Haberlandt, K. 6
Hakim, H. 98
Halgren, E. 82–86, 88–90, 94, 138
Halliday, H. E. 110
Harbluk, J. L. 110

Harper, M. A. 20–22, 25–26, 39, 47, 52, 61,
    63, 67, 69–70, 82–84, 86, 92, 96,
    98–101, 104, 192
Harper, M. 25, 33, 82–83, 101, 103
Harriman, P. L. 12, 47, 95
Harrow, M. 19
Hartocollis, P. 100
Harvey, J. H. 20
Hasher, L. 184
Hashtroudi, S. 150
Hawley, K. J. 194
Hawthorne, N. 123, 150
Head, H. 97
Hearn, L. 12
Hennessy, M. J. 83–84
Henzler, A. 129
Hermann, B. 6
Herring, A. 82
Herrmann, D. 3, 82, 91, 103, 108
Hes, R. 155
Heymans, G. 20–21, 28–30, 47–48, 53, 94,
    98, 100, 103, 106, 109, 174
Hilgard, E. R. 149
Hill, A. 153
Hill, D. 82, 96
Hintzman, D. L. 161
Hirshman, E. 129
Hoch, P. H. 106–107
Hodgson, S. H. 75, 116, 164
Holmes, O. W. 12, 28, 116, 118, 142, 155, 157
Holyoak, K. J. 6
Hornstein, S. L. 194
Horowitz, L. M. 162
Horowitz, S. 83
Horton, D. L. 6
Houston, J. P. 6
Howard, R. 110
Hughes, R. C. 83
Hulbert, K. R. 20
Hulse, S. H. 6
Humphrey, G. 12, 110, 142, 155–156
Hunt, R. R. 6
Hunter, I. M. L. 103, 107–108, 155
Huppert, F. A. 161
Husband, T. H. 159
Huston, H. I. 119
Hyman, I. E. 159

I

Ide, M. 88, 93

Ikawa, N. 93
Inoue, Y. 89
Irwin, H. J. 24, 61, 77, 101, 103–104, 106, 114

J

Jääskeläinen, S. K. 93, 190
Jackson, J. H. 11, 81–83, 85, 87, 94, 103, 105,
    109, 133
Jacoby, L. L. 6, 109, 140–141, 163, 177–179,
    192–194
James, W. 12, 155–156
Jansen, J. 52, 70
Jasper, H. H. 89
Java, R. 190
Jeavons, P. M. 83
Jensen 12, 116, 142
Jessen, P. 155
Johnson, M. K. 130, 150–151, 157, 165
Johnston, W. A. 183, 194
Jones, E. M. 67
Joordens, S. 179
Jordan, T. R. 155
Joshi, S. 23, 25, 114
Jung, C. G. 118

K

Kafka, J. S. 156
Kahan, T. L. 157
Kahn, R. L. 97
Kato, M. 28, 61
Kauff, D. M. 6
Kausler, D. H. 6
Keegan, M. 153
Keller, N. J. A. 92
Kelley, C. M. 109, 163
Kennison, R. F. 177
Keschner, M. 83
Ketcham, K. 159
Kim, J. K. 165
Kimura, M. 28, 61
King, M. D. 19
Kinnier Wilson, S. A. K. 42, 82, 98, 105–106,
    124, 169, 184
Kirshner, L. A. 75, 95–97, 122, 191
Kintsch, W. 6
Klatzky, R. L. 6
Klein, J. 158
Knight, B. 149–150

Knowlton, B. J. 151
Kohn, S. R. 58, 65, 117, 123
Kohr, R. L. 20–22, 38–39, 61, 68, 70, 74–76, 114–116
Kolers, P. A. 130, 154
Kraepelin, E. 11, 47, 61, 95, 116, 141, 180
Krijgers Janzen, E. 11, 47, 51, 55–56, 75, 83, 103, 116, 174–175
Kuiper, P. C. 47, 100
Kulik, J. 28
Kumar, V. K. 27
Kunst-Wilson, W. R. 167

L

Labiner, D. 82
Lalande, A. 11, 61, 70, 116–117, 174–176
La Lorrain, J. 155
Lampinen, J. M. 160–161
Langdon, R. 98
Lapie, P. 155, 157–159
Larwill, L. K. 140
Leeds, M. 19–22, 27, 29–30, 39, 42, 47–48, 52–54, 70, 83, 155–156, 174, 189, 191
Legrand, J. A. 20
Lennox, W. G. 83, 89
Léon-Kindberg, M. 132
Levin, D. T. 183
Levin, J. S. 61, 66
Levitan, H. 100, 124, 155, 170
Lewis, D. O. 98
Light, L. L. 148, 177
Lindsay, D. S. 3, 150–151
Linn, L. 48, 166
Linszen, D. H. 9, 54, 95–96, 100–101, 103, 106, 113–114, 116, 119, 155–157, 165,
170, 192
Loftus, E. F. 6, 159
Loftus, G. R. 6
Lowenstein, R. J. 107
Luauté, J. P. 98
Lucas, D. 23
Luciano, D. 83

M

MacCurdy, J. T. 47, 54–55, 61, 75, 98, 122–123, 148, 155–157, 166

Mack, A. 181–182
MacKay, D. G. 28
Maeterlinck, M. 12, 118
Mandler, G. 151
Marcovitz, E. 116, 124
Marcuse, F. L. 153, 194
Marková, I. S. 10, 47, 98, 116, 142
Marsh, R. L. 110
Martindale, C. 6
Martinez-Mustardo, Y. 98
Marvin, S. L. 92
Mathieson, G. 87
Matlin, M. 6
Matsuda, K. 89
Maudsley, H. 82, 142
Mayer, B. 126, 166–167
Mayer, R. E. 6
McClelland, J. L. 170
McClenon, J. 20, 33, 74, 114–116
McCready, W. C. 20, 22, 39, 61, 63
McDermott, K. B. 3, 67, 134, 147, 155, 158, 160
McKellar, A. 110, 116
McKellar, P. 19, 21, 25–26, 76
McLaughlin, D. R. 110
Medin, D. L. 6
Mensh, I. N. 12, 20–22, 26, 33, 40, 61–63, 67–71, 73, 76, 148, 158, 192
Merckelbach, H. 126, 166–167
Merikle, P. M. 158, 179, 181, 194
Metcalfe, J. 4
Meurs, E. J. 155
Mihara, T. 89
Milford, G. 27
Milner, A. D. 143
Mitchell, D. B. 163
Mizukami, K. 87
Morgan, J. J. B. 103–104, 108, 155
Morris, C. D. 154
Montañes, P. 89
Mullan, S. 83–85, 87–88, 106
Mulligan, N. W. 194
Multhaup, K. S. 67
Murdock, B. B. 6
Murai, T. 83
Murnane, K. 151
Murphy, D. R. 110, 149, 155
Murphy, G. 11–12, 48, 163
Myers, D. H. 19, 21, 25, 33, 70, 100, 103, 106–107, 122, 124, 166
Myers, F. W. H. 11–12, 116–118, 134–135, 142, 148, 157, 175–176

Myers, W. A. 97, 123

N

Neath, I. 6
Neisser, U. 3
Nelson, K. 149
Nelson, T. O. 4
Nemiah, J. 100
Neppe, V. M. 9–12, 16–17, 20–23, 26–27, 30,
        33, 45, 47, 61, 65, 67, 75–76,
        82–84, 90, 95–97, 103–106, 110,
        113–114, 118, 122, 152, 161–162,
        192
Newport, F. 19–20, 23–25, 63, 65, 67, 69–70,
        77–78, 114
Niño, C. R. 19
Nisbett, R. E. 27
Niwa, N. 93
Nix, L. A. 163
Norman, D. A. 6
Nurnberger, J. 20
Nyberg, S. E. 6

O

Oberndorf, C. P. 48, 61, 100, 103–104, 123,
        155
O'Connor, W. A. 103
Öhman, A. 167
Olivier, A. 83
Oommen, K. J. 82
Osborne, H. F. 12, 21–22, 48, 75, 94, 116, 142,
        148, 150, 154–155, 157–158, 174,
        185, 192
Otsubo, T. 89
Ouspensky, P. D. 65, 118
Owen, A. M. 110

P

Pacella, B. L. 123–125
Pacia, S. V. 83–84, 106
Pagliaro, L. 102, 164–165
Palmer, J. 20–24, 33, 38–39, 61, 63, 67–70,
        74–76, 92, 114–116
Palmini, A. 83–84, 87–88
Parish, E. 47, 61, 75, 132, 141–142, 170
Parkin, A. J. 6, 128

Pashler, H. 130
Passchier, J. 158
Paterson, J. M. 27
Paul, I. H. 160
Paulsen, J. S. 20
Pekala, R. J. 27
Penfield, W. 82–85, 87–88, 90, 94, 103,
        105–106, 138
Pentland, J. 159
Perot, P. 87–88, 94
Perrine, K. 83
Pethö, B. 98
Peynircioglu, Z. F. 177
Phillips, D. E. 11
Pick, A. 42, 98
Pickford, R, W. 11, 55, 95, 100, 118, 122–124,
        151
Pickrell, J. E. 159
Piercy, M. 161
Pillsbury, W. B. 11–12, 118, 155
Pine, F. 160
Poetzl, O. 48, 100, 160
Posner, M. I. 6
Post, R. M. 20
Pribram, K. 156
Probst, P. 52, 70
Prull, M. W. 177
Prytulak, L. S. 162
Pulido, E. 19
Putnam, F. W. 102, 107

Q

Quaerens 48, 82
Quesney, L. F. 83

R

Rapaport, D. 54
Ravdin, L. 83
Raye, C. L. 157
Read, J. D. 108
Reason, J. T. 28
Reber, R. 165
Reed, G. 51, 54, 61, 103–104, 106, 108–110,
        116, 155, 163–164, 168, 183
Reed, S. K. 6
Reisberg, D. 6
Retterstøl, N. 98
Reynolds, A. G. 6

Rhine, L. E.   116, 158
Ribot, T.   174–175
Richardson, E. D.   20
Richardson, T. F.   20, 22, 33, 48, 61, 63, 67–70, 73, 82–83, 91–92, 97–99, 191
Richardson-Klavehn, A.   147, 158
Riley, K. C.   101, 107
Risinger, M. W.   83–84, 89
Risse, G.   165
Rivera, D. B.   19
Roberts, R. J.   20, 27, 40–41, 103–104
Rock, I.   181–182
Roediger, H. L., III   3–4, 6–7, 109, 130, 134, 147, 154–155, 158, 160
Rosen, D. S.   118–119
Ross, B. H.   6, 107
Ross, C. A.   23, 25, 27, 114
Roth, M.   25, 33, 82–83, 100–101, 103–104
Ruiz, E.   89
Rummelhart, D. E.   170
Rypma, B.   184

S

Salthouse, T. A.   144
Sander, W.   61, 116, 168
Santa, J. L.   6
Schacter, D. L.   2, 6, 10, 110, 134, 141, 147, 155, 158–159
Scheyer, R. D.   87–89
Schilder, P.   48, 100
Schneck, J. M.   48, 75, 113, 122–124
Schneider, G. E.   143
Schwarz, N.   165
Scott, W.   48, 155–156
Seamon, J. G.   6, 160, 167–168, 193
Searleman, A.   3, 6, 103, 108
Sebel, P. S.   158
Sengoku, A.   83–84, 87, 105, 107
Serpa, A.   98
Shelley, P. B.   116
Shepherd, J. S.   30
Shevrin, H.   160
Shiraishi, H.   87
Silberman, E. K.   20, 27, 33, 82–84, 98–99, 103–104
Silbermann, I.   75, 103–104, 106, 122
Silverman, D. K.   160
Silverman, L. H.   160
Silzer, H.   11, 87, 95–97, 103–105, 138, 161, 191

Simmons, M. B.   11
Simons, D. A.   4, 183
Simpson, L.   19, 21, 25–26, 76
Siomopoulos, V.   48, 100, 103, 164–165
Slamecka, N. J.   2
Slater, P. C.   107
Slochower, H.   123
Smilek, D.   181
Smith, S. M.   119
Smith, T. L.   10, 48, 109, 113, 149–150
Sno, H. N.   3, 9, 11–12, 21, 28, 30, 45, 48, 54, 58, 61, 63, 70, 82, 95–96, 98, 100, 102–104, 106–107, 109, 113–114, 116, 119, 155–157, 192
Soares, J. J. F.   167
Sobal, J.   25, 66, 77–78, 115
Solso, R. L.   6
Spatt, J.   58, 138–139
Spencer, D. D.   87
Spencer, S. S.   87
Springer, J. A.   20
Squire, L. R.   107, 151
Stanford, R. G.   61
Stein, A.   91, 114
Stern, L.   6
Stern, W.   10, 54, 103, 106
Sternberg, R. J.   6
Stevens, J. R.   84–85, 138
Stevenson, I.   118, 191
Stijnen, T.   158
Stoltzfus, E. R.   184
Strauss, I.   83
Strayer, D. L.   183
Strickland, S. E.   160
Strömgren, E.   82, 91
Struchen, M. A.   20
Stuss, D. T.   111
Sugarman, L. A.   97
Sully, J.   12, 118, 149, 157, 159
Surprenant, A. M.   6
Sutherland, S.   12
Suzuki, T.   87
Swan, C. M.   20

T

Taiminen, T.   93, 190
Takaoka, K.   93
Takekawa, Y.   28
Tarpy, R. M.   6
Taylor, G. R.   103–104, 106

Teler, J. 160
Theodore, W. 20
Thompson, D. M. 109
Tiffin, J. 103–104, 106, 174
Titchener, E. B. 12, 48, 51, 116, 158, 165, 170,
 174, 179
Tobacyk, J. J. 27
Toichi, M. 83
Torem, M. 107
Tottori, T. 89
Tucker, G. J. 20
Tulving, E. 109, 128, 131
Turnage, T. W. 6
Turner, J. 93
Tusques, J. 111

U

Underwood, B. J. 129

V

Vanegas, C. J. 19
Van Paesschen, W. 19–20, 82–84, 88
Varney, N. T. 20
Vazquez, B. 83
Verma, N. P. 98
Verrienti, D. 58
Vokey, J. R. 108

W

Wade, E. 28
Walter, R. D. 83
Walter, W. G. 12, 114
Ward, J. 10, 12, 116
Warren, H. C. 12
Warrington, E. K. 151
Watkins, M. J. 177
Weinand, M. E. 82–84, 87–88, 94, 142
Weinstein, E. A. 92, 97, 128, 148, 191
Weizkrantz, L. 143, 151

Welch, K. R. 6, 179
Weldon, M. S. 154
West, D. J. 48, 116, 180
West, L. J. 48
White, K. D. 27
White, R. 58, 65, 113
White, R. M. 6
Whitehouse, K. 6, 177–179, 192–193
Whittlesea, B. W. A. 163–164, 179
Wickelgren, W. A. 6, 157
Wigan, A. L. 11–12, 48, 133–134, 142, 174
Williams, L. D. 163–164
Wilmer Brakel, L. A. 100, 124
Wilson, T. D. 27
Wingfield, A. 6
Winkielman, P. 165
Winokur, G. 20, 22, 33, 48, 61, 63, 67–70, 73,
 82–83, 91–92, 97–99, 191
Wohlgemuth, A. 83, 160–161
Wolf, H. 48
Wolfradt, U. 77, 103–104, 106
Woloshyn, V. 163
Wolters, G. 158
Woodworth, R. S. 12, 103, 106
Worthley, J. S. 28
Woulfin, J. R. 160
Wyler, A. R. 82

Y

Yager, J. 48, 103
Yagi, K. 89

Z

Zacks, R. T. 184
Zajonc, R. B. 166–167
Zangwill, O. L. 16, 42, 82–84, 87–88, 91, 96,
 122–123, 148, 150–153, 155, 159,
 193
Zechmeister, E. B. 6
Zeidenberg, P. 122, 155, 164–165
Zuger, B. 19–20, 22, 61, 63, 76, 157

Subject Index

A

Academic achievement 69
Adrenaline 141
Affect 164–165
Age 38, 61–67, 78, 189–190, 192
Agoraphobia 25
Alcohol 93
Alzheimer's disease 144, 190
Amantadine hydrochloride 93
Amnesia 92, 148, 161, 190
    Childhood 148
    Source 110
Amphetamine 93, 142
Amygdala 89, 128, 138
Anesthesia 158
Anxiety 47
Attention
    Diminished 180–181
    Inattention 181–183
Aura (pre-seizure) 83–85, 105, 138, 170

B

Behaviorism 2
Belief, in déjà vu 77, 114–116
Benzodiazepine 190
Bipolar mood disorder 93, 98
Brain structures 89–91

C

Capgras' syndrome 110–111
Carbamazepine 93
Castles 47, 148, 150–151
Castration anxiety 122, 125

Context, of déjà vu 48–51
Causes of déjà vu 46–48
    Activity 49–50
    Physical setting 49
    Social setting 50–51
Change blindness 183
Chronophrenia 98
Clonazepam 93
Collective unconscious 118–119
Consciousness
    Dual 133–134
    Parasitic 133
Consolidation 139
Cryptomnesia 12, 110, 149
Cue dependent forgetting 109–110

D

Daydreams 76–77, 158, 180
Demographic variables 61–75
Depersonalization 25, 28–29, 100–101, 106
Derealization 25, 100
Diagnostic and Statistical Manual (DSM)
    102
Dissociation 101–102
Dopamine 93, 190
Dreams 29, 75–76, 138–139, 157–159
Dreamy state 81
Drugs 92–94
Duration (of déjà vu) 51–52

E

Education 67–69, 78
Ego defense 121–122
Electrical stimulation 85

Electrical recording 85
Electro-convulsive therapy (ECT) 191
Emotions during déjà vu 54, 184
Epilepsy, temporal lobe (TLE) 81–91, 138
Episodic forgetting 148

F

False memory 159
Familiarity 128–129
    Gestalt 168–170
    Single-element 154–160
    Multiple-element 160–161
Fantasy 77
Fatigue 47, 53, 141, 160, 180
Feeling of knowing (FOK) 4–5
            Flanker task 194–195
Flashback 12, 165
Flashbulb memory 28
Fluency, processing 162–165
Frégoli syndrome 111
Freqency, of déjà vu 38–41

G

Gender 70–72, 78
Geons 170

H

Handedness 88–89
Hemispheres, cerebral 86–89, 138, 142
Hippocampus 89–91, 138–139
Hologram 156
Huntington's disease 144, 148, 190
Hyperaesthesia 141
Hypnosis 151–153, 193–194

I

Illusion 3
Imagery
    Eidetic 175
    Hypnogogic 25, 191
    Hypnopompic 25, 157, 176, 191
Inattentional blindness 181–183, 195
Incidence 31–43
    Subjective 31

Income 70
Intermetamorphosis 111
Illness 47

J

Jamais vu 103–111, 128
Judgement of learning (JOL) 4–5

K

Korsakoff's disease 148, 161, 165

L

L-dopa 190
Lateral inhibition 183, 185
Literature 58, 149–150, 158–159

M

Marital status 79
Mere exposure, subliminal 167–168, 193
Metacognition 4–5
Micropsia 98
MINERVA 161
Multiple sclerosis 190

N

National Opinion Research Council
        (NORC) 20, 23, 39, 62–66,
        68–71, 73–75, 114–115, 190
Negative priming 183–184
Neurosis 98–100

O

Occupational status 70
Oedipal conflict 122

P

Paramnesia 10–11, 161–162
Paranormal 22–25, 27, 33, 65

Parapsychology 5, 113–119, 189, 191
Parkinson's disease 144, 148
Perceptual
    Fluency 140
    Gap 174–177
    Inhibition 183–184
Phenylpropanolamine hydrochloride 93
Physical response, to déjà vu 56
Platonic reminiscence 118
Poetzl phenomenon 160
Political orientation 74
Precognition 12, 116–117, 143, 189
Psychodynamic 5, 121–126, 191

Q

Questionnaires 19, 27, 101–102, 107, 115,
        190, 192

R

Race 72–73, 78
Recency, of déjà vu 38
Redintegration 161–162
Reduplicative paramnesia 98
Regression 124–125
Reincarnation 118
Reliability, of self report 26
Religious preference 74
Reminiscence 10
Repression 122–123
Reticular activating system (RAS) 166
Retrospective reports 19
Revelation effect 176–177

S

Sampling, unrepresentative 21–23
Schizophrenia 22, 29, 95–98, 100
Screen memory 123
Seizure 138
Semantic satiation 109, 111
Socioeconomic class 69–70, 190
Source memory 150–151
Space 57
Split brain patients 191
Stress 47
Stroop task 183–184
Subjective interpretations 184–185
Survey
    Retrospective 30
    Prospective 28–30
Synchronicity 118–119
Synesthesia 25

T

Tape recorder metaphor 130
Telepathy 117
Temporal lobe 89–93, 138, 190
Temporal aspects of déjà vu 52–54, 56–58
Time gap 183
Tip of the tongue 3–5, 28, 192
Toluene 93
Transfer appropriate processing 154
Tumor 91
Travel frequency 73–74

W

Wish fulfillment 124